ONE MAN'S MEXICO

A Record of Travels and Encounters

JOHN LINCOLN

Introduction by Nicolas Cheetham

CENTURY PUBLISHING
LONDON

Printed in Great Britain by
Richard Clay (The Chaucer Press) Ltd,
Bungay, Suffolk

Contents

MEXICO

To the Tigress & the Raven of Chihuahua

Introduction

I am very glad that John Lincoln's *One Man's Mexico* is being reprinted after fifteen years, for it ranks high among the many perceptive studies of Mexican life which have been produced by British writers since Mexico won its independence. It takes an honourable place alongside such widely differing classics as the Scotswoman Fanny Calderón de la Barca's *Life in Mexico* (1843), D. H. Lawrence's *Mornings in Mexico* (1927), Rodney Gallop's *Mexican Mosaic* (1939) and Patrick O'Hea's *Reminiscences of the Mexican Revolution* (1966). Indeed, if my own reactions can serve as a guide, the serious foreigner travelling in Mexico or, better still, living there for any length of time, can hardly resist the urge to add his or her own literary tribute to those already paid to the variety and grandeur of the country's landscapes, to the massive heritage of its ancient cultures or to the fantastic vicissitudes of its history. If he is bold enough he may even attempt to interpret the baffling contradictions of the national character.

Lincoln's travels date from the years 1958 to 1964, a period when the pace of change in Mexico—economic, demographic and cultural—was accelerating but not yet threatening to become uncontrollable. They also coincided exactly with the presidency of Adolfo Lopez Mateos, a singularly selfless and enlightened head of state. Under his leadership Mexico was enjoying a well-deserved reputation for political stability and economic progress, and in both those respects it was acknowledged to be ahead of most other Latin American countries. Its political system, resting as it did and still does, on an autocratic presidency backed up by a single party organisation permeating and controlling all sectors of the national life, hardly satisfied the standards of North American or Western European democracy. Yet the Mexican citizen, seeing his country more peaceful, prosperous and respected than at any time within his recollection, was content to judge by results. The evils of urban squalor and rural backwardness were too obvious to be ignored; so were the corruption and raw abuses which too often cropped up in public life. On the other hand there was no denying the government's very real concern with improving the lot of the Indian peasantry, with developing welfare services and with promoting popular education. Its aim was to provide every village with electricity, piped water, an approach road and a school as basic necessities. The interests of the industrial workers were guaranteed by strong trade unions entrenched within the official party.

Above all, the economy was booming and there seemed to be no reason why the boom should ever end. Impressive programmes of public works were in hand. Mexico was not only feeding its swelling population but exporting foodstuffs. Industry was expanding with the aid of copious foreign investment. Huge reserves of oil and gas were coming to light. Tourists provided an increasing income and confirmed the Mexicans' pride in their own cultural achievements. In short the national mood was one of buoyant optimism, although the prevailing euphoria did not exclude scathing public criticism of the blemishes which marred the general picture.

Against this background Lincoln explored Mexico in all its fascinating variety, from the border with California in the north to that of Guatemala in the south. Reading his book, I was delighted to find that I had in the course of six years myself managed to visit many of the places which he describes. While I only wish that I could have wandered as far as he did from the beaten track, I cannot help stressing that the 'real' Mexico is not exclusively to be sought in its rural recesses as opposed to its bustling cities or its little provincial towns where the sleepy rhythm of life recalls the spacious era of colonial and creole rule. Lincoln's vivid accounts of his adventures in odd corners of the land reveal a decided penchant for the weird and inexplicable, for grotesque situations and strange people and for all the eerie aspects of Mexican life which are usually concealed from the foreigner. Most of his contacts were with the underdogs rather than with the rapidly multiplying *mestizo* middle class. To each man his own Mexico, and Lincoln's tale had to be told by a writer of his special talent before his Mexico disappeared. I think that to some extent he has harked back to an older Mexican tradition. His portrayal of the sleazy side of provincial life and of strange occurrences in the backwoods remind me strongly of the blend of fact and fantasy in certain picaresque novels of the early nineteenth century such as *El Periquillo Sarniento* (The Mangy Little Parrot) of Fernandez de Lizardi or *Los Bandidos de Rio Frio* of Payno. He himself faithfully records the crudity and violence of popular life while hinting at the simultaneous existence, as it were behind a veil, of a whole world of subtle mystery.

Mexicans, as Lincoln soon discovered, make the best and most generous friends in the world, and he clearly possessed all the right qualities for winning their confidence. Nevertheless he seems to have found this difficult at first, for he insists, in his own Introduction, on their basic xenophobia which so often disconcerts the foreigner. But in most cases the hostility is passive and seldom erupts. On one sole occasion I narrowly avoided a swipe with a machete, but I honestly believe that in six years I never heard a nasty word spoken to my face by any Mexican. Even bandits can be exquisitely polite in stripping their victims of all their possessions. In general the foreigner has little to fear unless he behaves discourteously himself or encounters a dangerous drunk on a feast day. Whenever a Mexican wishes to see him off he retreats, as Lincoln explains, behind a barrier of impenetrable reserve, a display of blank incomprehension which may be genuine or simulated but is invariably effective.

The streak of cruelty in the Mexican character, together with the fatalistic acceptance of violence and death, no doubt owes its origin to history and pre-hispanic religion. However, it has been much less frequently displayed in hatred of the foreigner than in lengthy and ferocious outbreaks of internal strife, as during the struggles which led to national independence, the wars of the Reform in the mid-nineteenth century and the bloody agonies of the Revolution in the early twentieth. The country was left exhausted by those conflicts but in a sense purified, and they were followed by half a century of peace and reconciliation under the present political system. We must hope that the old passions have been finally spent. So far as the foreigners are concerned, no particular resentment is felt against the French for having sent an army to occupy Mexico in the 1860s, and much less than one would think against the Americans for having seized California, Arizona, New Mexico and most of Texas twenty years earlier. Mexicans are indeed inclined to decry all that the 'Yanquis' say or do, but the truth is that they have become more deeply influenced than they would care to admit by the American way of life, with the result that they are apt increasingly to think and behave like Americans (a statement which they would, of course, passionately contest). Also the old complex love–hate relationship with Spain is being superceded by a new feeling, on the Mexican side, of tolerance and affection. Thus the traditional dislike for the gringo and the Spaniard is on the way out for the reason that the modern Mexican shares too many characteristics with them both for it to persist. Finally there are many aspects of his Spanish colonial past in which he is no longer ashamed to take pride. After all, that era lasted for 300 years and bequeathed a rich cultural legacy to the nation.

I suspect that the schizophrenic Mexican of Octavio Paz's *El Laberinto de la Soledad* (1950) is no longer typical. His successor appears to me to be a simpler creature, less haunted by the ghosts of the past but now, alas, plunged into doubts about his future. When he least expected it he learnt that his country was bankrupt. The setback to its material progress has been shockingly abrupt and it would not be surprising if the distress and bitterness which it has caused were manifested in political and social unrest. Yet it is probably wrong to predict a second Revolution and that Pancho Villa will ride again. The real trouble surely is that Mexico has not had time to adapt itself to the unbelievably rapid changes of the last century. To take only one striking example, when I first arrived in Mexico in 1941 about one million people lived in Mexico City and about twenty-two million in the whole country. The corresponding figures today may be as much as twelve million for the city alone and well over seventy million for the country. They pose problems which would be horrific enough even without a financial catastrophe. But the Mexicans, so grossly maligned by foreign caricaturists, are in reality a gifted, resilient and hardworking race. It is not too much to expect of them that they will soon get over any loss of nerve and surmount their present crisis.

Nicolas Cheetham, 1983

Introduction
The Foreigner in Mexico

The life of Mexico is fascinating and mysterious and so impenetrable that after a few months the foreigner usually becomes resigned to living on its surface. But even this is not easy, for the surface itself has two quite different aspects. In one it is like thin ice through which he is always in danger of falling, in the other like a sea so salt that he cannot sink into it. The ice can be delightful so long as it holds. The sea troughs are gloomy but the crests magnificent.

Whatever his reasons for being in Mexico, he will soon realize that no matter how much kindness he may receive from individual Mexicans, he is only accepted in their country on sufferance. The mistrust and hostility which Mexicans feel towards foreigners, however illogical, are a result of their experience in history.

The sixteenth-century conquest by the Spaniards of the old Indian civilizations is counted by modern Mexicans, in all its greed and savagery, as the first foreign outrage against the race, even though the majority of the people may now possess as much Spanish as Indian blood. Early in the colonial period friction arose between the settlers and the bureaucracy imposed on them by imperial Spain. The straitjacket in which the vice-regal system and the Catholic Church gripped creoles* and mestizos† alike thwarted their material and intellectual development. At the beginning of the nineteenth century the impulse towards freedom exploded into war, and the inhabitants of New Spain (as up to that time the country had generally been called) transferred their identity and became Mexicans.

---

* Pure-blooded Spaniards born in Mexico.
† People of mixed Indian and Spanish descent.

9

This was the name by which the Indians of the central plateau had been known before the conquest. The fact that it was borrowed from them to christen the new nation did little to improve their status. As in other Latin American countries independence left the mass of Indians relegated to the serfdom in which they had existed throughout the colonial period. But their part in the struggle had been significant enough to offer them the possibility of improving their position in the future. This might not have been so if the great landowners had joined in the attack on the government when it started. Instead they remained loyal because they mistrusted the social character of the revolution and hoped for the triumph of reactionary elements in Spain which could be relied upon to support their feudal interests. Had they fought with the rebels they would have insisted on the Indians being treated as conscripts. But the leadership was left to men lower down the social scale: Hidalgo and Morelos, both country priests, Allendé, a cavalry officer, and Dominguez, the mayor of a provincial city. The army which sprang up at Hidalgo's call in the little town of Dolores was already twenty-five thousand strong when it reached Guanajuato, only twenty miles away. It consisted in the main of Indian peasants. After an initial success against the loyalists it was defeated. Hidalgo was taken prisoner and hanged.

The final break with Spain was achieved ten years later in 1821 mainly as a result of the landowners changing sides in opposition to the liberal policy of the Spanish government. But the path to political power already lay open to the Indians and they did not hesitate to follow it. Thus by the middle of the century it was possible for a pure Zapotec, Benito Juarez, to become president. The greatest figure in the history of modern Mexico, he introduced the first liberal reforms, frustrated the intervention of the French and executed their abandoned puppet, the Emperor Maximilian.

A few years earlier in the 1847 war with the North Americans the country had suffered a violation almost as traumatic in its effect as that inflicted on the Indian civilizations by the Spaniards. It is an episode which has received little attention outside the western hemisphere and yet it should be remembered if only as one of the most unjust and rapacious wars in history. By the terms which the victors exacted, the Mexicans lost almost half their territory, the area which is now made up of the states of Texas, Arizona, New Mexico, Nevada and California, in return for which they received fifteen million dollars.

The French had been interested in Mexico for some years. In 1838 they had backed a French baker, who claimed he had been robbed of seventy thousand cakes, by sending a naval squadron to Veracruz. They were bought off with an indemnity of six thousand dollars, but not before the Mexican general, Santa Anna, had lost his leg to a French cannon-ball. The leg was embalmed and a monument was erected in its honour.

Failure to pay debts owed to the governments of Britain, Spain and France provided Napoleon III with the pretext for sending an army to Mexico in 1862. Briefly supported by Spain and Britain, the French intervention lasted tenuously until the execution of Maximilian in 1867. Of all the attempts of foreigners to gain control over the country, by invasion from without or exploitation from within, the French was the most easily forgiven by the Mexicans,* not only because it was ultimately defeated by the patient strategy of Juarez, but because it provided Mexico, at the battle of Puebla, with the one undisputed military success in its history, an occasion still celebrated by a great national fiesta.

Four years after Juarez' death in 1872, one of his dissident generals, Porfirio Diaz, an Indian from Oaxaca, became president and set up a dictatorship which lasted until his overthrow in the revolution of 1910. Using the same ruthless methods by which he had obtained his supremacy, he curbed the factious spirit of his countrymen and imposed a state of order as beneficial to the rich, who supported him, as it was oppressive to the poor whose liberal champions he would not tolerate. He encouraged the foreign investments which were needed to convert Mexico from the most backward of Latin American countries into one of the most materially progressive. The investors themselves, convinced that the old anarchic liberalism of the country was dead, set upon the corpse with

---

* Even today the French is still the most popular and privileged foreign colony in Mexico.

confidence and rapacity. Among them the North Americans and, to a lesser degree, the British predominated. This was the 'golden age' to which elderly foreign residents, who remember it, look back with nostalgia; the age which the revolution exploded into chaos and bloodshed.

There were two characteristics of the rule of Porfirio Diaz which contributed to his downfall. He refused to allow any form of political opposition, so that rebellion was the only means by which he could be overthrown, and he encouraged the great landowners, many of them foreign, without doing anything to relieve the misery of the peasants who still worked as serfs on their estates. His opponents, whether idealists or self-seekers, inevitably took to violence, and found it easy to raise followers among the hungry and dispossessed. These were for the most part Indian peasants. Thus in the revolution, as in the war of independence, the Indian population took an important part in the fighting and produced some of its most spectacular leaders.

After twenty years, when from physical exhaustion rather than the will to peace the country subsided into a makeshift order, the Mexicans again became concerned with the question of their identity. After the horror and turmoil of civil war, they had somehow to assure themselves that they could still hang together as a nation. Although their wounds had been mostly self-inflicted, they were convinced that their real enemy lay without. As after the independence they had denied Spain, now after the revolution they denied all forms of foreign interference from whatever source. Thus, in the last spasm of revolutionary violence, Calles was able to make his rabid attack upon the Catholic Church. Cardenas, an Indian from Michoacan, who followed him as president, restored freedom of worship and initiated an important programme of agrarian reform. But the act for which he will always be remembered, the most popular single measure carried out by any Mexican president, was the expropriation of the British- and American-owned oil fields, an event commemorated by a public monument and a national holiday.

As a result of the xenophobia which grew out of the revolution, the people now saw themselves, despite their share of Spanish blood, as having roots in a continuous past which reached back to the Indian civilizations before the conquest. With this new conception of 'the race', the violations of Spain and North America became the highlights in a long history of foreign intrigue and aggression. Thus the idea of foreigners, at least in the abstract, came to rouse in the Mexican mind a hostile reflex and, in extreme cases, an explosive impulse for revenge. If they were to be tolerated it was only for their money, knowledge or technical skill. But they were needed for another reason which Mexicans are still reluctant to admit; that is for their friendship.

And so the foreigner in Mexico soon learns that just as the thin air of the mountain capital, in spite of the almost perpetual sunlight by which it is transfused, can treacherously turn a mild cold into pneumonia, so the thin ice of Mexican tolerance may at any moment split open and plunge him into the depth below.

What makes the ice break? And what happens to the foreigner who falls through it?

There are many answers to the first question. An insignificant detail is found to be missing from his papers, the fault of the clerk who instructed him how to fill them in, or the result of a new regulation, announced so surreptitiously that there is no chance of his having heard of it, or, perhaps, never announced at all, or dug up from some code which has been dead for half a century, or simply invented at the whim of the official who stares at him impassively from behind his desk.

He drives down a one-way street, following the direction in which, until the day before, an almost invisible arrow pointed; but overnight it has been switched round, and at the next corner a superlative living symbol of Mexican male virility is waiting for him, a broad, plump policeman in a brown uniform, helmeted, with a revolver at his hip, his expression inscrutable behind a black moustache and black glasses, and his legs straddling a powerful motor-bicycle in a stance which suggests that the roar from the exhaust is an audible extension of the sexual potency between his thighs.

If the foreigner is a woman, over-anxious to get to know the city for herself, she too may take a wrong turning. This time the policemen (for there are sure to be not less than three together in the area into which she has strayed), who come nudging up on either side of her to demand her prostitute's licence, will be wearing dark blue uniforms. They, also, will have revolvers at their hips or even in their hands, and if, with their pudgy, pock-marked faces, they can be said to be symbolic, it is not of anything specifically Mexican, but of corruption, which lurks in every country within the shadow of the law.

Impecunious or energetic (it is more likely to be a man this time) the foreigner decides to hike from the port at which he has disembarked to the capital. He stops in a village full of drunken Indians who fall in love with his white skin until, imagining an insult in his failure to understand them, they move their hands to their *machetes*.* Or when he has arrived safely in the capital, the politico sitting opposite him in a bar decides he doesn't like his face, or, perhaps, that his girl friend likes it too much, so he pulls out his gun and fires.†

Now to come to the second question: what happens when the ice has broken?

Weeks, even months, passed in government offices. Bribes and fines and counter-bribes. Summary expulsion over the frontier. Prison and more bribes and fines and lawyers' fees. Ambulances, hospitals, bribes and fines and doctors' fees. Or, if the Indians were drunk enough or the politico was sufficiently sober, a shallow grave in the desert, a corpse rotting in the gully of a *barranca*.‡

If taxed about their xenophobia, the conduct of officials and police, and the national tendency towards violence, Mexicans might reply with justice that while it may be true that they do not like foreigners in general they have nothing against individuals who behave themselves. The same laws apply to both Mexicans and foreigners. The consequences of law-breaking in any country are likely to be unpleasant. As for crimes of violence, is the situation in Mexico so very much

---

* The Mexican *machete* is sword-shaped and between two and three feet long. It is carried in a leather scabbard attached to a belt round the waist. Its principal uses are agricultural.

† These examples of ice-breaking are based on incidents which occurred while I was in Mexico. Happily they are becoming increasingly rare. Although the murder rate is still high very few victims are foreigners.

‡ A deep precipitous valley. Those in Mexico City are often the haunts of criminals. They are also convenient for the disposal of corpses.

worse than in such great centres of civilization as London, Paris or New York?

Any foreigner who has experienced the generous warmth of Mexican hospitality would agree that good behaviour alone would be a low price at which to obtain it. But to behave well, according to the varying demands of the inhabitants, is an acquired art, while to transgress, even innocently, may prove disastrous. If this is true of the foreigner's relations with individuals, it is even more so when he comes up against the nation collectively in the shape of the law.

For most foreigners the law is a thug with a plastic-covered card and a gun. The Mexicans at least have the advantage of having had experience from birth of the accepted ways of contending with the lawless aspects of their own legal system.

Violence is, of course, not unique to Mexico. There are plenty of murders in every country and every large city. What often makes them unusual in Mexico is their motive. It is as well to know what playing the wrong tune on a guitar, refusing the offer of a drink or having a disagreement with another motorist may lead to. The fact that most people in Mexico carry a gun, and most of those who do not, carry a *machete*, may increase the satisfaction of the adventurous traveller in a journey successfully accomplished, but this is not likely to be the view of the ordinary visitor.

If travel in Mexico involves hazards, what are the compensations which make it worth while or even enjoyable?

There are obvious answers to this question: the beauty of the landscape, the picturesque appearance and intriguing character of its inhabitants, the exotic birds, animals and flowers, the ruins of the ancient civilizations, the crumbling churches and monasteries of New Spain, the new-world architecture of modern Mexico, the markets and festivals of the countryside, the jaguar- crocodile- and turkey-hunting, the playground pleasures of Acapulco, its sun, sex, high divers and deep sea fishing. With such a wide range to choose from no visitor should be left unsatisfied, providing, to take an example, he is prepared to enjoy the hunt although the jaguar fails to show up. Even when he realizes that there is little hope of finding his chosen quarry he may still return to Mexico year after year just for the excitement of the quest. For there are pleasures related to the very hazards of a journey which can make Mexican travel for some people, especially if they stay in the country long enough, an obsession. To understand this more completely it is necessary to return to my opening paragraph. So far I have only dealt with the surface, on which the foreigner moves, as thin ice; now it must be considered in its other aspect, as a sea into which it is impossible to sink.

If he travels to Mexico by air the European visitor will land first at the capital. Although it may be larger than he expected, he is not likely to find it very different from other great cities which have expanded rapidly in the last thirty years. There is something of Cairo in the dusty suburbs around the airport and the crowded pavements of the poorer quarters. There are streets in the commercial section not unlike those in certain districts of Milan; even a touch of Paris still lingers about the great avenue of the Reforma. On the whole he will find himself comparing more often than contrasting, but as the journey from Europe will have lasted less than twenty-four hours, this may not surprise him.

If he travels to New York by ship and thence by rail to Mexico City it will take between nine and twelve days according to the speed of the liner on which he crosses the Atlantic. If he goes all the way by sea to Veracruz, the voyage cannot take less than a fortnight. Either route entails a long journey by modern standards and the traveller from the old world may feel, on crossing the frontier at Laredo or disembarking from the Gulf, that he has the right to expect to find himself in a country which looks very different from any part of Europe.

To approach Veracruz by sea on a clear day when the frozen tooth of the volcano of Orizaba glitters in the tropical sky is a dramatic experience. But once the ship has anchored in the harbour, the town must surely impress the European with its familiarity rather than its strangeness. It is, after all, little more than a shoddy, though attractive, piece of old Spain, peopled by a race a shade darker than most southern Europeans and of a temperament about as languid as a Sicilian's in mid-siesta. Even the natural setting, perhaps because its vast scale minimizes the particular, is not strikingly exotic.

Approached from the north by train after the glass and steel beauty of New York and the neat cold-hearted towns strung out on the line, ephemeral-looking as huts shacked-up round building sites, the first glimpse of the Mexican fringe of a Texan city can produce in a European with a taste for the south the unlooked-for sensation of an actual home-coming. For these vivid, dark-thronged suburbs have a strong Mediterranean atmosphere by contrast with the orderly brick and chromium business blocks at the city's centre.

By the time the frontier is reached it is likely to be dark. The first view of Mexico will be at dawn the next day when the traveller is jolted awake by one among a score of unscheduled stops. Turning over in his sleeper he pokes up the blind and looks out. The rails run through the centre of a desert village. In the middle of a dirt square a man, wrapped to the eyes in a blanket and wearing a wide-brimmed hat, leans motionless against the trunk of a pepper tree. A figure so conventionally Mexican can hardly come as a surprise. It is the familiarity of his surroundings which astonishes. The mud brick houses bounding the square have their counterparts in thousands of villages on the shores of the Mediterranean, while the little whitewashed church, with its dome and twin towers, has a European distribution stretching from Cyprus to the Straits of Gibraltar. Even the pepper tree, itself an import from Peru, has also travelled east and may be remembered in Athens, if in no other place, where it droops its elegant form and casts its inadequate shadow over many of the principal streets of that city.

As the train moves south, it will be the same. For any one object which is new to him there will be a dozen which are familiar either because the influence of Europe is evident, as in most of the buildings, or because, as with the flowers, they have crossed the Atlantic to flourish in European soil. This discovery, consoling or disappointing according to temperament, will be confirmed when the traveller reaches the capital.

There are, of course, many reasons why Mexico should be reminiscent of Europe. It was not only colonized by Europeans, but with the destruction of the old civilizations it had to be re-invented by them as well. Naturally this process was carried out by the settlers as near as possible in the European

17

image. At first Spain served as a model, but when it fell out of favour France, in spite of the war of the cakes and the Maximilian episode, took its place. The evidence of French influence, now chiefly confined to the capital, still survives in elegant neo-classic façades, scattered over the city, and in the Reforma itself which was planned by Maximilian* as a Mexican counterpart to the Champs Elysées. Subsequently many different styles have been introduced, including that of fascist Italy, which continued to inspire, consciously or otherwise, the architects of government offices and public monuments long after the fall of Mussolini. North American influences strengthened with the Second World War, and today most construction is carried out in steel, glass and poured concrete, techniques to which Mexican architects have made outstanding contributions.

Modern Mexico, then, from the first had its face turned towards Europe. What was true of architecture was equally so of art, literature, science, philosophy, politics, dress, manners and social customs. Even the great Indian presidents, Juarez and Diaz, were both European in their political outlook. Although in many ways European influence may have been no more than a veneer, up to the beginning of the present century most of the country's man-made outward aspect and its people's articulate cultural development could be traced back to its re-invention in the mould of Europe.

But European civilization, as it came to Mexico, was already the outcome of influences and counter-influences which had shuttled backwards and forwards between east Asia and the Atlantic seaboard since the first stirrings of the human race. Pre-Hispanic Mexico was, in this respect, very different. The main tide of immigrants from north-east Asia, which peopled the North American continent, came to an end at the close of the last Ice Age when it was cut off by physiographic changes in the Bering Strait. The tribes of mixed Mongolian and Alpine stock brought with them a palaeolithic heritage which was sufficient to account for most of the Asiatic affinities to be found, particularly in religious concepts, among the civilizations which flourished in Mexico before the conquest.

---

* Or possibly by the Empress Carlotta as a replica of the Avenue Louise in Brussels.

There may have been more recent arrivals from Asia, but they can hardly have been on a large scale since they did not introduce such obvious technological developments as the art of writing or the wheeled vehicle. Most likely their intrusions were accidental, but it is not impossible that individual arte-facts brought with them may have influenced American craftsmen. Although some authorities attach great importance to post-Ice Age contacts with Asia, until they can produce more conclusive evidence it can be assumed that the civilizations of ancient Mexico arrived at their highest achievements without significant interference or inspiration from outside the American continent.

It would have been remarkable if peoples isolated at such an early stage had not developed differently from the Asiatics and Europeans who had the advantage of comparatively easy over-land routes between centres of culture, which automatically facilitated the cross-fertilization of ideas and techniques. If the original immigrants to the new world had any knowledge of agriculture, it was not until they reached central Mexico, where the conditions were favourable, that they could have applied it. Even then, the development of the maize plant, which provided their basic diet, must have taken them over a thousand years. Cut off, as these early agriculturists were, and subject to the inroads of nomads from the north less advanced than themselves, it is not surprising that their progress should have been retarded. At the time of the Spanish conquest their technology was still that of the Stone Age and their one great scientific achievement, the invention of an accurate calendar, had been put to the service of beliefs which blocked all hope of further intellectual progress.

This obsession with chronology illustrates the lack of interest in practical discoveries which appears to have been common to all the Indian civilizations. Although the computation of time may have had its origin in the need to determine the correct periods for the planting and harvesting of crops, it was de-veloped into an abstract study to which the mythology and religious conceptions of the race were attached. Thus in the end the people became the victims of an astronomically-controlled ideology, which dictated, according to the hour and day of their birth, not only their daily actions but the way in which they would die and what happened to them after death.

In other aspects of their culture they seem to have put their knowledge and skill to ends which, in the European view, appear to have missed the obvious practical application. The Maya invented a system of hieroglyphic writing which they used, so far as is known, mainly for the esoteric calculations in time to which I have already referred. The development of religious architecture in Europe and Asia was concerned with the need to provide a covered space for the worship of the deity. Although the climate of southern Mexico could have provided the same incentive, the Indians developed their architecture to exactly the opposite conclusion. Their great ceremonial sites, planned on a magnificent scale, were laid out in vast agglomerations of stairs, platforms and terraces, open to sun and rain, and dominated by huge pyramids set with flights of precipitous steps. The vaulted shrines usually amounted to no more than a few square feet of dark and windowless gloom.

Their failure to develop the use of the wheel is another example of this characteristic; for having discovered it they restricted its application to mobile toys for the amusement of their children.

Related to their negative attitude towards practical advancement was their extreme conservatism. Both characteristics must have had roots in the fatalistic nature of their religious concepts. Although ceremonial centres of the Mayans were abandoned and in some cases appear to have been destroyed, the essential character of their beliefs did not change, only the rites required by them became ever more rigorous and horrific. In the western world there have been long periods in which superstition has arrested man's development, but not quite to the same degree as in ancient Mexico. The apparent absence of any dissenting voice among the people is all the more remarkable when it is considered that, in addition to regulating almost every action of their daily lives, their priests demanded a vast toll of human sacrifice, culminating under Aztec rule in holocausts at which as many as twenty thousand victims were immolated at a time. Even the after-life offered little compensation. The best that could be hoped for by the Aztecs, and then only by warriors who died in battle, was to be transformed into humming birds; the worst which, through no fault of their own, awaited the majority of the population, was a long journey to oblivion through 'a wind of obsidian knives'.

Without going further into their beliefs and customs, it is clear that the Indians developed very differently from the descendants of their palaeolithic or early neolithic ancestors who remained on the other side of the Bering Strait. Their neglect of technological progress, their passivity under the fearful exactions of their priesthood, their courage and resignation in facing the horror of ritual warfare or the sacrificial knife, and above all, their hopeless but passionate obsession with time and death, whether they arouse our admiration or disgust, are racial characteristics which remain largely incomprehensible to the European mind.

For Cortés and his followers there was never any doubt that the Indians were worshippers of Satan, while the Indians on their side were quickly convinced by the sadistic cruelty of the Spaniards and their insatiable hunger for gold that they had been conquered by a race of devils. Few of the Spaniards concerned themselves with going deeply into the customs or beliefs of the people they had enslaved. Avid for personal gain and intent on the creation of an image of their own country in which to enjoy their prosperity, they had only one use for the Indians: to provide the labour with which to achieve these objectives.

As new towns sprang up all over the country with Spanish names, and churches and palaces built in the Spanish style, the invention of New Spain went forward rapidly. But what the Spaniards could not consciously invent or control was the character of the new race which their presence in Mexico was to produce.

The immense cleavage in temperament between the two people out of whose coupling the race was conceived, made its birth sordid and painful. It was, in the first instance, the produce of rape, and the childhood which followed was a long and melancholy one. As might have been expected, adolescence brought with it violence and confusion, but also, in the fight for independence, the first strains of nobility. The torment of a divided personality, struggling to find itself in the process of growing up, is reflected in the century of chaos which followed independence and which, after the brief deceptive calm of the

21

Diaz dictatorship, culminated in the blood bath of the revolution.

Today the young adult race which has emerged still exhibits the unease of its divided origin. Among the urban population, only the snobs or the politicians claim pure Spanish or Indian descent. The true Mexicans are a mixture and, if they think about themselves, they cannot help being aware of it. The great gulf of incomprehension and incompatibility which separated the two peoples of whose blood they are compacted has made the achievement of a comfortable synthesis difficult if not impossible. The race exists, however, in its own right, with characteristics which, though they may be hard to define, are surprisingly easy to distinguish, especially when the size of the country and variety of its climate are taken into account. Seen in a crowd anywhere between Monterrey in the north and Comitán in the south the people in the towns look and behave alike. Even among the peasants only the tribal Indians stand apart. The split occurs not in the race as a whole but in each individual. It is this which makes them unpredictable in outlook and reaction, which accounts for their instability in thought and conduct, and which makes possible their extreme and rapid changes of mood, so that a man who appears to be withdrawn at one moment into an almost sub-human torpor can be roused for no seemingly adequate reason to a sudden act of brutish violence or uncalculating humanity.

To return to the hypothetical foreigner who, however deeply he may have been impressed by the beauty of the country through which he has passed or the attractions of its cities, is still disappointed that here, in the heart of the new world, he should find after so long a journey so much to remind him of the old; thus far his reactions have been prompted only by outward appearances. They are not likely to be very different in regard to the first Mexicans with whom he comes into contact. Some may be polite and friendly, others sullen and hostile, but they will not strike him as very different from southern Europeans. Once his relations with them begin to develop he will quickly realize that he was wrong.

This discovery may stimulate him into hatred or affection, but even the most vapid and dollar-insulated tourist cannot travel in Mexico and remain indifferent to its inhabitants.

Once he has made himself in the smallest degree dependent on them, he will be subject to the vagaries of their mood and the mysterious logic of their actions. Although verbal communication with them may, for linguistic reasons, be difficult, even their silences are too formidable to be disregarded, while their presence alone, whether it exasperates, alarms or attracts, once noted (for sometimes they are so much part of the landscape as to be almost invisible) cannot be overlooked. Even when their profession demands subservience to a tourist's wishes, the appropriate mask fits them uneasily. If they feel themselves pressed too hard they may whip it off to reveal almost anything, or simply vanish. In either event the effect can be disconcerting, especially if the atmosphere is already hostile or the terrain desolate and remote.

To get on well with Mexicans requires care and discretion. Apart from self-interest, the trouble, if it is felt to be so, is worth taking. A smile is not their immediate response to an approach by a foreigner; but the appearance of two perfect rows of white teeth (the product of a diet of maize flour) in a soft copper-dark complexion, may be found a reward in itself. The amiability which follows may take odd forms, incur immense delay and end in total misdirection, but it is warm and genuine. Even in the most casual circumstances an actual break-through into friendship has the feel of an adventure and, if pursued, will lead to experiences, often enjoyable, sometimes with an alarming twist, but seldom dull. Frequently the traveller will emerge from them moved by the kindness and generosity with which he has been treated, especially by the very poor; but whatever his reactions, bewilderment will almost certainly prevail. There will have been unexplained comings and goings, answers which appear to bear no relation to questions asked, questions so mysterious as to have left him gaping for an answer, moments of optimism followed by moments of despair, an obvious solution, turned down without reason at the outset, belatedly produced with an air of the miraculous, and, at the end, a fabulous invitation or a vague backing away, a silence when there should have been speech, the solitude of an empty road stretching to a remote horizon, or the back-seat company of half a dozen old women and a gaggle of livestock.

After such initial contacts with the inhabitants, the foreigner will find that he begins to see the country itself differently. The things which struck him as familiar gradually become unimportant. The landscape is not only beautiful but strange. His earlier comparisons appear false. The vast horizons and exotic detail are like nothing which he has known before. Once he has dropped the habit of comparing, his untrammelled sensibility lies open to their full impact. The skies, clear or magnificently clouded, intoxicate. The splendid scenery and weird vegetation lure him on. Soon he leaves the tarred highway for the hazards of rutted tracks. Abandoning his car he hires a pony and takes to the mountain paths or the green clefts which lead off into forest and jungle. He must see everything, because he is convinced that somewhere in this country is a paradise which, once discovered he will never leave. Time and again in the grassy streets of an Indian village, beside a waterfall which comes tumbling out of the rain forest, its spray drifting among orchids and giant ferns, on some crescent of white sand shaded by palm trees, or at the edge of a jungle lake where the egrets skim in white arrows over the surface, he thinks that he has reached the end of his quest.

He is seldom right. On the first day everything is perfect. On the second he grows restless. The midges, which he hardly noticed when he arrived, swarm over his hands and face. He picks up his shoe in the morning and a tarantula scuttles out of it. The barking of a score of dogs keeps him awake or cockroaches run races over his pillow. Indians from a nearby village settle round his camp, silent and evasive. The air smells of decaying vegetation or human excrement. Wild cries outside his hut disturb him at night and in the morning there are bloodstains on the sand.

Even when he suffers no such vexations or alarms, by the third day he will feel the impulse to move on. The truth is that for most foreigners Mexico, with all its beauty and fascination, is a country to explore but not to inhabit. It is as if there were something hostile to settlement in the soil itself, something which the people who are born to it acknowledge, so that after four centuries of Christianity they continue to pay their furtive respects to the hierarchy of nature gods which terrorized their ancestors and by which they, themselves, can still be made to tremble as the night wind rasps by over the desert or the jungle creaks and shuffles round them in the dark.

Peasants always seem odd to the visitor from a country which possesses no true peasantry of its own. When their past is taken into account it is not surprising that peasants in Mexico should seem even odder than in most other places. But what of the educated Mexicans of the cities, the doctors, the university professors, the businessmen, are they really so different from their own kind in other countries? And if so, in what way do they show it?

The first question is hard to answer because of the difficulty of getting to know Mexicans well enough to discover what they are really like. The second is easier for it is in this very quality of unknowableness that they differ most from other people. The traveller hardly hopes to make real contact with the peasants, for their world is so evidently remote; but often he is surprised to find, once initial mistrust has been broken down, the extent to which they may reveal themselves if only by the questions they ask. The educated townsman is far more wary and his defences are almost impregnable. Above all he wants to avoid the feeling that he may have given any part of his real personality away. So he has to present a façade to protect himself not just from foreigners but from his fellow Mexicans as well. He does not care if its falseness is apparent so long as it remains intact. The more educated the Mexican, the more elaborate and misleading the façade.

But why do they feel the need to protect themselves? What is it that they have to hide? Is it an energy so violent that it must be screened off or only a vacuum which has to be kept sealed? The answer lies, I believe, in the racial duality which has already been discussed.

Every Mexican is aware, subconsciously or otherwise, that he is not one person but two: the aggressive Spaniard and the proud but passive Indian; the eternal conqueror and the eternal victim. The façade covers the split. For a Mexican to feel secure against the weakness of his own duality he must protect it against the probing of friend and enemy alike.

That each Mexican is a fortress armed against other Mexicans as well as against foreigners is not easily understood. Faced with defences which are too threatening to be ignored or an inscrutableness too contrived to be discounted as reserve, once again, as with the ever-present hostility of the countryside, the foreigner may feel himself rejected. He can make friends with Mexicans and enjoy their inexhaustible kindness and hospitality, but he can never get to know them. The guns may be lowered but the barricades are never down. If a chink does appear it usually reveals something so strange that he is left dazed with incomprehension. In a second it will be closed again. The façade will be as intact, mysterious and unreal as before.*

Like other foreigners I can only claim to have lived on the surface of Mexican life. I found its insecurity as stimulating as a drug and its impenetrability a challenge which I was incapable of resisting. This book is the record of journeys and encounters in a country by which I was fascinated to obsession. It is certainly among the most varied and beautiful in the world, as its people are among the most mysterious and, in their odd prickly way, the most likeable and attractive.

---

* A brilliant analysis of the Mexican character is given by the great Mexican poet, Octavio Paz, in his book, *The Labyrinth of Solitude*.

I
By the Pacific

There are three main roads from the United States border to Mexico City: through Eagle Pass along the central plateau, and from Brownsville down the east and from El Paso down the west coast. They are eight hundred, seven hundred and fifty, and one thousand four hundred and ninety miles long respectively. Two main roads continue south from the capital through the isthmus of Tehuantepec. The one in the east curves up through the peninsula of Yucatan and turns south again to reach the Hondos river, the frontier between Mexico and British Honduras. It is one thousand two hundred and seventy miles long. The road in the west is four hundred miles shorter. After leaving the isthmus it climbs through the Chiapas highlands and crosses into Guatemala at Ciudad Cuauhtemoc.

These figures are given because distances in Mexico are important. On journeys up and down the country north and south they may seem even greater than they really are since the scenery changes gradually and any one type of landscape may continue for hundreds of miles at a stretch. Cactus forests and mesquit plains, however fascinating at first sight, are so uniform that after a few hours they become tedious. Even the mountains, though more varied, can wear out the traveller when after interminable windings from one valley head to the next he still sees in front of him layer upon layer of corrugated crests receding to a remote horizon.

Journeying across the country east and west the distances are not so great. From Acapulco on the Pacific through Mexico City to Veracruz on the Gulf is only five hundred and forty miles. Moreover the changes in scenery are frequent and dramatic. This is specially true of the descent from the central plateau to the Gulf. Starting out from San Luis Potosí, for example, the road leaves the mine-scarred mountains, the source of the city's wealth, to cross a mesquit plain which quickly changes to a cactus desert. The land begins to drop and within a few miles the cacti are replaced by oak woods bearded with Spanish moss. Another fall and the road passes through a belt of cloud forest where giant ferns loll under the pines. At this level the lip of the mountains forms a barrier against which the Atlantic clouds roll in and anchor. Here and in the region below the rainfall is heavy and occurs at all seasons. A few more downward twists and the vegetation becomes tropical, a forest of vivid green crested with orchids and looped with creepers. The mountains sink to wooded hills. The valleys are rich with coffee and banana plantations. Beyond lies the low flat jungle stretching to the lagoons and oil wells on the Gulf.

The central plateau which can be dull in the north has some splendid scenery in the belt between Guadalajara and Puebla. Here the great snow-capped volcanoes of the high sierra rise from mountains flanked with pine forest. Lower down the terraced hillsides of maguey, an aloe-like cactus planted in formal rows, gives a mathematical beauty to the contours and perspective of the land. The air is thin and clear. Magnificent cloudscapes drift over swaying plains of maize. There are sudden drops where the vegetation becomes tropical. Its best season is the autumn when the colonial cities of soft yellow stone rise from fields of burnished stubble and the lakes are still full after the summer rains.

To the west the descent from the plateau is gradual at first and less spectacular than the fall to the east. But between Nayarit and Guerrero there is no flat coastal belt and the mountains drop directly to the sea. The forests which cover them are bright with flowering trees and flocks of parakeets. The white rim of the ocean sweeps in wide curves below broken by few bays or inlets secure enough to shelter even the smallest craft. Manzanillo and Acapulco are the two large towns on this mountainous coast. The tourist resorts of Zihuatanejo and Puerto Vallarta are limited in size because they depend on air transport. Only a few of the scattered fishing villages are accessible even by road. Since they are relatively unspoilt 'a tropical paradise' is often the description given of them individually in guide-books. The reservations, which follow, are rounded off by the prophecy that before long they will have acquired all the amenities of more popular resorts.

The road to this one such paradise winds down the mountains between trees submerged by waves of rose- and saffron-coloured creepers. A mile or so from the sea it plunges into a belt of palm forest, a world of green twilight under a thatch of fronds which shut out the sky. Lower down, it crosses a mangrove swamp which provides some of the best jaguar hunting in Mexico.

It was evening when I crossed this swamp and found myself among the stick huts and palm trees of the village. The adobe buildings beside the quay glowed in the sunset. I opened the door of the car and put my sandalled foot on to the track. Within seconds the gnats had descended on it in a seething, blood-sucking mass. I withdrew my foot and slammed the door. After dabbing insect repellent on the exposed areas of my skin I opened it again and stepped out. For half an hour, the gnats would keep their distance.

On the quay a reed awning sheltered the terrace of a deserted café. I sat down at one of the tables and watched the sun sinking over the bay. Some fishermen lounging on the opposite side of the track glanced in my direction without appearing to see me. I was just another *gringo** and they had decided to behave as if I did not exist. Nothing had been changed by my arrival. No one wanted to know anything about me, to sell me anything or to show off with a few words of English or a tune on a guitar.

The sun set, the glow slipped from the buildings and the stifling dusk came down like a bolster. A fishing boat drifted in from the bay. The crew, after tying it to a post, plunged into the water and waded ashore. Drawn by the sound of their splashing feet, the café-owner loomed in the doorway of his hut. All that showed of him was the white of his pants and the gleam of sweat on his torso. Although I was sitting at one of his tables, he, too, decided to ignore me. After nodding to the men as they went by he drew back into the darkness. Content, as so often in Mexico, to be the invisible man, I sat on until the whine of a gnat warned me that my half-hour of immunity was up.

---

* A contemptuous Latin-American nickname for North Americans, although it is frequently used in reference to other foreigners. Its origin is doubtful. Possibly a corruption of *hablar en griego*, to speak Greek, i.e. to talk unintelligibly.

I walked back to the car. It was time to cease being invisible and find somewhere to spend the night. I stopped at a hotel sign and walked in through the open door. It was built round a courtyard with a swimming pool in which there was a foot of water. A door close to the entrance had a 'bar' notice to one side of it and 'Joe's Cabin' written in gothic letters over the top. Inside there was a man who might have been Joe himself. He gave a welcoming grunt, but the shock of being seen for the first time was too much for me, so I turned and walked out.

A boy had stopped to inspect my car. When I asked him if there were any other hotels he looked as if he was going to bolt, but once he realized that I was talking Spanish, he grinned amiably and directed me down a track. At the end of it a single-storey building loomed among the palms against the last wash of the sunset. When I had stopped the car and switched off the engine I could hear the shrilling of crickets all round me and the clucking of bullfrogs in the swamp. I walked into the hotel and found that it was built on the same plan as Joe's Cabin, but on a larger scale. Beyond the open end of the courtyard I could hear the thump of Pacific rollers breaking on the shore. The courtyard itself was planted with bushes and a cluster of palm trees. The entrance hall and dining-room opened on to it without any dividing wall. The dining-room must have been equipped to seat a hundred people, but it was out of season and the whole place was deserted. Somewhere inside the building the trill of a single cricket went off with the urgency of an alarm clock. The sea thumped away in the darkness beyond the bushes. Suddenly a wave crashed down so loudly that I expected the surf to swirl in and carry off the chairs and tables. It withdrew with a heavy sigh and the cricket was once again left in command of the silence.

I went up to the reception desk to look for a bell, or if I could not find one, to use it as a sounding board for my fist. There was no bell, so I raised my hand, but just as I was about to bring it down, I noticed a clump of straight black hair resting against the desk on the inside an inch from the spot where I was about to strike. Lowering my hand I tapped the wood sharply with my knuckles. The hair moved in a half-circle, bobbed up and revealed a dark sleepy face beneath it. As the eyes opened wider they expressed faint surprise touched with derision. How did the *gringo* get in? What the hell does he want!

'Can I have a room please?'

'Yes, señor. We have fifty rooms.'

'I'd like one looking on to the sea.'

'They all look on to the sea, señor.'

'Just give me any room then.'

Without looking round he reached up to the key-board and took down the first key his fingers touched. After glancing at its number he moved out reluctantly from behind the desk. His shirt was very white against his dark skin but his black waiter's pants were rusty with stains. His complexion was a shade paler than the copper of the pure Indian or the reddish mahogany of the Negro half-caste. The inhabitants of the Pacific villages are often of mixed race or come from other parts of the country. Francisco, as I learned later, was a native of Veracruz. I followed him, weaving round the furniture in almost total darkness. We crossed into the courtyard among the hibiscus bushes beyond the bar. The surface of a small pool reflected the sky. Something jerked up in the middle of it.

'What's that?' I asked.

'An alligator, it's only a baby. There're plenty of big ones in the swamp.'

'Does it bite?'

'Only if you go close to it.'

'Can it get out of the pool?'

'Yes, of course, if it wants to.'

The key he had chosen fitted a door in the middle of the right-hand wing. The room looked out on to the bushes and the pool.

'But I want a room facing the sea.'

'None of the rooms face the sea, señor.'

'You told me they all did.'

'Yes. They face on to the courtyard and the courtyard faces on to the sea.'

The room smelt of mould as if it had not been occupied for months.

'The electricity'll come on in a minute.' Francisco struck a match and lit a candle which stood in a saucer on the table. At some time there had been an attempt to make the room attractive, but now the bed cover was stained, there were holes

31

in the mosquito mesh over the windows, and the veneer on the furniture had cracked. A curtained doorway led to a lavatory and shower. Water dripping from the cistern had made a pool on the floor, but by candle-light it looked clean, and the lavatory worked.

Somewhere at the back of the building a generator started up. Gradually the bulb hanging from the ceiling took on an inward glow. Soon it had brightened enough to make a mock of the candle flame. This was luxury. There was nothing wrong with the room which a day's airing, a good scrub and a dose of insecticide would not put right. Then why was it all so depressing? Perhaps because, like many other hotels of its kind in Mexico, it had obviously aimed high at the start. Whoever had built it had believed in the theory of the tropical paradise. But, for some reason, the expected tourists had failed to turn up. Probably the midges were too much for them or the road south rushed them on to pleasure grounds with established reputations. Whatever the cause, the village, on its strip of land between the swamp and the sea, was, even metaphorically speaking, in low water. But from what I had seen of it so far, armed as I had been against the gnats, I was inclined to think that it probably was a paradise of a kind. Even if the hotel depressed me, I could put up with it for a few days while looking for somewhere more congenial to live.

I unpacked, took a shower, changed into a clean shirt, and set out for the restaurant. Rather than risk a false step with the alligator, I kept to the path which ran along the side of the block. On reaching the hall I found that the place had brightened up. Francisco was behind the bar wearing a white jacket and a black tie. Red and blue bulbs glowed in the hibiscus bushes behind him. There was still no sign of other guests, but three waiters stood among the tables gossiping.

'Good evening, señor, everything all right?'

The proprietor came towards me from the reception desk.

'Fine, thank you.'

'Are you American?'

'No, I'm English.'

'My first English visitor! You must have a drink.'

We sat down at the bar and Francisco served us. I learned that the man who built the hotel had run out of money and had been forced to give it up. His successor had also failed but this was not surprising: he had had no idea of how to run the place.

'I've only been here a couple of months myself, but once I've put it in order and people get to know about it, it's bound to be a success. You haven't seen the beach, have you? Miles of sand and the safest bathing in Mexico. Excellent fishing, too. I haven't got a boat yet but I can get one for you from the village. Then there's the lagoon. That's really beautiful. If I wasn't so busy I could spend hours coasting about under the trees. It's good for hunting, too. If you give me a few days I can fix you up with a jaguar.'

I was feeling hungry so I thanked him for the drink and sat down at one of the tables. When I had finished dinner he was still by himself at the bar.

'Francisco was telling me that our baby in the garden gave you a fright. You needn't worry, we always keep it on a chain.'

I did not think a chained alligator could be either happy or secure, but I did not say so.

'Are there many in the swamp?'

'Very few. They keep shooting them.'

'I'd like to see one in its wild state. Would that be possible?'

'It's rather difficult, but if you take a boat out before sunrise you might be lucky.'

'I think I'll do that.'

With the excuse of an early start I went to bed.

In spite of the humidity and the smell of mould I slept soundly and it was already beginning to grow light when I woke up. I dressed quickly and drove to the point where the road crossed the swamp on the outskirts of the village. There were dozens of canoes moored along the bank. As I got out of the car a boy approached and asked me if I wanted to go fishing. I told him that it was not fish but alligators that interested me. Nothing easier! He knew several places where we'd be sure to find some. I followed him down to the water and he pulled one of the canoes close to the bank. I was about to step into it when he asked me if I had forgotten my gun. I replied that I had no gun to forget.

'My uncle has a rifle. He'll lend it to you for twenty pesos.'

If we delayed longer the sun would be up. I explained that I did not want to kill an alligator but only to see one. His astonishment turned to suspicion. Screwing up his eyes he backed away. The wish to see an alligator without killing it was too eccentric to be convincing. Perhaps he thought that, once out in the swamp, I planned to knock him on the head and steal his tin cross from round his neck.

Pulling a notebook from my pocket I told him that I was an artist and wanted to draw an alligator in its native haunt. Fortunately I had made some sketches in the book. When he saw them he was reassured. The canoe had drifted away, but now he pulled it in again. It was a long narrow dug-out. He directed me to sit three feet from the stern and placed himself just behind me. We glided across a clear stretch of water and entered a tunnel which opened into the mangroves on the other side. The enclosed air was so cold that I began to shiver but the boy, who wore his shirt open to the navel, did not bother to button it up.

The stems of the mangroves rose above us in a dense tangle through which the early light had scarcely begun to filter. Silent at first, the swamp was soon loud with bird calls. An egret slipped off a branch and swooped in a low glide over the water. We turned into a narrower tunnel. The canoe slowed down, its bow nosing to the edge of a pool, and stopped. The boy pointed at the mud bank on the other side. I stared at it with straining eyes but could see nothing. After a few minutes he shook his head and paddled on. The next time we stopped I made out a long dark object lying half submerged in the water. When it did not move I told the boy to paddle closer. It proved to be a log.

The sky had now turned to a pale brilliant yellow. Every leaf and twig of the intricate network above us was etched against it. At any moment the sun would be up and there would be even less chance of seeing an alligator. Clumps of pink lilies were now visible among the mangrove roots. A belted kingfisher let us pass within a few yards without moving. The sun rose and the dark foliage began to glitter. There was a sudden imbecile screeching in the air. I looked up as a volley of green parrots swept by over the trees. A splash sounded behind us and the boy gave a yell: *'Caimán!'**

---

* Alligator.

34

I jerked round rocking the canoe. Large rings spread out over the water.

'It doesn't matter, señor, it moved so quickly you wouldn't even have had time to get out your pencil.'

Back at the hotel I decided to go down to the beach for a swim. The sand was muddy and a line of refuse lay along the rim of the tide. The sea was flat for a hundred yards, then there were breakers. I waded towards them and was more than half-way out before the coffee-coloured water had reached to my knees. Invisible creatures kept scuttling round my feet. A sudden sharp nip sent me leaping forward. As soon as my foot touched the bottom it was nipped again. I gave up and plunged back to the shore.

In the hope of finding a more attractive place to bathe I started walking along the sand. As it curved away from the village it became cleaner. The line of breakers receded and the intervening stretch of water looked clear and deep. I had just decided to go in again when I noticed some turkey vultures sitting on a black rock. I had never seen these birds close to, so I walked on more slowly hoping for a good view of them before they flew off. To my astonishment they let me approach to within twenty yards. Their occupation was puzzling. Were they sharpening their beaks, or cracking shell-fish on the rock? Or were they actually—but this was not possible!—tearing large hunks out of the rock itself?

When I was only a few paces away they glanced up resentfully and flopped off with a couple of wing beats to some near-by scrub. But my attention was fixed on the perch they had just left, for now I saw that it was not a rock they had been sitting on but the recently washed-up carcass of an eight-foot shark. I walked round to its head and inspected the jaws. They were ten inches long and had a formidable battery of teeth.

I moved away, and the great birds, looking like diseased and ill-disposed barnyard turkeys, flounced back to their feast. Although I no longer intended to bathe, I continued my walk. Far ahead I could see a stretch of sparkling white sand backed by palm trees. I was determined to go on until I reached it but the shore curved inland and I was confronted by an outlet from the swamp. The water was yellow and in contrast to the pure air of the swamp that morning, it stank like a sewer. It was impossible to judge its depth and I had no wish to experiment. After a lingering gaze at the white beach and the palm trees I turned round and walked back to the hotel.

Tired from my early excursion I slept until late in the afternoon. I was hungry when I woke up but fearing that I might discourage the proprietor if he trapped me into a description of my visit to the beach, I set out to find a restaurant in the village. On the outskirts I stopped at a hut to buy some bananas. The girl who served me had smooth dark skin, and the fine bones and demure expression of a Madonna in a Flemish primitive. When I asked her where I could eat, she could only suggest Joe's Cabin or the café by the harbour. I walked through the village and sat down at the same table in the café as on the previous evening. It was the same hour, the sunset glowed on the buildings and a fishing boat came gliding in with its catch. A cloud of gnats descended on me and had to be warned off with repellent. The same men ignored my presence from the other side of the road, and the café owner came to the door of his hut without a glance in my direction.

Tropical paradise or not, I realized, as I munched through the bananas, that I had fallen in love with the place, with the alligators I would never see, and the strip of white sand I would never reach and above all with the slow torrid rot of the existence which it offered and from which I would inevitably turn away. I imagined the easy sloughing-off of responsibilities, the carefree decline into depravity and the final stages of physical degradation, my evening walk to the café turned to a shuffle, the gnats clustered on my skin when, immune to their bites, I would no longer bother to brush them away.

But the bananas had not satisfied my hunger. As I could not bring myself to break the spell of my invisibility by asking the café owner if he could give me something to eat, I decided to return to the hotel. I took a path which led behind some shacks on the seashore. As I passed one of them, a little white-shirted figure came out from the shadows and caught my arm.

'Hi! Johhny! What are you doing here?'

Peering down I recognized Francisco. His hair was even more tousled than when I had roused him from behind the reception desk. But now he was very much awake.

'Going back to the hotel. What are you doing?'

'It's my evening off. Let's have a drink.'

We crossed the plank verandah of the nearest shack and sat down at a metal table. 'What d'you want? Beer?'

'Yes, but I must eat.'

'That's all right.' He turned and shouted an order into the black opening of the doorway behind us. There was no reply—but a generator was turned on and a string of bulbs overhead bloomed into a light bright enough to extinguish the last glitter of the sunset. A moment later the sound of the waves was banished by a blast of *mariachi** music from loudspeakers set in each corner of the verandah roof.

Francisco's mouth was opening and shutting, but I could hear nothing of what he said. A boy came out with the beer and I bawled for food. Blank-faced he gaped at me. I pointed to the loudspeakers and put my fingers to my ears. He looked astonished and then crestfallen, but he went back into the café and turned down the volume. It had already been apparent to me that Francisco's mouthings were repetitive. Now, as his words became audible, I found that I had not been mistaken.

'You want girls? Beautiful girls? You want them? I fetch them down? Right?'

'Down from where?'

'From up there. Beautiful girls! Beautiful!' Eager-eyed, he leaned forward and pointed over my shoulder. I turned and saw that in the corner behind me a flight of wooden steps led up to a hole in the verandah roof. The structure of the café looked hardly strong enough to support a second storey. I had a vision of a flock of little dark Madonnas, sisters of the banana girl, gliding down the steps out of the night sky.

The pad of bare feet sounded over the boards. Turning I saw a tough-looking character with gold teeth and a broken nose sauntering towards us. Francisco jumped up, gave him an *abrazo*†

---

* Troops of musicians who can be hired for parties or serenades. Their instruments include fiddles, guitars and trumpets. They wear *charro* costumes. This is a kind of superior cowboy outfit: leather jacket and tight suede trousers with silver studs and embroidery, a vast hat usually decorated with gold or silver braid, gun-belt, pistol and spurs.

† A friendly embrace. Each man puts his arm half-way round the other and pats his back.

and muttered excitedly into his ear. The man nodded and moved closer holding out his hand. Francisco introduced us. 'My friend, Juanito, champion boxer of Nayarit.'

Juanito's grip clamped on my fingers like the slam of a door. 'You want girls,' he said. 'I'll get them.'

'What I really want is something to eat.'

'Girls first, eat afterwards.' He strolled over to the steps and shouted up through the hole in the roof. Harsh cackles broke out in the darkness above. Grinning, he came back and sat down at our table. 'Three times champ!' He pulled his shirt-sleeves up to the shoulder and tensed his biceps. The muscles popped up like croquet balls. I expressed my admiration. Francisco ordered another round of beer. This time six bottles arrived. As the boy put them down, the wooden steps creaked loudly. I looked round and saw a pair of elephantine legs descending from out of the roof. As the thighs appeared, perilously restricted by a skirt wrinkled to the crotch, the ladder shuddered again and a second pair of vast fleshy pillars began their descent. These were followed by yet a third only a step behind. When all three women had reached the floor, I saw that the promise of their lower limbs was fulfilled in the rest of their bodies. Female mestizo giants, they waddled towards us, sporting with a give-away nonchalance under splitting envelopes of black and purple satin enormous buttocks, breasts and bellies. They settled themselves between us, but continued to cackle at each other over our heads. Their dog-jowled faces were pasty with powder, and the dye on their greasy hair was streaky.

I intended to finish my drink and go, but the boy brought another round before I was half-way through the bottle.

'Drink up!' Francisco shouted. 'Fine *muchachas*, eh? Which one do you like?'

The music had stopped and in the pause, while the boy was changing the record, I could at least be sure that I was heard.

'This one,' I said, giving a squeeze to the trollop on my right. 'But I must get something to eat first.' I pulled out a note to cover the beers, 'I'll be back.'

But Francisco was not listening. His gaze, fixed on the other side of the café, had taken on a lunatic glee. I turned and saw three enormous men, the perfect counterparts of our women, glaring at us from under wide felt hats from the edge of the verandah. They lumbered forward menacingly, but halted after a few steps and slumped down at a table. The boy abandoned the pick-up and ran to serve them.

'Who are they?' I asked.

'The biggest bastards in Mexico!—They think they can run the whole place and rob every poor bugger of his last peso! But they're out of luck this time. We've got their women, see! My! They're going to be mad at us!'

The music blared again. 'Come on!' he shouted. 'Dance!'

'But I don't want to dance!'

'You've got to! If you don't they'll come and get your girl. Understand?'

I did not; but assumed that there must be some polite convention which would hold them back from wrenching the women out of our arms while we were actually on the floor. Francisco's malice was infectious. They were an ugly-looking trio. I caught hold of my woman and launched out with her. She was nimble for her size. As we wheeled round, her body melted over me like hot butter. The record seemed to go on interminably. When it stopped we had only time to gulp down another bottle before we were on our feet again. By the end of the third dance I was out.

'Look here, Francisco! This is your quarrel, not mine. They can have this old cow if they want her. I'm giving up.'

He began to protest but, catching sight of a man riding past on a bicycle, broke off and shouted at him to join us. The cyclist swerved, bounced his wheels up on to the floorboards and stopped by our table. He was already very drunk but he picked up a bottle and emptied it. When the music started again, he took my partner and tottered off with her round the floor.

Left alone I glanced across at our rivals and saw that all three were staring at me. They were drinking hard and their table was already covered with empty bottles. I gazed at the moths circling the light bulbs overhead, but I was mentally weighing our boxer's muscles against the chances that the others carried guns. When the dance ended my stand-in refused to stay. Without a word he mounted his bicycle and wobbled off into the night.

There was no alternative but to keep going. I lunged round half a dozen times. Then the cyclist reappeared, took over for a dance and vanished again. But the pace had become slower. The boy, growing drowsy, left longer pauses between each record. The women too had begun to tire. Suddenly at the end of a dance they wandered, clutching each other, to the steps. Up they went on all fours, sighing and farting, until with a final creak the last pair of flower-pot ankles disappeared through the roof.

As I turned from watching them, Francisco's head banged down on to the table. The boxer caught it by the hair and shook it. When it fell forward again among the bottles, he got up with a grin and began to back slowly away.

'What're you doing? Don't go!'

I jumped up but already he was out on the sand. I ran to the edge of the verandah. 'Hi! Come back!' For a second I caught a gleam of gold teeth, then he was gone.

I went back to the table and shouted for the boy.

'How much?' I waved at the empty bottles.

'What for?'

'The drinks, of course!'

'But they've been paid for.'

'Who by?'

'The gentlemen over there.'

I turned round. Two of the trio had collapsed over the table. The third, still upright, gave a slight bow in my direction. I walked slowly towards him. He half rose and held out his hand. 'Professor Rogerro Flores de la Gracias y Montaña at your service.' I took his hand, thanking him and protesting at his generosity.

'It's nothing. Sit down and have a last bottle before you go.' As I pulled up a chair beside him he waved towards his unconscious friends, introducing the one as chief of the Fish Co-operative and the other as Captain of the Customs House. His voice was thick and unsteady, and he kept closing his eyes.

'And you, Professor, what do you do yourself?'

'Well, I'm just a professor, and you?'

'I'm a professor too. What's your subject?'

He blinked first one eye and then the other. The pupils had gold flecks and the irises were yellow.

'History. I teach history.'

'The history of Mexico?'

'No, history. The history of our town.'

'Is it very old?'

His eyes were shut tight again and he paused before he answered.

'As old as anything can be.'

'Are there any pre-Columbian remains?'

This time the pause was even longer.

'I don't know, I've never heard of any. But I can tell you all about the Fish Co-operative. It's pure Marxism, quite, quite pure. The purest in all Mexico.' His voice trailed off and his great head rolled on to his shoulder. It looked as if it would be some time before he spoke again.

When I woke up in the hotel it was still dark. I knew at once that there was something wrong. At first I could not decide what it was. Then I noticed the smell. I got up and opened the door. The wind had changed. It was blowing straight off the outlet of the swamp. I slammed the door and got back into bed, but I could not sleep. The yellow eyes of the professor haunted me, and every minute the smell became stronger and more sickening. At last I got up, dressed and packed my suitcase. I moved quietly through the empty hall of the hotel and left an envelope with some notes in it on the reception desk. Then I went out to the car and drove away. Crossing the swamp I again regretted the alligator I had not seen. Although the sudden urge to get out of the place had been irresistible, I knew that whenever I thought of it in the future I would want to go back. Swinging up through the palm forest my head-lights caught a pair of eyes, as yellow as the professor's, in the undergrowth. When the car came out into the open I rolled down the windows and let in the pure mountain air.

2

San Juan
under the Volcano

No mountain air could have had a purer tang than that of the Toluca highlands on the day of my first visit to San Juan. Don Julian had told me how to reach the village but I was soon lost and had to stop to ask a peasant the way. He pointed to a track which split off from the paved road like a tapering scar across the cornfields. The entire bed of the valley, scooped out between the Desierto range and the Nevada, was planted with maize. Only here and there the acres of plumed stalks were broken by a line of pepper trees or a mud brick village.

'It doesn't look a very good road.'

'Don't worry, señor! The bus goes along it every day.'

As I turned down the track, dust billowed out from under the wheels and drove in through the floorboards. Swallowed up by the corn, I lost the circling sweep of the plateau. Straight ahead the land heaved into foothills overhung by the splayed apex of a volcano. Against the brilliant sky the colour of its flanks ranged from blue to brick-dust. The upper rim of its crater was tipped with bright snow. At the first village the houses hemmed the car so close that I had to reverse to take a corner. Beyond, the track became less certain and the rocks jutting out from it more formidable. The corn brushed the wings of the car and camomile flowers scented the air as the tyres crushed over them. I overtook groups of peasants on foot or on horseback, all heading in the direction of San Juan. I had to concentrate hard to keep the car on the track. Once when I glanced too long at the volcano, a stone ripped through the exhaust and its roar scattered nearby horsemen into the fields.

'Is it much further to San Juan?'

'No, señor, you're almost there.'

Several times I had to stop to clear large rocks from the

surface. With the engine switched off the only sound was the slapping of the breeze in the corn stalks. Soon I had to ask the way again.

'To the right, señor. Up there in the valley. You'll see the church tower in a moment.'

I kept glancing ahead but could see no building of any kind. I was coming close to the foothills and the track, which had been climbing steadily, began to swoop and plunge. The corn-fields broke into patches cut off from each other by tracts of waste-land and covered with rye grass and horned poppies. Some straggling pepper trees marked the course of a river. The track wound beside it and then, with a twist, pitched down the bank and split into a net of narrow paths threading among the boulders.

I stopped the car and got out. From the tyre-marks I could see that the bus had been high enough off the ground to clear dozens of large rocks. In the river it had sloughed up to its axles through a mud bank. It would have been useless to try to go any farther in the car, so I went back and locked it up. As I turned I heard a shout and saw Don Julian and his eldest son, Saturno, riding down the bank on the opposite side. They crossed the water and dismounted. Don Julian greeted me with an *abrazo*.

'I thought you wouldn't be able to get across. It was all right up till a week ago, then we had a storm. Even the bus couldn't get through for a couple of days.'

Released from his bear hug, I shook hands with Saturno, who offered me his pony. When I had mounted, Don Julian swung himself into his saddle and we set out across the river with the boy splashing behind us.

The snow on the crater had only been there since the storm, Don Julian told me. In the valley hailstones had fallen inches thick. The crops had been damaged, but most of the villagers, following his advice, had insured with the government. The few who had not done so were ruined. It was often difficult to get the people to do what was best in their own interests.

On the opposite bank we joined up with peasants who had come by another route. They were friends of Don Julian. Soon they were all talking fast in country accents which I found difficult to follow. We climbed on through the hills into an upper valley where the volcano rose directly above us and pine-covered spurs curved down on either side. Here, marigolds crowded the verges of the track. Beside the stream there were banks of blue lupins. At the far end of the valley the sunlight, slanting from above the volcano, caught the flat roofs of houses and shimmered on the dome and bell tower of a church. From a distance the village looked impressive, but as we came closer, it turned out to be a simple collection of mud cottages which filled the hollow as if they had subsided into it after an earthquake. The baked bricks were crumbling and there were fewer walls intact than those in decay. The crowd so thronged the narrow streets that they appeared in danger of cracking open. Children scampered everywhere. Galaxies of young men and girls paraded up and down past scarcely less volatile groups of gossiping elders, while through them all, cavorting, sun-dark cowboys pranced their ponies on little puff-balls of smoking dust. In the church tower the bells jangled. Showers of fire crackers burst above the dome.

As we rode along the main street, a rutted track like the rest but slightly broader, Don Julian was greeted from all sides. Although he was a peasant himself with nothing in his appearance or manner to set him apart, he clearly drew from his friends not only affection but respect. Riding behind him I received, because I was his guest, almost as many smiles as he did.

San Juan was a small village with a population of not more than five hundred. The crowd, apart from the actual inhabitants, had come in from neighbouring villages no bigger than San Juan itself. This, then, was not one of those important fiestas which drew buses from the towns, wayside merchants, feathered dancers, swings, switchbacks and ferris wheels. Here, only a few old women sold *tacos** at makeshift stalls and the only mechanical amusement was a minute children's roundabout worked by hand. The chief enjoyment which the people so far seemed to be taking in the day was that of finding themselves together. There was a sustained babble of talk as friends

---

* Meat, chicken, cheese or vegetables wrapped up in tortillas and fried in oil. Tortillas are maize pancakes which take the place of bread in the diet of most Mexicans.

44

were sighted and greetings exchanged. Although there were few raised voices and little laughter, everyone was gay and smiling. Some of the young men carried guitars. Early drunks staggered about clutching at the tolerant sober for support. White teeth gleamed in reddish-brown faces, new hats shone like haloes and silk *rebozos** glistened in the sun. Then we came to the soldiers.

There were only two of them. They stood with their backs against the mud bricks of a cottage. A space had been left clear on either side of them across which people passed quickly, keeping close to the houses opposite. I first glimpsed their smooth helmets, dome shapes of olive green, above the sea of straw crowns and curling brims in front of us. Their incongruity alone was sinister, but it was the expression on the little dark faces, framed by the curving metal, which shocked. The two men, evidently recruited from the same Indian tribe, were almost identical in appearance. Their near-black skin fitted smooth and firm over their high cheek-bones. The upper halves of their faces under the helmets were blacked out by bands of shadow as by masks through which only their white eye-chinks glistened. But it was the set of their mouths, the lips curled back a little from the teeth, which expressed what was only dormant in the rest of their features, a bristling animal brutality. Their short bodies were packed tight into canvas battle-kit and from under each right arm a sub-machine gun poked out horizontally, its breech stuffed with a loaded magazine.

When we had passed them, keeping like the rest of the crowd as far away as possible, I caught up with Don Julian and asked him why they were there.

'They always send them when there's a fiesta. They're supposed to prevent trouble, but if there is any, they're usually the cause of it.'

'Are there only two of them?'

'Oh no. A dozen or more. They're posted all over the village.'

'What do they expect to happen?'

---

* Long woven shawls worn by the women and frequently used as a carrier for their babies.

45

'Nothing. They're just hoping for a chance.'

'What for?'

'To let off their guns, and see what they can get out of us before they stop.'

While talking we had turned down another track and now on the fringe of the village we halted outside Don Julian's house. Saturno took the ponies and we walked into a small yard. Flowers grew everywhere, flourishing on disorder. A rose bush sprawled over a dung heap, dahlias sprouted from the spokes of a discarded wheel and some piglets had made their home in a clump of geraniums. The mud brick cottage had only one windowless room. The kitchen was in a little shed propped against the wall. From its open end Don Julian's wife, Eleonora, came out to welcome us. A small, frail woman, she looked young for the size of her family. The eldest daughter, Guadalupe, a girl of twenty-four, and Roberto, a younger brother of Saturno came out with her, while other children, three boys and a little girl carrying a baby, peered out from the shelter of the kitchen. Eleonora withdrew at once to get on with her cooking, but Guadalupe brought some chairs and Roberto fetched a bottle of tequila* and some glasses. Don Julian poured me a drink but refused to take one himself. We sat down in the sun with the family watching us.

This was the last day of the fair. The day before there had been cock-fighting. Don Julian pointed to a little red, stream-lined bird which was pecking viciously on the dung heap. It had won him two hundred pesos. He never gambled at cards or bought lottery tickets, but he always kept a few cocks and usually one or two turned out champions. This afternoon there was to be steer-riding and Saturno was to try his skill. As he spoke the boy himself came in from tethering the ponies. I wished him luck and his red face became even redder.

A girl, whom I had not seen before, emerged from the kitchen. Taller than the others, she was fair-skinned and had mild, brown eyes. Her parted lips gave her an easy docile look. She was pregnant and her domed belly lifted the front of her skirt above her knees. Don Julian ignored her. I was curious and asked who she was.

---

* Made from the maguey cactus. It is usually drunk with salt and lemon.

46

'That's Celia. Saturno's wife.'

I had met Saturno several times with his father in the town. He looked a young sixteen, I had never thought that he might be a husband.

'They've got a child already.' He waved towards the baby which his own small daughter was holding. 'And now, as you see, they're going to have another.'

'How about Roberto?'

'He has a *novia*.* They'll be married at Christmas.'

'And Guadalupe?'

'She must wait a little. We haven't found the right husband for her yet.'

The girl blushed. Her figure was already growing dumpy. At twenty-four she would soon be past marriageable age. In her father's patriarchal view, her brothers could marry and breed as young as they liked, but the girls could have no such freedom. He needed Lupe to stay at home and work. He loved her more than his sons and he depended on her. It did not occur to him that she had the right to a future outside his own wishes. Recently, a young man had asked her to marry him. He had agreed to wait six months for an answer. She realized it was her last chance, but she was too afraid of her father to tell him. If Don Julian was stuck in the old ways as regards his children, in anything which concerned the welfare of the village he was passionately progressive. He had persuaded the farmers to take to new methods and to plant new crops. The fruit trees which flourished lower down in the valley had been bought cheap from the government at his suggestion. Without his efforts there would have been no track for wheeled vehicles and no bus. He had told me of other plans which he hoped to realize. I asked him how they were getting on.

'Slowly; but we'll have the water fixed by the New Year. They brought the first load of pipes last week. They're up by the spring. It's a nice spot under the trees, but it makes a long trek to fetch water. We can go there if you like.'

We rose from our chairs and he directed Lupe with a nod to come with us. We walked up through the village between

---

* The girl to whom a young man is betrothed. The word is often used simply for a girl friend.

47

crumbling walls overhung by trumpet vine and bougainvilia. Open doors led into yards full of flowers and refuse, or little dark rooms in many of which the only furniture was a chair and a sewing machine. In this upper part of the village there were few people about. When we reached the open space in front of the church, it was deserted. The bell still clanged in the tower turning over and over on a horizontal beam. Three little boys sat below it. One tugged the bell-rope while the others set off bangers which burst with a scarcely visible flash against the midday sky. The door of the church was open. As we passed it, Lupe asked me if I would like to see the decorations; she had helped with them herself. Don Julian said that they were not worth seeing. I'd much better take a look at the school. He pointed to a near-by shack. It was distinguished from the neighbouring cottages by its windows, but they had neither glass nor frames. Didn't I think it a disgrace that children should have to be taught in such a hovel? He was trying to get the government to give them one of the new pre-fabricated buildings and to appoint a teacher who would live in the village instead of coming up for a few hours daily in the bus.

Leaving Don Julian with his shoulders hunched in disapproval, I followed Lupe out of the sunlight into the black vault of the church. For a few moments the darkness clamped over my head like a shutter. The air was cold, but heavy with the musk of burnt copal* and the sweet sickliness of wilting flowers. Suddenly the bell stopped ringing. In the silence I heard a soft padding on the earth floor. Its rhythm beat into the darkness a pattern of sound which was powerfully hypnotic. As my sight began to come back I made out a group of small white figures, apparently suspended a few inches from the ground, struck in frozen stillness at the steps of the altar. The padding was all round them and with it a movement of dark jerking shapes. But my blindness lifted rapidly and I soon saw that the motionless figures were young girls wearing long white dresses and white scarves on their heads. Their brown feet and ankles were bare and hardly visible against the earth floor. Behind the altar a wall of white flowers reached to the roof.

---

* The resin extracted from the copal tree. Used as incense today as in ancient times.

Children at their first communion, I thought, but I soon realized that I was wrong. The tall candles were unlit and there was no priest before the altar and no congregation. Except for the girls who stood ranked behind each other, two by two, and the six dancers who pranced up and down on either side of them, the church was empty. The girls were absolutely still and looked straight ahead towards the altar. The dancers were men. They wore dark clothes and their faces were hidden by masks. Some of these were cut out of rabbit's fur. Others were of crudely carved wood, stained black, with tufts of fur outlining the features. One man held a long stick with a snake's head carved at the end of it. When he pulled a wire, which ran down the length of the stick, the wooden jaws snapped. All the dancers moved to the same rhythm, their feet drumming with rapid intricacy on the beaten floor. Although their steps never faltered, their bodies had a drunken reel and the sour smell of sweated pulque* reeked through the sweetness of the decaying flowers. As they danced they plucked at the girls' dresses and the man with the snake snapped its jaws round their ears.

'It took us all day,' Lupe said, leading me towards the flower-backed altar.

'I'm not surprised. It's beautiful.'

Although we spoke very quietly the snake-man heard us. He turned and without breaking the rhythm of the dance came slowly towards us waving his stick. The little girls looked round and stared with solemn brown faces. But when the snake snapped close to my nose they began to giggle. As we retreated towards the door the man pursued us prodding and snapping. The children's laughter rose in a shrill chorus, but was drowned as the bells clashed out again and a salvo of fire crackers burst above the roof.

Outside in the sunlight Don Julian stood waiting, a solid, square-set figure under his cocked sombrero.

'What were they doing?' I asked Lupe. But her father cut in before she could answer.

'A lot of nonsense!' Turning abruptly he led us forward again on our walk.

'Was it some kind of religious ceremony?'

---

* Beer made from the juice of the maguey cactus.

'No, of course not. Just a game.'

'But doesn't the priest object?'

'We haven't got a priest. We've done very well without one since the revolution.'

'Then you don't have any services in the church?'

'Only once a year. On the feast of San Juan a priest comes up from Tenango to say mass.'

We had taken a path which ran uphill beside a stream. At the top where the village straggled to an end, there was a grove of cedars. In the shade under their branches women stood gossiping. They carried buckets and earthenware pots. A pile of iron pipes was stacked on one side. Don Julian walked up to them and made them ring with an affectionate tap from his boot.

'They're going to make a difference to our lives,' he said. 'It's all right up here on a fine day, but it's not so pleasant in a rainstorm or when it's snowing in winter. But the water's good. You must try it.'

We walked in under the trees to where the women were standing. A wall built against the hillside was pierced by three holes from which the spring gushed into a stone trough. I stopped and cupped some of the ice-cold water to my lips.

'There'll be six taps in the village, so no one'll have far to fetch it.'

'They have a lot to thank you for.'

'No. Everyone's joined in and the government's helped. What we want now is electricity.'

'You'll have to wait a long time for that.'

'Not so long. The plan's been agreed to. If we raise half the money, the government'll raise the other half. We've already got a good sum towards it. After the harvest we ought to be able to find the rest. Life's never going to be easy for us up here, but there's no reason why we shouldn't make the best of it.'

When we got back to the cottage Don Julian's friends, who had been invited to eat with us, had already arrived. After I had drunk a glass of tequila with them, Lupe announced that the meal was ready. We all went inside but only the men sat down at the table. The cottage had an earth floor. The mud brick walls were thinly plastered. Apart from the rough country-made chairs and table, the only piece of furniture was Don Julian's matrimonial bed. A recent purchase from a shop in Toluca, it was encased in an elaborately veneered frame, which only just fitted into the width of the room. A pile of rugs and mats, to be spread out on the floor at night, provided the bedding for the rest of the family. The only light came through the open doorway.

Once we were settled at the table, the girls brought in a huge dish of *mole*,* piles of tortillas and plates of beans, rice and green chiles. Saturno walked round with a jug from which he filled our tumblers with pulque.

The talk was mostly of village matters: the crops, the effects of the hailstorm, the price at which things were selling or at which they could be bought in the markets of Tenango and Toluca. Then they wanted to know if the same crops were grown in my country and what price was paid for them and how the people lived and what I thought of the way things were done in Mexico. They were proud of Don Julian and his schemes. Did English villages have light and water? Did we have roads like the great new motorway from Toluca to the city? What did I think of Don Fidel and the Americans? What was it like to be governed by a queen? Did we have fiestas in our villages? Was there cock-fighting and steer-riding and did the government send soldiers to keep order?

This last question made everyone laugh.

'But they're not as bad as they used to be,' Don Julian said. 'There was a time when even at the sight of one soldier the whole village would have fled into the forest.'

'Yes, they're better these days,' one of his friends agreed. 'They haven't shot anyone yet. The trouble is they always come from the poorest families and have no education.'

'Poor devils!' Don Julian said. 'It's not much of a life. We ought to get together and give them something when they leave.'

The others nodded. 'Yes, that's true. They deserve it. After all, they've behaved decently.'

It was half-way through the afternoon by the time we had finished eating. Outside in the yard the sun had lost its strength

---

* Chicken prepared with chocolate sauce.

and the mountain air was beginning to grow cold. From lower down in the village came the rumble of hooves and wild shouting as the steers were driven in for the fiesta. It was time for us to go. Don Julian went back into the cottage and came out carrying two *sarapes*.* He gave one to me and put on the other himself. They were very thick and woven in a rich pattern of white, black and reddish brown.

A stockade had been fixed up for the contest on a piece of level ground at the bottom of the village. By the time we reached it a large crowd was already packed against the rails. Most of the men wore the same kind of *sarape* as Don Julian's. The women had their *rebozos* drawn close about their heads and shoulders. Inside the stockade the competitors were showing off. They were mostly young boys wearing hats with curled brims, fringed jackets of cow-hide and cowboy boots. They charged about on their ponies in a haze of dust, leaning out of their saddles as they chased the steers to catch them by their tails. Children ran perilously among the stampeding animals. A drunk who staggered into the arena had to be dragged out by his friends.

Most of the crowd had been drinking, but they were not rowdy as Europeans would have been. Their condition only showed itself in the slight sway of their movements and in bemused smiles which made them seem, perhaps, more gentle and friendly than they really were. The soldiers, grouped at one end of the stockade, had also had their share of pulque. Although in a potentially more dangerous state, they looked, with their helmets pushed back and their guns swinging loose from their shoulders, less terrifying than the grimly alert couple we had passed that morning. The whole scene, in spite of the animation of the horsemen, had melancholy calm. The sun had swung low over the western spur of the volcano. Doused in its glow the reds and browns of the *sarapes* deepened to even richer tones and the tanned highland faces which poked through them became ruddy. Forming a background to the scene the valley lay stretched away in a gold haze above which a remote mountain range basked pink and arid under the blue sky.

---

* A thick woven blanket worn round the shoulders as protection against cold and rain.

The contest took some time to get started. At last a steer with a rope round its neck was dragged up against the inside of the stockade. A boy jumped from the top rail on to its back. He grasped the rope with both hands. As soon as the men who were holding the animal let it go, it bucked off into the arena hitting the ground with all four hooves simultaneously. With each bounce the boy was jarred a foot into the air. For an instant a triangle of light appeared between his thighs. Then his fork thumped down on the nubbly bone ridge beneath him. Half-way across the ring the animal changed its tactics. Flicking its hind legs in the air, it shook its body into a violent twist which shot the boy over its head. He hit the ground on his shoulder and went rolling into the dust. The next half-dozen competitors were no more successful, but contrived, by sliding off instead of being thrown, to make less perilous landings. The first boy to get near to completing the course beat the bucking with a grip which kept him wedged like a peg to the animal's back. Then his rope broke and he was pitched off sideways. About twenty others followed, but only four made the full circuit and tamed their mounts to a standstill. Whatever their antics, the crowd watched them with intense, hushed concentration. There was little shouting or laughter and scarcely a cheer or a handclap. The contest seemed to be viewed more as a ritual than a sport. Perhaps because emotions were so little expressed or because of the drinking which had gone before, the tension in the crowd took on an existence of its own, independent of the spectacle.

Don Julian had found a place for us close to the rails, not far from where the soldiers were standing. As in the street, the crowd had left an open space round them. Suddenly a small boy belted across it, pursued by an angry comrade who threw a stone at him. The stone missed and hit one of the soldiers. Turning, he lunged out, caught the runaway and held him. The boy yelped and struggled. A woman at the edge of the crowd screamed and at once the people near by surged round her. The scream alerted the rest of the soldiers. Jerking down their helmets, they clamped their guns under their arms and pointed them across the open space. Don Julian left the rails and tried to force his way to the front but the crowd moved forward ahead of him. Except for the boy's yells there was

silence. Gradually the space round the soldiers narrowed. Don
Julian had almost reached it when the sergeant in charge of the
troop, his gun still slung on his shoulder, lounged up to the boy,
and taking him from his captor, pushed him off into the crowd
with a cuff. Then he walked round with the same casual stride
in front of the levelled weapons of his troop. As he passed, the
people drew back. The crisis was over. When another steer was
released, they turned to the arena. The soldiers relaxed but did
not lower their guns.

There were only a few more competitors and when the last
of them had been thrown by his steer, the crowd moved and
became articulate. Some climbed through the rails into the
ring, others drifted in groups towards the village. The cowboys
who had been successful, amid shouts of encouragement,
demanded *abrazos* of their chosen girls. Don Julian gave a
laughing welcome to Saturno, who had fallen after the first
few bucks, and watched with a tolerant smile when Lupe was
picked out for an embrace.

The sun had now sunk behind the mountains and it was time
to leave if I was to reach the paved road while it was still light.
We turned back towards the village moving slowly with the tide
of blanket-shrouded figures. Blue coils of smoke hung over the
houses. Above us the volcano lifted its black summit like a
hunched shoulder into the darkening sky. Suddenly Don
Julian stopped.

'Are you tired?' he asked.

'No, but it'll be dark soon. I ought to go back.'

'Oh, that's all right; Saturno'll go with you to the road.
There's something I'd like to show you. It'll only take us a few
minutes.'

We cut off at an angle from the village and soon reached the
foot of the hill which rose to one side of it. Don Julian went
ahead leading the way up a path which wound steeply through
the pines. Soon the ground levelled out and we came to a small
cottage built in a hollow against the hill with a narrow terrace
in front of it.

'This is where I was born,' Don Julian said. 'No one lives
here now, but it still belongs to me.'

We crossed a strip of derelict garden to the edge of the
terrace. Below us the dusk had already fallen over the village

54

and fields of San Juan, but beyond, the great valleys, stretching away to the mountains above Mexico City, were swept by the last red flare of the sunset. In the distance shallow dips in the land lay like blue lakes under the mountains. The atmosphere was very clear and still.

'Was it worth the climb?' he asked.

I told him it was one of the finest views I had seen. If I owned the cottage I should live in it.

'Oh no, you wouldn't: not if you had to fetch water. It's a quarter of a mile from here to the spring. During the rains it's all right, but we could only collect enough to last a week or two after they had finished. All the same when I was a boy it had its advantages. We went through some bad times then.'

'In the revolution?'

'Yes, in the revolution. Once we had soldiers here for a fortnight. They were not really soldiers, just bandits. Most of the people fled into the forest, but they had no food. Some of them died of starvation. Of those who stayed behind a few were lucky enough to be shot trying to escape. Others hid themselves, but they were all hunted out in the end. It wasn't pleasant to be caught alive. We could hear them screaming.'

'Where were you?'

'Up here.'

'Didn't they find the cottage?'

'Yes, of course, but we were hiding. I'll show you the place.'

I followed him to the other end of the terrace. It was sealed off by a huge boulder, shrouded in the trees which grew on the slope above it. Its smooth bulging sides were at least fifteen feet high. It was surrounded by a thicket of cactus and prickly shrubs. We skirted up the hill for a few yards, then turned down and edged in through the bushes. At the point where we reached its base, the rock rose sheer above us, but with only a slight outward bulge. Don Julian felt with his hands and feet for familiar holds and heaved himself up. I followed and found the climb easier than I had expected. At the top a great chunk had been cracked out of the boulder when it had first fallen from the mountain. It had left a hollow, sheltered from above by the overhanging trees.

'I was the eldest, so I used to go down at night with my father to get food. We had some stored in a cave close by. Luckily it was during the rains so we could collect water from pools among the rocks. After the soldiers had gone, we never knew when they'd come back, so we slept up here for months.

'They were bad times all right. But for those who survived, it was worth it. We work the land for ourselves now and with a little luck we can make our living. There're many things which are still bad, but they're getting better. We're going to have the water laid on by Christmas and after that we'll have electricity, I don't suppose I'd get anyone to live in the cottage now, even if I were to give it to them. But I wouldn't part with it. You never know, it might come in useful again.'

It was five months before I next saw Don Julian. He was spending a day in Mexico City and came to visit me. When I asked after his wife and children he shook his head gloomily. He had had trouble with Guadalupe. She had run off with a young man and was going to have a baby. Of course he would see to it that they got married. I would be invited to the wedding.

I asked him about the water. Oh, yes, it had been laid on for a couple of months now. But there'd been trouble about the electricity. After the villagers had collected their share of the cost the government had tried to back out. Some visiting officials had been stoned and soldiers had been sent up to keep order. Luckily it was the same troop. They had even become quite popular in the village. Anyhow everything had been settled. He had gone himself to see the governor. Now they hoped to have electricity by the autumn. The governor was a fine man, a real son of the revolution. He had even promised to attend the inauguration.

'We shall have another fiesta. Of course you must come up for that too.'

3
A Lake by the Gulf

I woke early as the birdsong broke into a ringing chorus.
Every tree and bush seemed to be full of birds. They kept it up
right through the morning, long after I had left the lake shore
and was already deep in the jungle. Apart from their songs they
made every kind of call, cry and whistle. There were sudden
wild shrieks and chatterings or single flute-like notes which fell
through the air like drops of water. Whenever there was a
pause in the full flourish of song, the hush was filled by the
hollow cooing of doves.

And yet I hardly saw a bird. The jungle was not very high
but it was dense. The trees grew in vivid green mounds, their
contours repeated on a larger scale by the wooded hills which
formed a barrier between the lake and the sea. I had intended
to climb the hills and keep on until I reached the coast. If I
was lucky, I might see a jaguar or one of the smaller cats which
were plentiful in the forest. But I was distracted by the birds.

It was exasperating to hear and not to see them. I stopped
every few minutes to look up into the branches. At most I
caught the flash of a tail feather or a darting silhouette against
the sun. Once I climbed into a tree, but the birds which, from
all I could glimpse of them from the ground, might have been
caged inside it, now fluttered and sang on the outside, as if it
was I, myself, who had become a prisoner, walled in by the
leaves.

Towards midday the chorus died down a little. I had come to
a clearing in which there was a thicket of tall bushes. Cattle
browsed under the thin foliage. From somewhere in the thicket
itself or in the jungle beyond came softly resonant coos answering each other with the precision of a metronome. I listened
until I had fixed the direction of the sounds, but found it
impossible, even though they did not vary in pitch or volume,
to judge their distance. I was puzzled by the birds' identity.

57

All the doves I had so far encountered in central Mexico had calls of more than one note. A single-noted call was unfamiliar.

I began to walk round the clearing, keeping a few yards inside the jungle. The undergrowth was dense and slung with heavy creepers. I was half-way round before I had made quite certain that the birds were in the thicket. Taking a line which seemed to lie midway between the two calls, I started towards them. As I penetrated deeper into the bushes the sounds receded, then became louder again until I was directly between them. Neither bird could have been more than a few yards away, but now, for the first time, they cooed simultaneously. The notes boomed in my ears in such resounding unison that I was utterly confused. I swivelled my head from side to side, amazed that despite the sparse foliage the birds remained invisible. But now they were inaudible too; for the cooing had stopped.

Convinced that they could not be seen from where I was standing, I set off first to the right and then to the left, but did not glimpse even the flick of a wing. Next I tried walking round in expanding circles. Gaping into the leaves I stumbled over tussocks and fallen branches. A near collision with a cow made me decide to give up. I had been searching for half an hour. Although I had not seen them I was sure that the birds must have flown away. But just as I reached the edge of the clearing the cooing boomed out again, from exactly the same place as before. I hesitated, but I was too hot and thirsty to go back. I spotted a jungle tick on my arm and found several more on my legs. After I had extracted them, my whole body began to itch. I longed for a plunge into cool, clean water. Giving up my earlier plan, I took a path which led eastwards. By following it I counted on reaching one of the rivers which flowed into the northern end of the lake.

In this part of the forest the trees were taller and twined with philodendrons. The huge leaves overlapped each other to form a green fleece under which the encircled trunks were completely hidden. Upper branches sprouted with orchids and air plants. Some of these were in flower, carrying sharp pyramids of red and purple or foaming cream-coloured sprays like suspended waterfalls. The bird song became livelier again. A light wind hustled through the trees. At last beneath these sounds I heard a continuous murmur. It grew louder until, at a turn in the path, I came out on to the bank of a bright, fast-running stream.

I stripped, and wading against the current, soon found a pool deep enough to lie down in. Leaving my clothes on a shelf of rock, I splashed about until I was cool. Then I went back to the rock and dried myself in the sun. Almost at once I heard the burr of vibrating wings. Looking round I saw a large kingfisher perched on a branch above the pool. It had a fierce spear of a beak at least four inches long, a fine upstanding crest and a white collar. Its back and wings were blue and its breast reddish brown. It swooped away over the water and rose again to perch on another branch out of sight. I was still regretting its departure when a pair of black-throated orioles (black and white markings on brilliant orange) burst from a tree opposite. They were half-way across the stream before they saw me and flared round squawking for cover.

I got up and waded close in beside the bank to a spot where I was screened by overhanging leaves, but had a clear view of the trees opposite. From one of them a dead branch stuck out against the sky. A flock of euphonia (bright green and yellow, pointed with blue) settled on its bare twigs. As if this display was not enough, they were soon joined by a velvet tanager, a bird about the size of a jay, soft jet all over except for a scarlet tab on the lower back. The gathering dispersed and the bough remained deserted. The kingfisher dipped past flying in the opposite direction. A loud chattering came from a tree higher up the river and its leaves were shaken violently. Keeping under cover I waded towards it, but when I was quite close both noise and movement stopped. I stared into the dense mass of leaves in vain. It was only when I lowered my gaze that I saw, sitting on a branch almost level with the bank, that marvellous mixture of the beautiful and absurd, an emerald-green toucanet. About fifteen inches long, its body was a sleek ripple of jade, broken only by touches of chestnut about the wings and a white patch at its throat. Between the eyes of this elegant and brilliantly coloured creature was stuck, like the false nose on a carnival buffoon, a broad curved bill, striped in black and yellow. The chattering started again in the branches above. With an answering squawk, the bird soared vertically and vanished among the leaves. In that brief flight, with its bill thrust forward in line with its throat and streamlined body, it lost all its comic element, and I saw it in its other aspect: a slim rocket of green feathers, tipped by a golden cone, streaking through the shadows under the forest.

As I turned back, wading in the centre of the stream, a flight of parrots hurtled by overhead. Watching them I did not notice that I was being watched. In my absence the pool had been taken over. Absorbed in the jungle and its birds, it had never occurred to me that the river was not all my own. Now on the rock where I had left my clothes a huddle of old women knelt gaping at me over their washing. Still closer, in the pool itself, three young girls, sleek as jungle cats, their bodies a reddish gold in the sunlight, lay partially submerged and totally naked in the water. They must have been watching my approach for several minutes. At my astonished look they clutched each other and giggled in the high tee-hee of the southern Indians. Their shaking bodies sent out circling ripples across the pool. The sight of a stripped *gringo* (light-haired, pink-skinned, with an absurd white, pubic, sunbather's band round belly and upper thighs) was too comic for alarm, much less embarrassment. The shock was on my side. I plunged into the water. Had it been deep enough to swim, I might have proved myself, like the toucanet in flight, at least in one element worthy of respect. As it was I could only crawl painfully along the pebbly bottom until I was close enough to the rock to reach up and grab my shirt. When I had slipped it over my shoulders I climbed out of the pool.

The old women turned their backs on me and began to slap and scrub. As I pulled on my clothes, the girls became suddenly shy. Still giggling they sank down into the water until it lapped under their breasts. Their black hair was wet and hung straight against the curve of their cheeks to spread out clinging on their shoulders. Their noses were finely curved. Their parted lips showed neat white teeth. The eyelids from beneath which they watched me, laughing but furtive, were turned up at the corners.

As I laced my boots I tried speaking to the women. I asked them where their village was and if I could get food there. They did not answer. Not a head turned. Their broad backs remained set in a formidable barrier. At the sound of my voice the girls sank another inch or two. But the water was shallow. As their hair floated off their shoulders, their nipples became islands, and three neat black notches, like birds' nests, broke through the surface among the reflection of leaves and sky. One of the women abruptly turned and pointed across the river to a path which led into the jungle on the other side. 'Over there, señor,' she said. 'There's a village beside the lake.'

As I unlaced my boots again to wade across, I asked her how far away it was, but received no answer. The row of backs were set against me implacably. I walked into the stream, crossed it and took the track which wound off among the trees. Out of sight I stopped to put on my boots. Above the sound of the water I could hear the high chorus of girlish tee-hee-hees and now, raised with it, the old women's mocking cackle.

A mile on I came to the village. Its few stick huts were dotted about in a wide clearing bounded on three sides by banana plantations and on the fourth, beyond some palms, by the lake. A few chickens, the only immediate evidence of life, lay with fluffed feathers in the shade beside a hut. The place was sunk in the stifling somnolence of mid-siesta. Passing an open door I saw, in the striped light within, brown legs dangling from sagged hammocks. By the lakeside some fishermen had beached their canoes and lay sprawled under a palm-tree. Smoke rose from between two large stones close beside them. When they saw me they called and beckoned.

There were five of them, very dark and fat. They had plump round faces and even white teeth. Their noses were broad, almost negroid, but their hair was Indian, blue-black, straight and sticking out from their heads in a rough thatch. Their eyes were very black and hot, but without expression. Two had moustaches which drooped in wisps round the corners of their mouths. Their thick necks sank into heavy womanish bodies which were covered all over with an even gloss of sweat. They wore only white cotton pants, soiled and ragged and sinking in front under their overhanging bellies.

I walked up to them.

Who was I? Where did I come from? What was I doing?

I was English, not American. No, not from the United States, but from Europe.

Was it far away?

Yes, two weeks at least in a ship from Veracruz.

They nodded without understanding. Why was I there?

Orchid-hunting. I was a collector of orchids.*

They talked for a moment inaudibly. When they stopped they had come to a decision. They would help me. They would take me to a place where a tree overhung the lake covered in flowers which did not grow anywhere else. It was an hour away by canoe. But first I must sit down with them and share their meal.

They pointed to a pot in which some fish were cooking over the fire. One of them rolled a log towards me for a seat. I did not want to stop, but I was hungry and the fish smelt good. I sat down and at once they turned back to their sprawling circle and lay muttering among themselves.

Behind us the banana leaves parted and a small boy came out followed by an enormous pig. The animal headed for the shade under the palm-tree. After rooting among the fallen fronds it settled down with its rump jutting into the human circle. The boy squatted wanly some yards off. His rib bones made shadows on his chest and his legs and arms were laced with scars. One of his eyes was fixed in a hungry stare, the other had been dissolved by disease into a clouded jelly.

The man who was cooking lifted the pot off the fire and put it on the ground. Tortillas were brought in a cloth and placed beside the pot. At the sight of the food the boy shuffled closer. The cook split open a fish, slipped the top half on to a banana leaf and passed it to me with a wad of tortillas. As he turned he

---

* It is always advisable for the traveller to be armed with an explanation of his presence which will satisfy the country people. The truth is often best avoided. Such explanations as 'going for a walk' or 'admiring the view' are incomprehensible to most Mexicans and are likely to arouse their suspicions. Hunting is understood but sometimes resented. Foreigners who bag large quantities of game merely for amusement may be depriving the local inhabitants of a much-needed supplement to their diet. An interest in archaeology may be interpreted by Indians, who believe that they have the right to anything of value found among the ruined temples of their ancestors, as a marauding treasure hunt. Orchid- and plant-collecting are usually acceptable as the Indians are fond of flowers themselves and it is a pursuit they can appreciate. Perhaps the safest explanation of all is to claim to be a pilgrim. Since most Mexicans can recollect the reasons why they or their friends have set out on similar expeditions, they seldom ask for further explanations.

noticed the boy's hungry gaze. Smiling maliciously, he stabbed the knife into the pot and brought out a sizeable fish-eye on its point. Taking it between finger and thumb, he stuck it over the closed lid of his own eye. The resemblance to the boy's blind jelly set them all rumbling with laughter. The boy gave a forced grin which vanished when the man, after holding the eye out towards him on the knife point, snatched it away and stuffed it into his own mouth. The others laughed and guffawed so loudly that the noise roused the pig, grunting, on to its feet. Its tail twirled like the handle of a coffee grinder, then lifted to let fly a glittering golden gush which missed the pot by a few inches but liberally spattered its contents. With curses like cannon-fire two of the men grabbed its hind legs and hurled it, still pissing, snout over tail into the banana trees. It fled with hideous screeches and the boy flung himself after it. A shower of stones plopped round him as he vanished among the leaves. Still chuckling through their curses, the men settled down again and helped themselves with eager fingers to great hunks of dripping fish from the pot.

As I munched through one fish-plump tortilla after another, I watched some humming-birds diving like bullets at the flowers of a near-by shrub. As they touched their target they stopped short on wings which worked so fast that they appeared only as a faint disturbance in the air. Sucking the honey through cotton-thin beaks, they looked like small vivid buds trembling among the flowers.

The fishermen ate noisily but without speaking. When they had finished they washed out their mouths with lake water and rounded the meal off with sphincter-splitting farts, at each of which they guffawed in chorus. My seat on the log was wearing hard. I decided to go. While I was still wondering whether I should offer to pay for my food, they all swung towards me and began volleying questions with the same violence as they had broken wind. They had the usual straight curiosity about the country I came from which was difficult to satisfy with explanations they could understand. They wanted to know, too, what I thought about Mexico. When I told them how many of its states I had visited, they shook their heads at the idea of a foreigner having seen so much when they themselves had been scarcely out of sight of the lake. But my boasting set their minds on another track. Where had I found the money to travel so far? I said I was a teacher. Teachers were badly paid in England, but I had wanted to come to Mexico so much that I'd managed to save enough for the journey. Unconvinced, their inquisitiveness turned to calculation. They eyed my wrist-watch and boots and asked me how much I had paid for them. Fingering the material of my trousers they estimated their cost in the local market, had they been available. As they muttered among themselves, I began to sense that they were now regarding me less as a guest than a prize.

One of the men rose and walked to the nearest canoe. I took this as a sign that my interrogation was over, but when I started to get up, their gentle brown hands clutched at my clothes and pulled me back. I must drink with them. The man returned from the canoe with a bottle. It was passed round from mouth to mouth. They accused me of sipping at it and forced me to take a proper swig. The raw cane spirit exploded like a fire-cracker in my throat.

'What do you think of Castro?' one of them asked.

'Fine for the Cubans if he does for Cuba what the revolution did for Mexico.'

Among peasants I had found this a safe answer. It silenced the fishermen. The bottle made another round before anyone spoke.

Did I think Don Fidel would come to Mexico? No. The Mexicans didn't need him or any other foreigner to show them how to run their own country.

Was it true that Cuban soldiers had already landed in Campeche?

Almost certainly not, but if it was, I had no doubt that the President of Mexico would send them home. I asked them what *they* thought about Castro?

They answered without looking at me.

If the Cubans liked Don Fidel they could keep him. 'We don't want him over here making trouble. We went through enough of that under Calles. The churches burnt down or the doors nailed up. Not a Christian burial to be had, let alone a wedding!'

'But haven't you all been better off since the revolution?'

They shrugged and chuckled. No, a thousand times worse!

Officials lining their own pockets, blood-sucking *caciques**—and soldiers everywhere, killing just for the sport of it!

But nowadays? They couldn't complain that things were like that now?

More shrugs, but no chuckles. When they spoke it was among themselves. Gradually they turned back into their own circle. Soon three of them were on their backs snoring. The other two leant against the palm-bole and smoked. When their cigarettes were finished, they, too, closed their eyes.

This was the moment to slip away, but I hesitated. After all they had been friendly and had given me food and drink. Their inquisitiveness and their calculating had been only natural. The least I could do was to wait until they woke up so that I could thank them.

'Señor!'

I turned. The boy with the blind eye beckoned from the bush of humming-birds. When I did not move, he crawled closer.

'You mustn't stay. These're bad men, everyone knows it. When it's dark they'll kill you and take your money.'

'Nonsense!'

'It's true, I heard them talking.'

'How did you hear?'

'From behind the tree.'

'I don't believe it. What d'you want?'

'Only to warn you, señor. But if you wish I can show you a waterfall, high like that.' He pointed to the sky. 'People come all the way from Veracruz to see it, even foreigners. They're always pleased. "Thank you, Pepe," they say, "it's beautiful!" '

I hesitated. I didn't believe what he'd said about the fishermen. If I went with him it would only be because of the waterfall. I had seen a good many in Mexico: they were usually worth a visit.

'Is it far?'

'No, señor; just up in the hills.'

'How long will it take?'

'Half an hour.'

More likely an hour and a half. But still there was time. It would not be dark for a couple of hours.

---

* Indian village chief, or local political boss.

'Come!' Beckoning again, he backed towards the bushes.

I got up and slung my haversack on to my shoulders, trying not to make my movements look stealthy. At my first step the men leaning against the tree opened their eyes.

'Where're you going?'

As they spoke they were on their feet. Startled I looked at the boy. One of the men, following my glance, spotted him and pounced. Now they were all up and standing round me. Pepe was dragged passive into the circle. Unsmiling, they stared at us with their hot, button-blank eyes.

'He's going to show me a waterfall. They're usually good for orchids. It seems there's one quite close by in the hills.'

'You said you were coming with us to see the tree we told you about.'

'When you all went to sleep I thought you'd forgotten.'

'There's still time. We can reach it before dark.'

Across the clearing the village was waking up. Indians stood outside the huts staring at us.

'I'll come back. You can take me tomorrow.'

The suggestion gave them an idea. They drew away together muttering. Pepe, released, looked round, ready to run. But in a moment they were back beside us again.

I wasn't to trust the boy. He was a thief. Once in the jungle he'd try to rob me. But I needn't worry; Pancho, here, would go with me. They pushed the reluctant youngest of the gang forward. He would bring me back to the place on the lake shore where they would sleep that night. They would take me to the orchid-tree at dawn.

I could only thank them. We shook hands, all smiling. Then the three of us set off, Pepe leading and Pancho behind.

After half an hour we began to climb into the hills. Pancho was soon gasping. Canoe life had not made him an expert walker. At a track junction, where one fork led down to the lake, he demanded a halt. I asked Pepe how much farther we had to go.

'Half an hour, señor.'

Perhaps it was the only time unit he knew.

'Look, Pancho, you stay here. We'll pick you up on the way back.'

'No, I'm coming with you.'

We set off again. At the top of the next ridge he was a hundred yards behind. Pepe began to scamper. We dipped down into a valley and up the other side. There were shouts behind us but we did not turn. At last I, too, had to stop. Looking down I could see almost a mile of track winding below us. It was empty. We moved on at an easier pace.

'How much farther is it, Pepe?'

'Half an hour, señor.'

We were high now on the flank of a mountain. The sun had dropped behind a spur and it was beginning to grow dark. In the forest round us the birds called and sang as loudly as at dawn, but now their notes were lingering and melancholy. We descended into another hollow. Under the trees at the bottom it was almost night. Glancing up, as we began to climb again, I saw on a higher stretch of the track a procession of Indians, dressed in white, carrying lanterns already lit for a night journey. At the next bend I sighted them again. In a few minutes they appeared on the same stretch as ourselves, trotting quietly towards us, lanterns bobbing through the dusk. We stepped aside under the trees to let them pass.

They wore white cotton shirts and trousers and all, save one, high-crowned straw hats. The soft pad of their bare feet on the earth was broken by the rhythmical creak of rope on wood. The hatless man was at the centre of the left-hand file. He moved with more of a jog than the others, and his chin, fallen on his chest, jerked his head loosely up and down. His body was held very stiff and straight. It was only when he was quite close that I saw that he was bound. The rope coiled round him from shoulder to hip, pinioning his arms rigid. Its ends were looped to the waists of the men in front and behind so that they were linked together in a chain.

The men in the right-hand file carried a hammock. It was slung from a pole which rested on their shoulders. A bundle wrapped in old sacks sagged in the hollow of the net. The hammock swung from side to side. It was the straining of its cords on the pole which creaked so rhythmically. Not one of the men looked in our direction. They all kept their gaze to the ground. As the hammock came level I saw a human leg, white and hairy, sticking out from the bundle. It ended in a bloody stump where it had been severed through above the ankle.

The lanterns bobbed and disappeared round a bend. I could hear the drumming of bare feet on the path below and then only the creak of the hammock swinging on its pole.

I looked at Pepe for an explanation, but he merely hunched his shoulders. We started to climb again. As we came out of the valley on to high ground, it grew lighter. There was even a last sunbeam on the trees above us. The ground levelled out and we came to a clearing. On the other side the track stretched away at a slight incline. Down the tunnel which it formed under the trees, a boy came running. He was naked to the waist and as the dusk absorbed his dark skin he was visible only as a pair of animated white trousers. He stopped at the edge of the clearing and stood blubbering quietly. Pepe ran on ahead and spoke to him. I could not hear what they said but I could see their lips moving over their white teeth. As I came up to them, Pepe explained that the boy was his friend. They had to go somewhere together. 'You can wait for me over there, señor.' He pointed to a dead tree at one side of the clearing. 'I'll be back in a minute.'

I had not even time to protest. They cut off straight into the undergrowth. Visible at one moment, at the next they had gone.

I walked up to the tree and stood with my back against the trunk. Its bleached twigs and branches reached into a sky which was deep violet. A few late humming-birds purred in a near-by bush. The calling and singing had almost died away. Only a flock of melodious blackbirds fluted a last chorus. A chuckle in the tree-tops made me look up. The sound was repeated, coming closer. Wings clapped and a large hawk-like bird settled on a branch above me. As I watched it, the feathers rose on its breast, its beak shot forward and it let out a hoarse, ringing cry. It was a ferocious, yet despairing sound. It rang out again and again until it had silenced the whole forest. Then the bird's feathers sank on its breast, and stretching its wings it glided off across the clearing. The blackbirds started calling again, mimicking the hawk's cry. But their defiance lasted only a moment. In the silence which followed, the night fell.

Gradually the nocturnal life of the jungle began to stir. Invisible creatures rustled and tapped or let out sudden shrieks. There was a loud thump, repeated every few minutes, as if a heavy body had fallen from a high branch. After half an hour I decided I had waited long enough. The track was beaten hard and its pale surface showed up in the dark so that I had no difficulty in following it. Walking with my eyes turned to the ground I did not notice that the forest was growing thinner. Suddenly I was out on a bare rocky slope overhung by a mountain ridge above which the full moon had just risen. From somewhere to my left came a roar like sustained thunder. For a moment I was puzzled and then I remembered the waterfall.

I took a path which led in the direction of the sound. As I turned the shoulder of the mountain, the land dropped away almost at my feet. High up on the right the water came sliding over a lip of rock, smooth and solid, shining like metal in the moonlight. In its fall it spilled into a tall, smoking column with its base planted in the dark crotch of the canyon. All round me the moonlight fixed haloes in the spray. Far down where the canyon opened into a wooded valley, a cloud of vapour lolled like a sleeping god above the forest.

I returned to the village from which I had set out, at dusk the next evening. As I walked up from the lake, white egrets roosting in the zapote trees looked like giant magnolia buds or the outsize cocoons of cotton-spinning insects. Drinking beer on the verandah of the inn, I searched my bird book for a wailing hawk and a one-noted dove. The ruddy quail-dove fitted. 'Its presence in the forest is made obvious during the mating season when the males are calling with a soft deep coo, usually delivered when the bird rests upon the ground, a mournful sound often heard amidst the forest . . . so retiring a thicket-dweller is difficult to shoot.'

The hawk was a laughing falcon. 'Usual cry a loud far-reaching wail. The laugh which sometimes precedes the wail is not very loud.'

It seemed typical of the perversity of things in Mexico that a dove should prefer to sit on the ground to coo rather than in a tree. I had probably almost stepped on it as I walked round scanning the branches. And how strange, too, that the falcon should have received its name from its chuckle and not from its true jungle voice, that agonized shriek of savagery and desolation.

4
Seri Land

Progress, like so much else in Mexico, is explosive. Sometimes when the charge has been laid, the fuse fizzles out. Paradise hotels which fail to catch on are examples of this, or, in the richer field of public works, the shells of municipal buildings for which the funds proved insufficient or were otherwise appropriated, railway stations without rails, and dams which collect no water or which in doing so create deserts more extensive than the lands they irrigate. The explosions which come off, on whatever scale, are impressive. Certainly the six-year presidential term and the law against re-election spur the President and his ministers to leave great works to perpetuate their names. But the politicos are not always responsible for the projects which bring the most immediate benefit to the people. These are often the achievements of modest but dedicated men, doctors, engineers, and schoolmasters or even simple farmers and villagers like my friend Don Julian from the volcano above Toluca.

To the traveller in search of the Mexican past these un-predictable explosions which precipitate the most backward areas into the present can be disconcerting. Where, he has been told by a visitor of a year or two before, he can expect to find an Indian tribe untouched by civilization, a new road, a recently started industry or the activities of a go-ahead school-teacher will have changed everything: old customs out of use, traditional clothes discarded, a juke-box in the main square, and a bus rolling in or an aeroplane touching down loaded with peasants triumphantly bringing home all kinds of cheap, machine-made conveniences from the nearest city. To deplore such evidence of progress would be foolish and ungenerous. From the start the traveller has to accept that whatever he is looking for, whether a rare animal, a paradise by the sea or the surviving practice of a primitive rite, the chances are that he will not find it, but that what he does find while looking for it may prove to be, in its way, even more remarkable.

The city of Hermosillo in the north-west corner of the Mexican mainland, a hundred and fifty miles south of the United States border, offers little to attract the foreign visitor. Faced with a short stay there I searched the guide-books for something of interest to see in its neighbourhood. As on other occasions, it was the 1908 edition of Terry's Guide* which offered the most promising possibilities. My final choice lay between a stop at Ciudad Obregón to see the Yaqui villages near the coast or an inward journey from Hermosillo to visit the Seris on the island of Tiburón. Naturally I did not imagine that either would be living in the same conditions as it had been fifty years earlier, but of the two the Seris, because of their isolated terrain, appeared less likely to have changed. What Terry had to say about them was interesting and ended with a challenge to the curious.

'The island of Tiburón† is mountainous and culminates in a peak which rises seven hundred feet above the level of the sea. It is inhabited by a fierce race of Indians (Seris of the Youma family) with anthropophagous instincts. They shoot turtles and fish with great skill, using bows and arrows. Poisoned arrows are employed whether hunting game or enemies. Visitors to the island are unwelcome.'

Before leaving for Hermosillo, I read all the books and articles I could find on the Seris. It was Hardy's account‡ of his visit to Tiburón which clinched my determination to go there.

In 1825 Lieutenant R. W. H. Hardy, RN, was commissioned by the General Pearl and Coral Fishing Association of London to prospect for new pearl fisheries off the mainland shore of the Gulf of California. La Paz on the east coast of the peninsula was still at that period the centre of one of the richest pearl-producing areas in the world. Hardy's travels took him through

---

* Houghton Mifflin, Boston and New York, 1908, revised 1922. The modern edition, published by Doubleday, is an excellent guide-book but omits most of Terry's descriptive passages.
† Shark island.
‡ *Travels in the Interior of Mexico* by Lieutenant R. W. H. Hardy, RN, London, 1829.

the Yaquis' country at the time of their revolt under the leadership of Juan de la Banderas. He did not encounter any Yaquis face to face. Had he done so he would certainly have got the better of them. His participation in the war was limited to his attempts to calm the inhabitants and organize the defences of the threatened towns through which he passed.

With his unassailable phlegm and his nostalgia for roast beef, Hardy presents himself as a caricature of the Englishman of his time. He is as eccentric as an ex-naval officer should be. His chief pride (he recounts successes but no failures) is in what he refers to with a seaman's frankness as his 'knowledge of quackery'. On arrival at Mazatlán he found his host suffering from a cold and bilious attack. 'I set to work with an emetic which I followed up with five grains of Mr Abernethy's nostrum, the blue pill, and the next day he was on his feet again.' At Villa de la Fuente, after curing a child of a 'cutaneous eruption', he had a spectacular success with a woman who was ill after childbirth. Moved by her mother's grief, he was persuaded to try and blunder upon a remedy. 'Accordingly I sent out for the leaf of the zarila and, putting a portion of it in spirits to steep, I allowed it to remain two hours, at the end of which time it had assumed a colour very much like a pale rose.' After a spoonful or two the woman's condition improved, but she was left with a pain on her right side and paralysis in her right arm and leg. 'Having exhausted my ingenuity, I was about to abandon my patient to her fate, when I recollected my wonderful *gotas*!* I gave her a few, not knowing what the consequences might be, by way of experiment! Almost at once she was cured of both pain and paralysis. They all thought me a wonderfully clever doctor and I believe I myself nearly fell into the same error.'

It was his aptitude for quackery that made him such a success on Tiburón, where he was the first white man on record to be treated hospitably by the inhabitants. Certainly, Hardy's being the only exception, reports of the Seris from their first encounter with the Spaniards to W. J. Magee's ethnological study of 1898 give them an extremely black character. The only favourable impression the Spaniards had

---

* Drops. He does not say what they contained.

of them was of their handsome appearance and physique. In
1541 Rodrigues Maldonado, a member of an expedition
searching for the fabled seven cities of Cibla, captured an
Indian 'so large and tall that the best man in the army reached
only to his chest'. From that time onwards Spanish-Seri
relations were a disaster.

The Seri warriors combined fanatical courage with low
cunning and treachery. They fought on foot with bows and
wooden clubs. Their arrow-heads were poisoned and the flesh
of a living creature wounded by them quickly became putre-
scent. The ambush was their favourite tactic and they often
professed false friendship as a means of trapping their enemies.
Captives, especially if notable fighters, were eaten and their
scalps paraded in a ceremonial dance. The only edible creature
they spared was a species of desert rat which made networks
of shallow tunnels beneath the sand. These caved in under the
weight of the Spanish horses and brought them down. The
Seris had a taste for horse-flesh. In 1571 alone they were said
to have stolen four thousand horses and mules. They had no
use for them as mounts since they could not feed them. In any
case they were so swift-footed themselves that they could outrun
deer and kill them with their hands. Only at night they moved
clumsily, for their vision was impaired by the daytime glare of
the desert.

Although primitively armed they easily defeated the smaller
detachments the Spaniards sent out against them. Faced with
larger forces they retreated to the coast and, when pursued,
slipped off in their balsa canoes to Tiburón. If the army failed
to exterminate them, the Catholic missionaries were equally
unsuccessful in attempting their conversion. The Indians would
tolerate the Fathers for a time, but the relationship always
ended in a massacre. After the stoning to death of Fray Juan
Crisostomo in 1773 both Church and State left the Seris alone
for a century. But they did not lose their evil reputation. Their
hatred for strangers was not confined to the Spaniards and their
treatment of neighbouring Indians was ferocious. It was said
that their greatest tribal virtue was the shedding of human
blood and their greatest crime marriage into an alien tribe.

The horrific tales which Hardy was told about the Seris did
not discourage him from visiting Tiburón Island in his search

73

for pearls. Anchored off-shore, he took the precaution of loading his two cannons and distributing his small arms (a musket, a sword, a pike and two pairs of pistols) among the crew. Almost at once two Indians appeared, making signals. Covering them with his cannon, he sent a boat to fetch them on board. One of the men wore a hat, a Seri symbol of superior rank. He spoke some Spanish and, after announcing himself as the Captain Chico, explained that the Captain Grande's wife was sick and that he would give all the tortoise-shell he possessed to anyone who would cure her. To Hardy the challenge was irresistible.

Leaving the visitors as hostages, he went ashore armed with a pistol. He was taken to a hut about four feet high made of sticks covered with brush and tortoise-shell. Inside, the Captain Grande, surrounded by women and children, was shaking a small leather bag over the prostrate body of his wife. She was in great agony and lay groaning on the sand. Hardy examined her and found 'the cause of the difficulty'. He does not state what this was, but when he indicated it to the other women, they howled in despair.

Not without qualms as to what would happen to him if the woman died and the chief held him responsible, he set about performing the necessary operation, which he rounded off with a dose of senna. He then returned to his ship. A few hours later, while smoking a cigar on deck, he heard the women howling again. Although he feared his patient might be dead, he went ashore, this time unarmed. A crowd welcomed him and rushed him to the hut, where he found that the operation and dose had taken effect and the woman's condition had already improved. In the rejoicing which followed, the daughter of the Captain Grande, 'a young lady of sixteen of a most interesting countenance', forced him to sit down while she painted his face. Appropriately the colours she chose were red, white and blue. 'With the assistance of a painted stick, the tender artist formed perpendicular narrow stripes down my cheeks and nose at such distance apart as to admit an equally narrow white line between them. With equal delicacy and skill the tops and bottoms of the white lines were finished off with a white spot!'

On returning to his ship he was taken by his crew for an Indian. At this point he gives a surprising piece of information

74

about himself. I had imagined him a sober figure dressed in a frock-coat of naval cut. I was wrong: the crew's confusion was due not only to his painted face, but to the fact that the shirt and trousers he was wearing were of scarlet baize.

The next day a dose of tincture of bark completed the woman's cure. The grateful Indians called him 'Hermano* Captain Tiburón' and allowed him to wander all over the island. He was disappointed when they refused to tell him how they made the poison with which they smeared their arrows.

Satisfied that there were no pearls in the area, he sailed north but was driven back by a storm. The Seri greeted him with the smugness of foreknowledge. They had not wanted him to leave, so they had invoked the storm by their magic. The following morning as the chief's wife showed no sign of a relapse, his ship was allowed to sail away without further hindrance.

Influenced by his own experience, Hardy thought that the savagery of the Seris had been exaggerated. While agreeing that they were brave and warlike he found them so amiable and was so touched by their gratitude that he left them with feelings 'of real kindness'. Subsequent records of Seri violence in the nineteen hundreds do not support his view. Apart from carrying out countless marauding raids, they persisted in their murderous and cannibalistic practices. In 1851 they massacred a Spanish gentleman and his family with sixteen servants. So it went on until the end of the century, when in 1894 two San Francisco journalists who landed on the island were killed and eaten. Two years later the crew of a sloop which ran aground off the Seri coast were disposed of in the same way.

W. J. Magee was attracted to the Seris because he believed that their inveterate savagery constituted a missing link between the animal and human conditions. He based his theory on such characteristics as their reliance on fleetness of foot, their lack of tool-sense, preference for tooth and nail, and their violent opposition to marriage with alien blood. He failed to prove his case, but during the brief period when he was in touch with outlying scavengers of the tribe, he collected much evidence of their sub-human behaviour. One of their

---

* Brother.

more repellent practices, shared by a few of their desert neighbours, is known to anthropology as 'the Californian second harvest'. The fruit of the pitahaya cactus was an important part of their diet. They made it doubly so by preserving their excrement after they had eaten it. When dry, they extracted the undigested seeds of the cactus which then served them for a second meal. But more convincing, as regards Magee's thesis, than any of their established customs is his account of an incident he witnessed in a Seri camp. A pregnant bitch tried to snatch food from a woman's cooking pot. She gave it such a vicious kick that its womb burst open and the embryo puppies fell out. Children playing near by grabbed the embryos, stuffed them into their mouths and gobbled them up.

What had become of the Seris in more recent times? The latest report on them I could find was written by A. L. Kroeber in 1931. By then their marauding and murderous habits had been checked, but otherwise their condition had hardly changed. In his concluding paragraph he urged that a more thorough study of the tribe should be undertaken, but warned that this would involve 'much grinding physical hardship and possibly some danger'.

A final piece of information came from an Englishman living in Mexico City. Twelve years before, on a cruise up the Sonora coast, he had encountered an exiled Seri chieftain. He was wearing his hat of office and, most incongruously, a pair of dark glasses. With this hint that the Seris could not have remained quite out of touch with civilization, I left for Hermosillo.

The plane landed at Ciudad Obregón. Taking off, it flew low over the Yaqui villages described by Terry. He would have scarcely recognized them, still less the country round about. Here, where in the guide-book's day all had been desert, progress had exploded dramatically. The course of the Yaqui River where it flows into the plain had been split up into a network of miniature canals. The villages lay bedded in a vast patchwork of cultivation across which scores of tractors and lorries trailed ribbons of dust. The scale of the achievement was impressive. In the villages little of the old Indian life could have survived. I was glad I had not stopped off to visit them.

If the environment of the Yaquis had been so changed, I wondered what might have become of the Seris.

I could not find anyone in Hermosillo who had seen a Seri, although all the people I questioned agreed that a few of them still existed. I met only one man who had visited the coast opposite Tiburón Island. He tried to discourage me from going there. The few existing villages were wretched places where I would find neither food nor lodging. He thought there was a bus which went to them once or twice a week, but he did not know how I could cross over from the mainland to Tiburón. I would do much better to visit Guaymas, where there were good hotels and excellent swimming.

I was told that the bus left at six in the morning. Fortunately I got up in good time, for I was directed to a dozen places before I found it. Ancient and battered, it stood like discarded scrap on a strip of wasteland. It was empty and there was no sign of its driver. After twenty minutes I was joined by an old woman who told me she was not going all the way to the coast herself, but she believed that the bus did go there at the request of passengers. We both got inside and waited. Shortly afterwards the driver arrived. He looked doubtful when I told him my destination, but he took my money and we set off. A tarred road led out of the city into a scrub desert. We rattled along at a good pace. It was extremely hot, dust blew in through the glassless windows and the road, tapering ahead, shimmered in the glare. Twenty miles out the landscape changed abruptly. It was the scene of another explosion. At one moment the road was bounded by scrub and sand, at the next it had entered a world of green cornfields broken by lines of poplars. We stopped at a neat brick village where the old woman got out. On one side of the road stood a white granary with three red tractors and a combine drawn up in front of it. I drank beer with the driver.

'What're you going to the coast for?'

'To visit the Seris.'

My reply made him raise his eyebrows. He downed the rest of his drink in silence. As we turned back to the bus, I noticed wisps of steam trailing from under the bonnet.

'Oh, it's nothing! It always does that on a hot day.'

We drove on. The cultivation ended as suddenly as it had

77

begun. Looking back, I could see its green edge stretching away on either side to the horizon. The road ran straight and smooth, but the desert we had now entered was different from the earlier stretch. Blazing white sand rolled away to pink mountains. From its undulations a forest of giant cacti probed with multiple fingers against a backing of brilliant blue. The bus stopped with a jolt. Steam whipped from the bonnet and blanketed the windscreen. The driver jumped out. I followed him.

'No water!' He threw up his arms, grinning. From the back of the bus he took an empty tin. Swinging it by its handle, he walked off down the road in the direction from which we had come. As I watched his diminishing figure, the sun flashed on the windscreen of an approaching car. Driven at high speed, it swept past me within seconds, an immense American convertible towing a caravan and a motor launch. I waved but it did not stop.

After half an hour the driver came back with his can filled. He started the engine, replenished the radiator and set off again. The road stretched ahead as straight as ever. Blue lakes appeared in the desert only to vanish as soon as we came close to them. We had been travelling for four hours. I asked how much farther we had to go. 'We're already there, señor!'

I could see nothing but desert. Then, almost at once, we turned off on to a track which swooped away among the dunes and sank into a village. A few mud shacks ringed a dusty hollow. At their hub was the village lock-up, a pill-box with one minute barred window. There was no sign of the sea. I thought of Guaymas and imagined long cool drinks under a thatch of palms. Bony, flea-bitten dogs yelped at the wheels of the bus. As it stopped, a few shifty-looking villagers lounged up to the driver. I got out and asked one of them where I could eat. There was a store which sold fishing tackle over the dunes, he said: I might try that. Sometimes they could provide a meal. I started off with the dogs snarling round me, but he yelled at them and they scattered. At the top of the dunes I stopped. The sea, a dark vivid blue, cracked into foam at the bottom of the slope less than a hundred yards away. The sand curved to the south in a clean, dazzling crescent ending in a headland of shattered rock. Out at sea small rose-pink islands lay in the bay's mouth. A larger island to the north lifted a jagged peak above the sweep of the dunes. Although I could only see its southern half I judged that farther up the coast it almost touched the mainland. This I knew must be Tiburón.

A little way down the slope was the store. The proprietor stood in the doorway. He could only offer me a dish of turtle meat, and for that I would have to wait twenty minutes. I said I would come back. I had spotted some fishermen with their boats farther along the beach. I walked over to them and asked them if they would take me to Tiburón.

'For fishing?'

'No, to visit the Seris.'

They stood in silence looking down at their nets.

'How long will it take? How much will it cost?'

A man who was obviously not a fisherman was the first to speak. He muttered something to the others and after a pause they nodded in agreement.

'You see,' he said, turning to me, 'I didn't want to stop these fellows taking your money if they felt like it, but it so happens they're not interested. In any case the current's too dangerous at the moment. You'd have to wait until tomorrow and set out at dawn. When you get there you wouldn't find any Seris.'

'Where are they then?'

'Up on the mainland at Desenboque and Puerto Cueca.'

'Is that far?'

'Desemboque's fifty kilometres. Puerto Cueca's a little over twenty. It's on the Infernillo Strait.'

'How can I get there?'

'Well, if you really want to go, I've got a truck.'

I regretted giving up the visit to Tiburón but if the fishermen would not take me, there seemed no way of crossing to the island. So I fixed a price for the truck. The man's name was Pedro. He promised to pick me up at the store. I went back to the turtle meat. A place had been laid for me at a table inside the hut. After a few minutes an Indian half-caste came in from the kitchen carrying a plate on which some large brownish hunks protruded from a pool of oil. As he placed it in front of me I noticed that his fingernails were varnished a rosy pink. The fried turtle was revolting, but I managed to get through it.

79

The half-caste stood at the other side of the table. He wanted to know why I had come to the coast.

'To visit the Seris.'

'Why do you want to do that?'

'I'm making a study of Indian tribes.'

'My father was a Seri.'

I looked at him more closely. He was, perhaps, a little taller than the average Indian. Although he was not fat, his shirt and trousers appeared to have more inside them than they could comfortably contain. His black hair was straight and coarse. He was very ugly, almost a monster, with broad cheek-bones and a flat nose with wide nostrils. A few long, wispy hairs trailed from his upper lip and chin. The cheek-bones looked authentically Seri, but the nose was wrong and the face should have been hairless. I wondered if his pink finger-nails were a substitute for face-painting.

'Why are your nails coloured?'

'There was a fiesta here on Sunday. Fifty people came from Hermosillo. It was the most we've ever had. One of the girls painted them for me.'

As I was paying for my meal, Pedro's truck drew up outside. I got in and we drove back through the village on to the tarred road. I asked where the road went.

'Just to the sea. They say they're going to build a hotel on the beach, but there's no sign of it yet. Only a few *gringos* camp there for the fishing.'

Before we came in sight of the coast we turned off down a dust trail into the desert. In the back of the truck an old oil-drum full of water swilled over at every bump.

'That's for the Seris,' Pedro explained. 'It's the best present you can take them.'

'Haven't they got water where they live?'

'Not a drop! God knows why they settled in such a place. We send them over some barrels every week.'

We drove on for a couple of hours. I tried to get Pedro to talk about the Indians, but he was not interested. They were a dirty lot, was all I could get out of him. If they found an animal which had been dead for a couple of days, they'd eat it. He wasn't communicative about anything else, having to keep his mind on the track, which dipped and twisted viciously. At last, as we reached the top of a ridge, he pointed ahead. 'There they are!'

The white sand dropped below us in smooth undulations. One long tongue licked out for a quarter of a mile into the sea. The Infernillo Strait ripped round it like a river in flood. Beyond lay the island, a mountain of pink rock splintered with triangles of blue shadows. In the curve formed by the tongue of sand was a cluster of what I took to be low bushes.

'I don't see them.'

'Down there—by the shore.'

It was not until we were less than a hundred yards away that I realized, as figures began to appear as if out of the ground, that the bushes were really huts. We drew up at the edge of them. They were exactly what I should have expected from Hardy's description: low tunnels of hooped sticks covered with rags, tortoise-shell and dry brush. A crowd of women and children came out to meet us. They were the wildest and most wretchedly clothed people I had ever seen. The tall long-skirted women, even those whose dresses were all of a piece, looked as if they had emerged from a garbage dump. The children who lurked behind them might all have belonged to the same sex. Their black hair hung over their eyes and reached to their shoulders. They were naked except for a short blanket round their hips. They glared at us like savage animals. The women, who stood laughing and chattering to each other, were rather handsome. They had very dark skins and straight noses. Their full cheeks tapered to narrow chins. I realized that Hardy might not have been romancing when he described the girl who painted his face as possessing an interesting countenance.

When they saw me getting out of the truck some of the older women scuttled off, revealing in the second row three or four girls with painted faces. But the art had declined since Hardy's day. Instead of elegant lines and dots they had only white wing shapes outlined in blue on their foreheads and cheekbones. Soon the women who had gone off returned carrying baskets which they pressed on me with the persistence of keen traders. The baskets resembled, both in shape and pattern, those made by primitive communities the world over. I bargained, and bought a few to keep them happy. One woman, the most handsome and intelligent-looking, spoke a little Spanish. I asked her why the girls painted their faces. 'Ah, señor,' it was as if the idea had just come to her. 'It's because it's so hot.'

When I inquired about the men of the village, she told me they had left three days before to go fishing. I tried several other questions without success. The interest I had aroused was soon exhausted and, when they realized that I was not going to buy anything more, they began to drift away. I looked round for Pedro, but he had vanished. I felt that if this was to be the end of my encounter with the Seris, I had made a long journey for very little. I decided to take a look at the settlement itself.

I had only moved a few paces when I was confronted by a tall menacing figure. I did not see where he came from. He was suddenly standing directly in my path. Thin but sinewy, he was dressed in an American sweat-shirt and patched jeans. On his head was a high crowned hat and he wore not one, like the exiled chief, but two pairs of dark glasses, one on top of the other. Clearly he was the Captain Grande. I walked up to him and offered him my hand. He did not take it.

'This is my camp.' He spoke barely intelligible Spanish, 'I'm the head of it. What d'you want?'

Now that I was actually in a Seri settlement and confronted by a hostile Seri chief I could think of no justification for my presence. I answered with a half-truth.

'I come from a country thousands of miles away across the sea. Many years ago one of my compatriots came to Tiburón. The wife of the Captain Grande was sick. He cured her with his medicines. In return your people accepted him as a friend. They painted his face and allowed him to wander all over the island. He wrote a book in which he said that the Seris were a fine people and had treated him well. I came here to see for myself what had become of his friends.'

I could not tell how much the chief understood of this speech as his eyes were totally invisible behind his double dark glasses; but it did not produce any friendly response. I broke his silence by asking him a question.

'Why are you no longer living on Tiburón?'

'It's no good there now. How could we sell what we catch?'

'Whom do you sell it to here?'

'We have a shop.' He nodded towards a mud-brick hut which I had not previously noticed. It stood a little apart from the settlement.

'Is this a good area for fish?'

'No, we have to go a long way to catch anything. Down by the village it's better.'

'Then why didn't you settle there?'

'We tried to, but the Mexicans wanted to keep the well for themselves, so they drove us away. Now the only water we have is what they bring us.'

'How many people live here?'

'Six families.'

'Is that all the Seris who are left?'

'There are others at Desenboque.'

'Do you visit them?'

'No.'

'Why not?'

'They don't live as we do. They are not true Seris any longer.'

If being a true Seri necessitated living in the conditions which I saw round me, I could not blame the other branch for having defected. And yet it was the Seris' obstinacy, their refusal to change their way of life, to mix their blood with that of any other race or to submit to any form of alien domination which had ensured their survival as an independent tribe over hundreds of years. But what kind of independence could they claim now, when they had to rely upon the people of the village to bring them water? And what was it worth if the instinct which urged them to cling to it tied them to a huddle of stick huts surrounded by years of accumulated refuse? If they insisted on living in such misery, who could blame the Mexicans for giving them up, for sweeping them, so to speak, under the carpet?

As I gazed round the squalid disorder of the camp I caught sight of a tapering object sticking out from behind a hut. I recognized it from one of Magee's illustrations as the bow of a balsa-wood canoe. I walked over to it, followed by the Captain Grande. The canoe was about ten feet long.

'Do you use this for fishing?'

'No, it's a toy. The children play with it.'

'But you make larger boats of the same kind?'

'No. Our boats are of wood.'

'Do you paddle them with oars or do you use sails?'

'Neither. They have motors.'

If they had progressed so far as to have motor-boats, why had they refused to change in other ways? Why did they go on living in wigwams on a muck-heap? Why had they chosen a strip of waterless desert for their settlement, where even the fishing was poor? As these questions presented themselves, my sympathy for the Seris began to dwindle. Stripped of his role of tragic survivor, the Captain Grande no longer commanded my respect. I turned away and wandered off among the huts. At every step flies buzzed up from lumps of discarded turtle flesh or piles of human excrement. The latter reminded me of the Californian second harvest, but I did not ask if this was the reason why so much of it was lying about. The filth of the man-inhabited patch was accentuated by the pure white of the desert by which it was surrounded. With the courage of contempt, I stooped and looked in through the opening of one of the huts. Half a dozen women and children crowded its narrow space. Startled by my appearance they shrank into a squirming heap. As I straightened up I felt the chief's hand on my shoulder. I jerked away, but he was only trying to attract my attention. He pointed towards the sea. Three long narrow boats, very low in the water, were heading for the shore. Propelled by outboard motors, they left white scars of foam in the waves behind them.

We hurried down to the beach. The men were already pulling the boats up on to the sand. They were a wild-looking people with long hair reaching to their shoulders. Half-naked, they exhibited bodies which were lean and muscular. They had on the same kind of apron-like blankets as the children, but wore them over coarse-woven trousers. As soon as the boats were well clear of the water, they threw out the catch on to the sand. I had expected a large pile of fish, but their total bag, after three days at sea, consisted of four turtles. Four turtles! What did they need outboard motors for? Their ancestors could have done better in their balsa canoes. The last dregs of my sympathy for the Seris ebbed away.

I held out my hand to the chief. 'I must go now.'

This time his hand came out towards me, not grasping mine, but with the palm upwards. 'You pay me,' he said.

'What for?'

'For letting you see my camp.'

'How much do you want?'

'A hundred pesos.'

Eight dollars for being allowed to walk round a human dung-heap! I decided that Pedro would deal with the demand more effectively than I could, so I walked towards the truck.

'Or a shirt or a pair of trousers. The *gringo* fishermen always give me presents.'

I reached the truck but there was no sign of Pedro.

'He'll be up in the shop.' The chief pointed to the mud-brick shack at the edge of the settlement. We walked over to it. The single room inside served as a store and living quarters. Cans of motor oil were piled to the roof. Rope and cord hung from the rafters. One wall was stacked with bales of cheap cloth. On the floor were drums, crates, and sacks and, jammed among them, a primitive table and a chair with a broken back. In the middle of this confusion, but swinging gently a few inches above it, an enormously fat Mexican, wearing only a pair of cotton pants, lay sprawled in a hammock. Pedro, who was sitting on an oil drum at his side, introduced us. The man's name was Don Jorge. He offered me the broken chair. I accepted and sat down.

What had brought me to Puerto Cueca? I told him how I had become interested in the Seris through Hardy's account of his visit to Tiburón.

He was a lucky man, he said. Even twenty years ago they were still murdering strangers. Today it was safe enough but one had to be careful. A few months ago a fisherman from the village had been shot at. The police had raided the camp and confiscated all the rifles they could find. They had taken his stock of ammunition, too, without paying for it. He got on well with the Indians, himself, and had traded with them for years. When they came to Puerto Cueca they asked him to set up a trading store. At first they bartered their catch for whatever supplies they needed. Now they insisted on money, but they spent most of what they earned in the shop.

'How long have you lived here?'

'Six years. I was at Desenboque before. The Government collected all the Seris there about ten years ago and set up a fishing co-operative for them. That's how they got the motors for their boats. There's a school there, too, and they live in houses.

'Why did these families leave?'

'Because they didn't like the missionaries.'

'What, Catholic priests?'

'No, Protestant *gringos*. They stopped them singing their own songs and made them learn hymns in Spanish. They were forbidden to drink alcohol or smoke marijuana or paint their faces or dance. It was an end to all their old customs, but this lot wouldn't change. In the end they made off. First they went to Tiburón, but they couldn't sell their fish there, so they moved to Puerto Cueca.'

'Didn't the missionaries come after them?'

'No, they gave them up. Nobody bothers about them now unless they make trouble.'

'What about the Catholics?'

'There's never been a priest here so far as I know.'

'Have they a religion of their own?'

Don Jorge thought for a moment. It seemed that this was a question which had not occurred to him before. Some of the fishermen, surrounded by their families, were now standing with the chief in the doorway. Among them was the Spanish-speaking woman who had sold me the baskets. Don Jorge heaved himself up in his hammock.

'You're Christians, aren't you?' he asked.

For a minute no one answered. Under their wild manner and tough animal appearance, the men had become nervous and shifty. It was the woman who pushed herself forward and spoke.

'No, we're not Christians!'

Don Jorge was shocked. 'You mean you don't believe in the Virgin and the Saints?'

'No, we don't.'

'You worship the old gods of your ancestors,' I suggested.

She was silent for a moment, then: 'No!'

'What do you believe in?'

This time she did not hesitate and her answer came out with ringing pride.

86

'*Nada!* Nothing! Nothing at all!'

As we walked back from the store, the chief kept close to me. He followed me round to my side of the truck and, while Pedro was getting into the driver's seat, thrust out his open palm. Wheedling and threatening, he again demanded his fee. Furtively I fumbled a note out of my wallet and gave it to him. At that moment Pedro glanced round. The sight of the hundred pesos made him shout with anger; but the Captain Grande already had it in his grasp. Poker-faced behind his battery of dark glasses, he turned without a word and strode off.

'A hundred pesos! You're mad! They'll only drink themselves crazy!'

All the way back to the village his anger simmered. I guessed it was not the thought of the drunken Seris which bothered him but his own failure to have judged from my appearance the amount he might have got out of me for the trip.

I was dumped outside the village lock-up unforgiven. There was no bus. The driver had said he would not leave before I got back, but I had not really expected him to wait. With the dogs snarling round my legs I walked over the dunes to the store. The proprietor and his wife were sitting outside watching the sunset.

Oh yes, the bus had gone. They'd heard its warning hoot just after I had left. It might be back tomorrow. It depended on whether there were any passengers.

Was there a house in the village where I could sleep?

They shook their heads. All they could suggest was a hut at the back of the store, but it had no bed. Would I like to see it? If I thought it would do, they would send the servant to borrow a *catre*.* Not wishing to depress myself by a preview of the place, I said I was sure it would suit me very well.

'Juanito!' The Seri half-caste appeared at the door. 'Go round to Don Rafael and ask him if he can lend us a *catre* for this gentleman to sleep on.'

Juanito went off grinning. The old man brought a chair out of the kitchen and invited me to sit down. His name was Pablo. He came from Hermosillo. His wife, Natalia, was from

---

* A primitive form of camp bed.

farther south. After years of bad health they had decided to come to live in the desert by the sea. The dry air suited them. They had never been happier. They made a little money supplying fishing equipment and meals to the few visitors who came to the village. Sometimes an American would buy up all their stock. But they really did not need to earn anything: living was cheap, and they had saved enough to last out their lifetime.

I asked Don Pablo if he had ever been to Puerto Cueca. No, he hadn't. Sometimes one or two of the Indians came to the village. He didn't think much of them. They were a dirty, thieving lot.

'Juanito told me his father was a Seri.'

'Yes, it's true. He was one of their chiefs, but they threw him out, so he came to live in the village. He took up with the wife of a fisherman who had deserted her. They had three children. Then he decided to go back to his own people. When he left her, the woman went to Hermosillo with the family. But Juanito didn't like it. He came back here on his own. It's only possible to make a living as a fisherman, but he wasn't any good for that, so he did odd jobs about the village. When we took him on he was starving. He doesn't work any more than he has to, but he's never given us any trouble. The Seris can be difficult though. How did you find the people at Puerto Cueca?'

'It's a tragedy. Cut off and living as they do, they'll be finished in fifty years. They were offered a chance at Desenboque. With education they'd have soon become like other Mexicans. It was the only solution. The irony of it is that, from the tribal point of view, they threw it all up for the right reasons.'

I told them about the missionaries.

'Yes, the Protestants always make trouble. All the same the Seris can't become Mexicans like the rest of us so long as they paint their faces and worship their pagan gods.'

'But they don't even paint their faces properly. They just dab on a few patches of whitewash. And they don't believe in their gods any more, either. They still look like the descendants of warriors and hunters, but I don't believe there was a man among those I saw who would have the determination, even if he had the energy, to run down a deer and kill it with his hands.'

'Ah, if it's real warriors you're looking for,' his wife said, 'you should've gone to the Yaquis.'

'But they've changed, too. Now the river's been used for irrigation, they've turned into farmers.'

'That's only in the plain. Down there they've been quiet for a long time. When I was a little girl, my father had a store in a village high up in the mountains. That was in the real Yaqui country. It was at the time of the gold rush. What a life we had! It drew all the worst ruffians in Mexico and from over the border too. Our village was their headquarters. They were the wildest lot you can imagine. No woman could be out after dark. My mother wouldn't let me leave the house by myself even in day-time.

'If any of them did find gold, the whole place went mad. They'd come into the village swearing to keep it secret, but after a few drinks out it would come. Then the trouble started. Not many reached the coast with a quarter of what they'd found and some lost it all.

'There were others who went up into the Sierra and were never heard of again. The rumour would go round that the Yaquis had got them. The Indians were supposed to have a gold mine of their own. If a stranger wandered too close to it, the look-outs would kill him with bows and arrows. They were cruel, those Yaquis, but they were a fine people. I used to watch them going past the window of the store. They were proud and handsome. Real warriors they were, and they looked as if they thought us Mexicans so much dirt. The Seris may have been warriors, too, but nowadays they're nothing but a bunch of dirty sneak-thieves.'

While we had been talking the sun had gone down and the breeze from across the gulf had quickened. It was becoming chilly. We got up from our chairs and carried them into the kitchen. Natalia offered me eggs for supper. I said I'd take a walk before eating.

As I set off down the slope of the dunes, the sand was dyed crimson from the last flare of the sunset. I stopped to watch the glow as it deepened over the islands and the long sweep of the bay, but was disturbed almost at once by ferocious barking from above. I turned and saw a pack of the village dogs streaking towards me. It was too late to retreat, so I cut down towards the sea, thinking that if the attack proved as savage as it sounded, I could take to the water. They had almost caught up with me when there was another equally ferocious outcry and a second pack came swooping down from a point further along the dunes. I thought I was going to be set upon by both packs at once, but they swerved and headed towards each other. There was a brief snarling skirmish, then the first pack broke and ran. I continued my walk unmolested. Evidently I had crossed an invisible boundary between the territories of two rival packs; for they behaved in the same way when I returned.

Back at the store my supper was waiting and Juanito served me. He had borrowed a *catre* but there were no blankets. I told him I had one in my sack, but he said it would not be enough. At that time of year it got very cold during the night. He himself had no less than seven on his bed. Although I imagined that he was probably more susceptible to cold than I was, his warning did not make me feel happier at the prospect of my night in the hut. I decided to put off going to bed until as late as possible. When I had finished my supper I took a walk round the village. The dogs snarled but did not attack. Passing a cottage I was greeted by Pedro, the truck-driver. He must have forgotten about the hundred pesos, for he was now quite friendly and asked me in for a drink. I stayed for half an hour, then he began yawning, so there was nothing for it but to go back. As I came over the dunes the wind struck me in the face. It was blowing hard and had a sharp cut to it. Don Pablo, ready for bed himself, was waiting for me. Lantern in hand, he led me round to the back of the kitchen. The hut was tucked in behind it with the entrance facing towards the sea. Its flimsy cane walls, under a thatched roof, were lined on the inside with scraps of cardboard and sacking. It contained two beds. The one placed in the most sheltered corner had a pillow and rugs. The other was a *catre*, a primitive truckle frame covered by a strip of sagging canvas.

'Who sleeps there?' I pointed to the bed with the blankets.

'Juanito. He'll be turning in soon. He won't disturb you.' Don Pablo put the lantern down on an upturned crate which served as a table. Wishing me good-night, he withdrew.

One end of the *catre* was wedged into the corner at the foot of Juanito's bed. If I were to lie with my head at that end I would have Juanito's feet in my face. Making a roll of my towel to serve as a pillow, I placed it at the other end. The wind, which was still rising, whipped it up and flung it against the wall. I turned to close the door, but found that it did not exist. Only the post was there with a pair of rusty hinges attached to it. Clearly I could not sleep with the wind blasting round my head, so I picked up the towel and placed it at the other end in the corner. I took off my jacket and hung it with my rucksack from a nail in the wall close to where my head would be resting. After removing my boots and hanging them from the same nail by their laces, I lay down with the rest of my clothes on and pulled my one blanket over me. I was uncomfortable but so tired that I did not think I would find it difficult to sleep. I rolled on one side away from the lantern and at once I was dozing.

Suddenly I was awake again. The light had moved. Now I saw its beams creeping over the wall, growing brighter. Juanito must have come in and picked it up. But what was he doing? Keeping very still, I continued to breathe deeply. There was a slight knock against the *catre*. I half opened one eye to watch my jacket and rucksack for predatory fingers. None appeared. Two harder knocks made the rickety frame sway beneath me. It was as if he was making sure that I was asleep or was determined to wake me up. I deepened my breathing to a snore. The light moved on the wall and grew dimmer. Then the lantern clinked as it was put down on the crate. In the silence which followed, I became uncertain whether Juanito was still in the hut. This doubt worried me. I had to turn over and look. The hut was empty, but now I could hear him outside urinating on the sand. I pulled the blanket over my head so that when he returned he would not be able to see that I had moved; but I left a chink for a look-out.

He came in and sat down on his bed. As he bent forward to untie his sandals, the light caught the colour of his nails. He stretched out his hands with his fingers apart and gazed at them. The sight of the vulgar pink brought a look of rapture to his face. A Caliban enchanted by a lost Ariel's touch, he sat without moving until at last the spell wore out. Standing up, he slowly drew his shirt over his head. As it pulled free from his belt it rose over a stomach as lean and dark as the Seri fishermen's, but on reaching his chest it caught for a second, then with a six-inch jerk it lifted to expose in the lantern's glow a pair of plump full-nippled breasts. Between them were straggling hairs, matching those on his chin and upper lip. As his fingers moved to his belt, I watched with fascination to see what other curiosities he might reveal. He undid the buckle and took off his trousers. His legs were hairy, his hips rounded and feminine. The sum of these sexual ambiguities was as horrifying as it was pathetic. After lowering the wick of the lantern he got into bed and still wearing his underpants, settled deep beneath his seven blankets.

I soon dozed off again myself, but after an hour or two I was woken up by something bumping me through the canvas on which I was lying. The lamp was still burning. When I peered over the side of the *catre* I encountered snarls and the gleam of six pairs of glassy eyes and six sets of bared canine teeth. The local pack, sheltering from the wind, had bedded down beneath me for the night. That they needed shelter was not surprising. Outside the hut and, to a modified degree, inside, it was blowing a gale. Through the canvas the cold gripped me like an ice-pack. I reached for my jacket and put it on, wrapping it close round my body. The balance between cold and fatigue was even. At last fatigue triumphed and I slept. It was not for long. The next time I woke the cold had got deep inside me, striking into my spine with a continuous tooth-edged pain. The dogs were feeling it, too, for they kept shaking themselves and moving about beneath me, while, above, Don Pablo's roosters were tramping up and down on the leeward side of the roof like a patrol of pigmy police. I pulled my spare clothes out of my rucksack and stuffed them inside my shirt and trousers. Finally I sacrificed my pillow and wound the towel in a tight cummerbund under my jacket.

I slept, but soon the cold came knifing into me again and I woke shaking with its torment. I decided to get up and walk. I put on my boots, but when I thrust a leg over the side of the *catre*, there was a snarl and a ringing snap. I jerked it out of reach. Cowed into resignation, I hunched under my blanket again. How right Juanito had been when he had said that one would not be enough! And how soundly he seemed to be sleeping under his seven layers! Surely he would not miss one of them. Cautiously I grasped his top blanket with both hands and drew it towards me a few inches. He did not stir. I pulled again. It moved easily, too easily, for all the other blankets moved with it. I stopped pulling but the blankets came on and Juanito, leering as he loomed above their folds, came with them.

It must have been about three o'clock, the hour when curiosity is at an ebb and fear is the emotion most easily aroused. But it was less fear than horror which sent me leaping from the *catre* to the entrance of the hut in a single bound. I was scarcely out on the sand before the dogs were up and after me. I knew the trick now and made a dash for the invisible boundary. As I crossed it, the rival pack swooped. I still ran on, although I knew from the snarls fading behind me that I was safe. When I had jogged the cold out of my body I turned in under the shelter of the dunes, where I broke off some branches of scrub and laid them out as a mattress. It was luxury after the hazards of Don Pablo's hut. For the first time that night I slept soundly.

When I awoke the sun was already rising. I climbed on to the dunes and watched the pink light on the islands growing paler as the grey sea which surrounded them deepened into blue. All over the bay dolphins threaded the waves with black shining loops. A flight of duck shot out to sea in a broad arrow and in the channel between two islands a whale spouted. It was here, more than a hundred years before on just such a morning, Lieutenant Hardy had come sailing through the Infernillo Strait with the sun on his rigging and the wind in his whiskers as he balanced staunchly on the poop, resplendent in scarlet baize.

It was all very well to smile at him, but his had been real adventures. Released from the Seri spells, he had sailed north up the gulf and had grounded on a shoal in the Colorado River. For a week, as he waited for the tide to rise high enough to float him off, he had been surrounded by hostile Indians. Buoyed by recollections of roast beef and fortified with that enviable sense of superiority which belonged to the Englishman of his time, he was able to reflect of the hordes which threatened him that 'they were but Indians. A savage is only a superior kind of animal, the intermediate link between civilized man and brute creation'.

Not for him the uncomfortable thoughts which came to me as I walked back along the dunes to the village. Probably with justice he would have written off the Seris of my day as miserably degenerate, whereas an encounter with a half-caste hermaphrodite might well have urged him to attempt new marvels in quackery. For myself, I was determined that I would never again visit a primitive tribe unless I had some motive for going other than curiosity. I was also shamefully aware that neither curiosity nor horror had been justifiable reactions to Juanito's condition.

When I came close to the village I saw the top of the bus gleaming in the sun.

'You see,' the driver exclaimed as I approached him, 'I've come back for you.'

'But you said you'd wait for me yesterday.'

He shrugged his shoulders. 'You told me you were going to visit the Seris. How was I to know when you'd come back or if you'd come back at all?'

5

Mushroom Country

Seen from the air the new road east from Teotitlán del Camino splinters into the Sierra Juarez like forked lightning. After zigzagging two thousand feet up the rock wall, it thrusts on through the mountains in spurts which are longer but have corners which are no less acute. Probing round the heads of valleys and delving into canyons, it finally reaches the villages of the Mixteca Indians on the watershed between the Tonto and Quiotepec rivers. The embroideries worked by the Indian women are among the most beautiful in Mexico. Now that the road, though frequently broken by landslides, has linked the villages to the civilization of the plains, the embroideries have begun to disappear. Such casualties are an inevitable consequence of Mexican progress. But between the Mixtecas and the civilized world the traffic has not been all one-way, for the rediscovery of a Mixteca mushroom cult, itself a pre-Christian survival, has helped scientists in a new approach to the study of the mind, and the treatment of mental disorders. The Indians eat their mushrooms not as food but for spiritual enlightenment. They call them 'the mushrooms of superior reason'.

The relative accessibility of the area brought about by the new road, and the publication of an article by R. G. Wasson in *Life* magazine interested people other than scientists in the properties of the Mixteca mushroom. Within a few years, the Indians, realizing that the mushrooms had become a saleable commodity, brought them down in sacks from the mountains to hawk among clients in Mexico City. This commerce was restricted as only a few Indians were prepared to make the journey and the season during which the mushrooms flourished was short. Moreover the effects they produced were not always so agreeable that those who tried them wished to repeat the experiment.

I became interested in the mushrooms at a time when it was still necessary to visit the Indian villages to obtain them. I had friends in Mexico City who had made the journey and had eaten them under the guidance of a village witch. It seemed that the effects of the drug* could be either malevolent or benign according to whether the person taking it resisted or accepted its influence. Before distributing the mushrooms, the witch had conducted a religious ceremony, half pagan, half Christian, which was intended to calm the fears of the participants so that they did not resist the drug and entered more easily into the state of superior reason.

When my friends decided to make a second expedition to the Mixteca country, they invited me to go with them. As I was unable to accept, they agreed to bring back some mushrooms for me to try. The day after their return, they came to my house in the evening carrying the mushrooms in a bag and accompanied by an American who also wished to take them. When they had divided them up, following the witch's instructions, there were three portions. They gave the American and myself a portion each and advised us to eat them lying down in a darkened room. We must cover ourselves with blankets, as the first symptom was a sensation of extreme cold.

The room leading out of the one in which we were sitting had a sofa at either end. I suggested to the American that we should each take one of the sofas. He agreed and we settled ourselves with our blankets and mushrooms. The spare portion was placed on a table within my reach. The lights were turned out but the door into the adjoining room, which was lit by one lamp, was left open.

I picked up a mushroom and inspected it. It was brownish-grey with a thin stalk. It had not been washed, since, according to the witch, this would have destroyed its magic properties. Some small particles attached to it had the appearance of dried dung. I thought of the great wall of the Sierra Juarez which I had often seen from the Veracruz road rising out of the plain beyond Tehuacán. It was up there in some remote valley that this far from innocent-looking fungus had been picked. I imagined the brown Indian hand which had delved into the

---

* Psilocybine.

dung to pluck its stalk, and the wrinkled fingers of the old witch who had taken it from her store to give to my friends. Then I checked my thoughts and put it into my mouth and ate it. It had a vegetable flavour, unfamiliar and faintly disagreeable. I finished my portion and lay back on the sofa.

After ten minutes the American, who had only eaten half his share, told me that his hands and feet were getting cold. Almost at once he was seeing bright colours and patterns, 'just like abstract paintings'. These were followed by more realistic visions. 'It's the space age! Greek statues floating in space! I didn't know I had such things in my head!'

Twenty minutes passed and I still felt no change in my own condition. I knew from experience that I was resistant to drugs. I had smoked and eaten marijuana under different names in several countries and in Mexico had chewed through the head of a peyotl cactus. None of these experiments had carried me out of my normal state. Fearing that I was again going to be disappointed, I became impatient. I took the rest of the American's share and a few more from the untouched portion.

I realized almost at once that I had no need of this second dose. Before it could have possibly had time to affect me, my hands and feet became numb. I closed my eyes. Iridescent lines as thin as hairs drifted through the darkness. Soon they swelled into more solid shapes and formed vivid patterns of luminous colour. It was true that they did resemble some form of abstract painting, but they possessed the added fascination of movement. I watched them happily enough until I began to be distracted by a less agreeable sensation. Something moved in the inmost depths of my consciousness, the mere stirrings at first of an alien power which I recognized as immensely strong, and defined, because I was afraid of it, as evil. Gradually its strength gathered and welled up through me until it challenged the possession not only of my will but of the very essence of my selfhood. I opened my eyes. The forms and colours vanished. My gaze fixed on the gilt frame of a mirror which caught the light above my head. No inanimate object had ever struck me before with such an aura of menace. On the other side of the room the American was making gasping sounds which grated on my nerves. I got up and walked through the open door. As

97

I moved, every object I looked at without being either changed or distorted gave off the same menace as the gilt frame.

Suddenly I had to vomit. I lurched across the room to the lavatory, where I retched in violent spasms. When the bout was over, I straightened up and staggered back into the room I had just left. But I did not come alone. For in the doorway my being was wrenched apart and two replicas of myself, imbued with insane aspects of my personality, broke free from me and jostled at my shoulders. I felt that I was mad and would remain so until I could get these monsters under my control. I stumbled forward and collapsed on to a sofa by the fire. In the hope that by concentrating on the familiar I might regain my sanity, I stared from one piece of furniture to another only to find that they had all been overlaid with the same veneer of malevolent animation. Now all other preoccupations were driven from my mind. My pulse weakened. I lay back groaning and closed my eyes. At once I was back in the world of the mushrooms. The scene it presented was weird and gloomy but because of its resemblance to the grotesque in Gothic sculpture and the fantastic in the paintings of Brueghel and Bosch it was not unfamiliar. As with the abstract patterns, everything in the vision moved continuously. The most impressive sequence, and the one which most frequently recurred, centred round a range of buildings overhung by trees and submerged in massive undergrowth. Both vegetation and architecture were formed of a substance like liquid soap which, without losing its basic shape, seethed into rents and holes through which fantastic reptilian creatures wove and scuttled. Although I saw it not only in my mind but with my eyes open I did not believe in its reality, and I remained outside it without any sense of participation as is usual in dreams.

What was intensely real, however, was the lurking presence of the power with which I had already had a preliminary skirmish. Now it was gathering its strength again. Though external to myself, as before, it seemed to come surging up from the remotest, the most unexplored reaches of my being. This time the struggle was long and fierce. I found that I could still disengage from it by opening my eyes, but whenever I did so, out of sheer exhaustion, the menace in the reality by which I was surrounded proved more intolerable than the visionary horror from which I was trying to escape. At last the power began to weaken. Detaching itself from my will, it drew back over a twilit waste and was lost in the black void beyond.

I felt a great weakness and calm. I opened my eyes. It was as if I had returned from a long journey. I found that the flames of the fire gave me comfort. Wan and feeble, I stared at their flickering glow like an exile at the lights of his homeland across an impassable frontier. When I looked away again I was back with the trees and architecture and the reptiles scurrying in and out. As I watched it, the writhing architecture began to disintegrate and I found myself looking into a cave which grew larger and deeper. At its extremity a red glow, faint to begin with but gradually deepening, spread out over the roof and walls. From its centre the power, now visible as a black shapeless mass, loomed forward for yet another assault. I moved into the cave to meet it. At first it remained intangible but soon, although I could not actually feel it in my grasp, it took on the form of a large hairy animal. Slowly the violence of its wrestling diminished. It became gentle, even friendly, until all the urgency went out of the struggle and we locked languidly together as in a game.

At last it dropped away from me. Gradually the light in the cave grew brighter and I began to laugh. The whole secret of life lay in laughter and above all in laughing at oneself. I opened my eyes and I was still laughing. I tried to explain my discovery to my friends. I could not understand why they were not laughing too, for I did not realize that my words were unintelligible. As I talked the visions returned again. In a blue sky white pavilions floated among birds and clouds. The architecture, of an absurd bandstand variety, made me laugh. It was a false paradise by which even a child could not have been taken in. Then I began to feel uneasy and my laughter stopped. The vision faded and through it the objects in the room emerged hideous and menacing.*

I felt ill, far worse than before. I was racked with nausea but could not vomit. My body grew colder and colder. My pulse became so weak that I could not feel it. I heard my friends

---

* This must have been the moment, although it did not occur to me at the time, when my second helping of mushrooms began to take effect.

talking in low urgent voices. One of them stirred something in the bottom of a glass. The grating of the spoon tortured my nerves. The glass was pushed into my hand: 'It's only sugar, it'll do you good.' I lifted it unsteadily to my lips and drank. At once I felt physically better. My pulse strengthened and the nausea left me. But the mushrooms had not finished with my mind.

In my anguish I clutched my head. My fingers closed over the naked bone of my skull. But soon it moved out of my grasp and floated in front of me, a white knobbly mass which could only have belonged to a monster. It receded over the same grey waste I had seen before. As it vanished, the power, now hostile again, appeared on the edge of the horizon. But I was distracted from it by an intolerable sense of oppression which began to weigh on me from overhead. Soon it condensed into a black oval shape which murmured with voices. I asked if there was anyone talking upstairs. My wife told me that our two Indian maids had gone to bed, but she could not hear them. As I insisted that I could still hear voices, she went up to their room. When she came back she said that she had found them on their knees praying.

At this stage my mind was clear of visions but my nerves were painfully agitated. The American, whose murmurings I could hear from the next room now began to shout. I asked my friends to stop him, but they replied that he was still under the influence of the drug and there was nothing they could do. As his voice rasped higher and higher, I felt a vicious rage boiling up inside me. Suddenly it moved out of my system and, ceasing altogether to be a part of me, left my mind in a profound calm; then within seconds, it manifested itself beside the fireplace in the shape of a tall Chinese dragon, black all over but outlined in vivid green. As I watched, it turned and began to move towards me. I knew that if it entered me again, its violence would be beyond my control. I rose with a struggle and stumbled upstairs to my room, where I lay down on my bed.

Through the window I heard a roar of voices. Although the curtains were drawn and I was lying on my back looking up at the ceiling, I saw that the street was crowded with Indians. From the centre of the mob, as if squeezed out by the pressure of the bodies which surrounded it, an obscene pink shape erupted, banded and bulging like a caterpillar but with human features and a great tonsured head. I recognized this monster, although it bore no resemblance to him, even before the crowd began to shout his name, as the priest Hidalgo, one of the heroes of Mexican Independence. This was the last of the 'set-piece' hallucinations and by far the most convincing. Even when it was over I was still certain that some kind of disturbance had taken place outside the house.

I now sank into a twilit coma, from which I emerged only to find myself wandering over the same waste land as before with the power still lying in wait on the horizon. I was too exhausted to struggle with it again. As I came to accept its presence, the gloom which surrounded me began to brighten. The light was pale at first but quickly grew into a brilliant white ball like a sun, but without heat or glare. I sat up in bed (in fact I did not move) to meet it. The light was the truth. Touched by its splendour there was nothing I could not understand, but as my intellect rose to grasp at the gift which it offered, it was the authenticity of the truth itself which I questioned. 'Why should this light be the truth?'

At once the implied doubt became a truth as absolute as the truth of the light. I was in a state of intense intellectual excitement. The denial of the ultimate truth was itself the ultimate truth, but this was not all, for I found that the same aura of truth suffused any thought or image which came into my mind. I felt like a prophet, a figure from Blake with a long white beard. I put my hand out to touch my knee, but it was a hundred yards away and my arm stretched a hundred yards to reach it. I thought of a Chinese jade which I had not even seen, found by a man whom I had never met, whose name I had not heard mentioned for twenty years, and the jade became a symbol of ultimate truth. Soon my intellect seemed to be working on a dozen different levels of consciousness at once and I was chasing ultimate truths like rats in a haystack. It was an exciting but exhausting occupation. At last I fell back on my pillow (it was two o'clock: for six hours the mushrooms had held me in their power); and sank into a long dreamless sleep.

Before leaving Mexico I made two attempts to reach the mushroom country, but they both failed, the first for lack of time and the second because the road was blocked by a landslide. Even as far as I went the road was remarkable, from the ascent of the rock wall, with the plain of Puebla tilted crazily below, to the wild mountain scenery at the top where range after range, split by valleys and canyons, rose to the high peaks of the watershed. In such a fastness, which, before the road, must have been formidably remote, it was not surprising that, while taking to Christianity with customary Indian fervour, the Mixtecas should have continued to practise their ancient cult, substituting the Virgin in their ritual for the little stone mushroom god invoked by their ancestors.*

---

* My interest in hallucinogenic mushrooms was stimulated by the experiences of two friends, one living in Mexico, the other in England, who were both subject to hallucinations without having recourse to drugs. The friend who lived in Mexico was a writer. The hallucinations came to him in bed at night just as he was about to fall asleep. His hands and feet would grow cold and, soon after, the room would fill with weird shapes and monsters. He felt that he was being drawn beyond the normal boundaries of consciousness, but he was too afraid to let himself go. On the one occasion he did not resist, he reached what he described as 'the threshold of cosmic understanding'. His experiences left him with the conviction that he had crossed over into a world which, however different, was as real as our own. Un-connected with the hallucinations, he had a fainting fit. His doctor advised him, if he had another attack, to take sugar. Subsequently he discovered that sugar acted as a partial antidote to his hallucinatory state. When I read him an account of what happened to me as a result of taking the mushrooms, he told me that in almost all its essentials it corresponded to his own experience. A neurologist prescribed a drug for him which would act as an antidote to the drug produced in his own system. He tried it, but it had the effect of making him feel that his blood had turned to lead in his veins. The sensation was so unpleasant that he threw the pills away, preferring to live with his hallucinations.

The friend in England was a painter. He had been born a Catholic, but had lapsed as a young man and become a sympathizer with the extreme left. He had pronounced manic-depressive tendencies for which he had been treated by a psychiatrist who had given him shock treatment.

One evening he arrived at our house in England without warning. He was in a manic state, but instead of this taking its usual form of mildly aggressive exhilara-tion, it set him wandering through the rooms exclaiming about the colours of objects and their symbolic significance. He refused to eat dinner but throughout the evening kept asking for honey, which he took in spoonfuls out of the pot. The next morning when he was called with his breakfast, he was sitting up in bed with his face drawn and his eyes staring. Asked if he was feeling ill, he replied that there was nothing wrong with him, but that he had had a revelation during the night. He had woken up to find the Virgin standing at the end of the bed. She had been surrounded by a circle of light which he had recognized as the ultimate truth. Now everything in life was clear to him. Above all he knew he had been wrong to give up the faith in which he had been born. Some months later, after visions of a similar kind, he went to live in a lay monastery where, except for occasional visits abroad, he spent the rest of his life.

On my return to England I visited him at his monastery. I told him that while in

Mexico I had had an experience in which he might find some similarity to his own visionary state at the time of his conversion. He said that he would like to hear about it. First I asked him if he remembered how on the evening at our house when he had seen the vision of the Virgin, he had refused to eat anything but honey. He remembered neither asking for honey nor eating it. Then I told him the story of the mushrooms. When I had finished, he agreed that what I had described, apart from the horrors, closely resembled what he had passed through himself. 'You only avoided the horrors,' I said, 'because you submitted to the power which took hold of you.'

'Yes, I submitted to the will of God. He gave His revelation to me in one way and to you in another. It is for you to decide now what you are going to do about it.'

His comment had rather more application than I liked. What was I going to do about it? For the effects of the mushrooms were still with me. I had woken up on the morning after eating them, delighted to find that I had not even a headache and pleased with myself that I should have had the courage or folly to have eaten so many, and the luck or stamina to have survived their onslaught. It was not until some months later that I found myself sinking with increasing frequency into prolonged bouts of suicidal depression. At times it seemed that my will became stultified. I would sit for hours with my mind empty and my body pinioned by an inertia from which I found it impossible to break out. When my brain was active it revolved most often round themes of madness and death. The mushrooms of superior reason had not left me with any greater understanding of absolute evil or absolute good, of ultimate falsehood or ultimate truth, but I did feel that they had taught me more than it was healthy for me to know of what it is like to be mad, and to die.

6
The City

Glimpsed in the early morning from between pine branches where the road swings over the pass, Mexico City lies a thousand feet below, webbed in a light haze but with glass towers glinting under a brilliant sky. An immense litter of buildings locked in the clasp of the high sierra, its very size staggers. The sunlight floods over it as on almost every morning throughout the year and as always it is springtime, keen, limpid, translucent. Within a few hours the season may have changed, for at this latitude when the sun strikes at midday it is high summer, and at this altitude every cloud which blocks the sun brings with it its own winter. But for the moment it is spring and so clear, that, though fifty miles away across the valley, the snow crests on the volcanoes seem to float like scraps of white paper above the outskirts of the city.

Below the level of the pass a large bird, black and broad-winged, with primaries splayed like bent-back fingers, revolves slowly against the pink and grey patchwork of the foothills. A vulture, and the commonest of the species which skulk over the Mexican landscape, it may yet serve as a reminder that somewhere beyond and below it, at a point now lost among the houses where the shores of the lake used to be, seven hundred years ago a nobler bird, an eagle hunched on a nopal cactus with a snake in its beak, brought the nomad Aztecs to a final halt. Obedient to this sign predicted by their priests, they settled and built their city, Tenochtitlán, on an island in the lake. In 1521 the Spaniards destroyed it and built a new city which mirrored across the Atlantic the image of Spain. Among its crumbling, lopsided relics the modern Mexicans are still building. Size and beauty vie in their justified claims. That thin shimmering pencil is the tallest skyscraper in the Latin south. Shrouded under the mist lie the longest building, the largest bull-ring and the most spacious university campus in the world.

There, too, from churches to workers' settlements, bold, elegant, fantastic, are examples of contemporary architecture conceived in the most daring application of glass, steel and flexed concrete. Even if the wind were to rise and lift the web of mist, from up here on the lip of the pass none of these features, except the skyscraper, would be easily visible. What impresses is the area covered by the city and the scale and grandeur of its mountain setting.

The road drops in wide curves out of the pine forest. Over the years the tide-rim of houses has surged up on to the foothills to meet it. Abruptly the four traffic lanes slide in between twin ranks of trees. Flowers crowd the dividing strip. Beyond the grass verges villas, standing in open gardens, compete in size and prosperous stream-lined simplicity, or, by contrast, in the elaboration of stone and wrought-iron erupting round doors and windows in Spanish feudal or neo-colonial styles. Huge dogs, pets or sentinels, pad over lawns of sun-resistant grass still plashy from nightfall dowsings. Walls are wine-coloured with bougainvilia or aglow with the tigerish yellow of trumpet-vines. Overhead jacarandas fan out in a blue haze or leafless coral trees sprout petals like scarlet claws. From a flight of marble steps a stout businessman eases himself into the back seat of an ark-sized saloon. An Indian housemaid giggles through iron railings at a fruit vendor from the country. A young girl, neat and elegant, slams a sports car through an open gateway and cuts into the traffic swinging towards the city's centre.

At the bottom of the hill, where the avenue is crossed by a railway line, the traffic pulls up screeching. A funeral procession has launched out from the path beside the rails. The leader, who carries a little coffin with a fluted lid on his shoulder, dodges clumsily between the bumpers of the cars. He is followed by an older man, three women and a trail of ragged children. The crossing completed, they bunch briefly, then jog off beside the track.

The cars move on again. The road leaps a sunken through-way, circles a monument commemorating the expropriation of Mexican oilfields from exploiting foreigners, and dives dead straight between a double line of trees mature enough to form unbroken tunnels when in leaf. Today, as almost always, the effect is incomplete; for in this bizarre climate as often as one tree gives up waiting for an autumn which never comes, and drops its leaves in a single night, another, abandoning the austerity of a self-inflicted winter, bursts out at dawn in the full flourish of spring.

On either side of the avenue lies a park wooded with pepper, pine, eucalyptus and Mexican cedar. Scores of gardeners water the lawns and flower-beds. Each man grips his hose-pipe at a level with his crotch so that it appears that he is himself the source of the twenty-foot jet which falls battering on grass and flowers. Already the interlacing paths are dotted with early strollers, aimless Indians from the country, students spouting audibly from textbooks, or dog-owners exercising their charges. On an open field boys play baseball. Boats lunge with oars splashing across a lake. An art class, complete with camp stools and canvases, is concentrated, under the direction of a girl-teacher, on the intricacies of a flowering tree. Further off a retired *torero* takes his pupils through their passes, the bull mimed by a youth with a horned scalp on his head. A pair of lovers lie a few inches apart under a pepper tree, while a police officer peers at them from a bush, keyed to extract a bribe or impose a fine should they slip into an embrace.

Where the park ends, the road pivots on a bronze statue of Diana the huntress (round whose pristine nudity a towel has been added at the shocked insistence of a former president's wife) to open at double its previous width into the original stretch of the Paseo planned by the Emperor Maximilian as the city's challenge to the Champs Elysées. Here, on either side and along the farther reaches of the avenue, the Mexican passion for building is perennially active. Few of the old houses in the French style survive. Even apartment blocks of quite recent date are torn down to make way for towering cubes of glass which tangle interiors and reflections, sky and clouds with desks and filing cabinets, and clerks and directors with the image of the golden Angel of Independence prancing on a column a hundred and fifty feet above the traffic.

The skeletons of buildings not yet completed swarm with workers. While some manipulate electric hoists and drills, others haul up buckets hand over hand, or climb rickety ladders carrying petrol cans of cement. At night camp-fires flare among the forests of steel and timber props, and the watchmen, huddled in their glow, doze with faces hidden under plate-brimmed hats and with Indian blankets cloaked about their shoulders.

Beyond the Angel of Independence the Paseo is crossed by the Avenida Insurgentes, the other great artery of the city's communications. At this intersection, the nodal point of all traffic which passes from end to end through the capital, the modern Mexicans have erected a monument to an Indian, Cuauhtemoc, the last emperor of the Aztecs. He stands braced above a group of his own warriors wearing a plumed robe and holding a poised spear above his head. The hero of the ultimate resistance to the Spaniards, he was captured by Cortés at the fall of Tenochtitlán, tortured, held prisoner and finally hanged. There is no monument to Cortés in the city, but his treachery is commemorated in the scenes of torture and execution incised on the pedestal of Cuauhtemoc's statue.

To one side of the intersection, on a site of almost equal importance, stands the monument to the Mother. For generations Mexican women have been the victims of the *machismo* cult of the Mexican male, which encourages him to demonstrate his virility, among other ways, by breeding as many children as possible from a number of women at the same time. After a few years, irked by the mouths to feed and bored by multiple obligations, he abandons all his broods and moves on to beget others elsewhere. Left to fend for herself and her family, the role of the Mexican mother is, indeed, heroic. In her monument she is fittingly represented by a modest relief at the base of an imposing phallic column.

Beyond Cuauhtemoc's statue, as the avenue strikes through the shopping centre towards the heart of the city, the pavements become more crowded. The people are mostly of the middle class which has sprung up since the revolution. The cut and colour of their clothes are sober beside the holiday wear of the American tourists. As they parade past the displays in the shop windows they look aggressively self-assured. The mixture of races in the men is rarely a success. At the same time, though seldom handsome, they have a latent vitality which attracts. The women tend to coarsen early and grow fat, but in the young girls, especially the very young, Spanish-Indian permutations—Latin eyes set at a slant, magnolia skin over Mongol cheek-bones, or red Castilian lips parted in the maize-eater's ivory smile—produce ravishing hybrids, voluptuous and exotic.

Occasional knots of migrant peasants, indifferent to the glamour of the shops or the brusque elbows of their urban compatriots, press through the crowd as through their native forests, their limbs alert but their expressions vacant. As pure descendants as may exist of Cuauhtemoc's warriors and here encountered within a stone's throw of his statue, in the view of the mestizo clerks and business men who brush past them they are not touched by any reflected glory from the older civilization. For such people they are mere *indios*, a term which in itself can carry insult, implying a condition of illiterate poverty. Despite the privileged state of the Mexican Indian compared to his counterpart in other Latin American countries, only the Mexican who has made good can afford to boast of his Indian blood, for the backing of wealth, power or intellectual achievement is required to eclipse the association of four hundred years of serfdom and to impose on the reluctant mestizo the myth of a twentieth-century projection from the splendours of the Aztec past.

Here, also, close to her monument, the Mexican Mother may be seen edging unobtrusively along the pavement. She is small, dark and smiling. Her skin is smooth and her hair drawn tightly back. She is not more than thirty and looks even younger. Pregnant, she carries a baby at her breast and another on her back wrapped sausage-like in her *rebozo*. Four or five children trail behind her, of which the eldest is under ten. The offspring of several different fathers, they are all, for practical purposes, fatherless. It is their mother's life which is dedicated to an endless dogged endeavour to clothe and feed them. She moves along humbly intent on a mission which may take her from one end of the city to the other in the hope of a few pesos. She does not beg, though she will take what is offered. When the pavement becomes congested, she is easily hustled into the gutter. As she walks she turns every few yards to see if her brood is still safely following.

Each monument in the Paseo tells more than its own story. Next, the honours go to the discoverer of the New World.

Christopher Columbus was a servant of the King of Spain and by his discovery laid open the Americas to Spanish conquest. But Columbus is a hero and Cortés a villain. The Columbus memorial serves as an acknowledgement that not all that came out of Europe was evil. Among other things the Spaniards brought the Catholic faith and Mexico is still predominantly a Catholic country. Even the most chauvinistic and anti-clerical Mexicans have to admit that Christianity was an improvement on the religion of the Aztecs. Certainly there can have been few countries in which the basic Christian teaching was more acceptable than in Mexico at the time of the conquest. After centuries of passive adherence to the concept of human sacrifice as a religious necessity and when the Aztecs were employing on a horrific scale the rites which it involved as a means of dominating their neighbours, the news that Christ, the man-god, by his voluntary death on the cross had obtained redemption for all his followers, must have been precisely the kind of revelation for which the potential victims of the old religion had been waiting. But Cortés, who regarded the conversion of the Indians as the true justification of the conquest, has received no credit for his zeal, while Columbus, whose convictions in this respect were less convincing, is honoured in the company of the great missionary fathers. Of the four ecclesiastics stationed around his statue, two, Pedro de Gante and Bartolomeo de las Casas, were among the most revered of the early teachers and protectors of the Indians.

The last of the Reforma monuments, a magnificent equestrian statue of Charles IV, stands at the point where until recently the avenue came to an end. Though an arrogant symbol of Spanish domination, it survived both the independence war and the revolution. A plaque on its base states that it was erected on its present site, not out of respect for the Spanish monarchy but because of its importance as a work of art. More effective than the plaque is the nickname, El Caballito (the little horse) by which the Mexicans have blocked its true identity and taken the sting out of its associations.

Today the municipal laws exact that no monument or building of the colonial period can be torn down unless re-erected on another site. But the great churches which most deserve to endure are threatened by their own bulk as with lurching towers they sink ever deeper into the glutinous subsoil of the former lake. The four-square palaces, of less architectural merit, settling evenly have withstood this process unimpaired. They survive, often as sordid tenements, to inflict savage garrottings on the city's traffic. The preservation of these obstructive memorials to the colonial past illustrates the oddness of the Mexican attitude to Spain and the Spaniards. Although the Franco régime is not recognized by the Mexican government, Spain is the country with which Mexicans feel the strongest affinity. Paradoxically, the republicans who were welcomed as refugees after Franco's victory and are now established in positions of affluence in commerce and the professions are perhaps the most disliked of all foreigners in Mexico.

Beyond El Caballito, bulldozers are churning out from one of the seediest of the old quarters a splendid new extension to the Paseo. But it is the Avenida Juarez, branching off right-handed from the statue, which leads on towards the heart of the city. At its far end it is overhung by the glass cliffs of luxury hotels dominated in turn by the one hundred and forty-seven stories of the Torre-Latino-Americano. Opposite the hotel lies the Alameda park, a countrified haven in spite of the traffic which swirls around it. Planted with trees and crossed by paths with fountains at their intersections, it imposes the tempo if not the elegance of earlier times when it was a fashionable resort. Today the people who loiter in it are mostly country folk resting from the bustle of the streets, labourers taking time off in the sun, or shop girls flirting away their dinner hour with clerks and office boys. Because the young predominate, the atmosphere, though relaxed, is lively. But here, too, strict moral standards are enforced, and a couple who start kissing on a bench are promptly parted by a policeman and fined.

The park was not always such an orderly place, nor was conduct in it so vigorously controlled. Until only a few years ago its shrubs and creepers flourished in an unruly tangle. Even at seven thousand feet tropical vegetation, unless checked, quickly gets out of hand. The same appears to have been true of the inhabitants of the capital when given a jungle instead of a park for their recreation. By day the behaviour of those who frequented it was barely decent, but by night it provided cover for an orgy. Such were the conditions when D. H. Lawrence, walking there one morning with a friend, was stirred to a fifty-minute outburst against the horrors of sex starvation, after being confronted by the statue of a naked lady (it can be identified by the inscription 'Malgré Tout' on its base) crouching on the ground with uptilted buttocks liberally encrusted with sperm.

However sordid the human antics sheltered by the Alameda in its jungle period, they were child's play compared to the solemn horrors conducted by the Spaniards on the same spot after the conquest. For it was here, not a hundred yards from the site of the sacrificial pyramid and skull-racks of the Aztecs, that the Inquisition erected its stakes and scaffolds. Whereas the pagan priests drugged their victims before cutting out their hearts with a single blow, their Christian counterparts made sure that the wretches they condemned were fully conscious and suffered as lingering an agony as could be contrived.

Though the Indians may have deplored the method, they could hardly have been shocked, accustomed as they were to the Aztec holocausts, by the scale of the Christian executions, since in all a mere fifty heretics were burned. What really horrified them was the sadistic cruelty with which the Spaniards punished the most trivial misdemeanours, ecclesiastical or secular. It was the policy of the friars to introduce their religion by the mildest means possible, but their example was not followed by all the clergy. In the *auto-da-fé* conducted by Bishop Landa* in Yucatan, three hundred and fifty-nine men and women were tortured and a further six thousand, three hundred and thirty were flogged, shorn and fined. Among the tortures listed are the following: binding arms and thighs and twisting the cords tight with rods; filling the victim's belly to bursting point with water and then trampling on him till water and blood gushed out of his ears and nostrils; hanging by the wrists with heavy stones attached to the feet; scorching the tenderest parts of the body with wax tapers or scalding them

---

* The author of *Relación de las cosas de Yucatan*, an account of the Maya people at the time of the conquest. In this book he gives an invaluable description of the pagan customs he set out to eradicate so mercilessly.

III

with boiling water. Many of those so treated succumbed or were permanently maimed.

It can be no surprise that the mingling of these two peoples, Spanish and Indian, both such staunch believers in murder and mutilation as the most effective means of satisfying their respective gods, should have produced a race for whom the attributes of death—the skull, the skeleton, the tomb*—became companionable symbols, while life itself was of such minimal consequence that it could be taken as casually as it could be engendered.

The sunlight may rarely fail in Mexico, but the country's history casts, even today, shadows over the human spirit. The city itself, for all its trees, fountains and statues, the vitality of its architecture and the panache with which it wears the outward aspects of its leap into modernity, still nurtures squalid enclaves, relics of its leprous past, in which these dark elements of the Mexican character erupt among the destitute inhabitants—although far from being exclusive to them—in outbursts of unpremeditated violence, casual, pointless and extravagant in human life.

The traveller will see nothing of such districts, though the evidence of their existence may sometimes obtrude—a lone mother with her ragged children, a slum family's trotting funeral—on a drive into the city through one of the wealthier suburbs and along the monumental stretches of the Paseo. Other incoming routes, though less agreeable, are in this respect more instructive. Until a few years ago (by now the merciful crusade of new roads and buildings may have swept the whole sad shambles into the past) had he chosen to arrive by the overnight train from Guadalajara and, as the engine braked in the periphery, chanced to pull up the blind of his carriage, he would have looked out on to a morass of miserable hovels, made out of every kind of discarded or pilfered scrap: packing-cases, cardboard, beaten-out petrol cans and the like, tottering against each other for support and allowing only sufficient space between them for twisted alleys scarcely wide

---

* The sugar skulls given to children with their names inscribed on them, the popularity of toy skeletons, and the graveyard feasts on All Souls' Night illustrate the Mexican attitude to death.

enough for two people to pass, while in the foreground on the waste beside the track the light from the window would have picked out inmates of the slum, men, women and children, shitting promiscuously in the nippy dawn.

Such squalor is not confined to the outskirts. A few hundred yards from the Alameda, near the very heart of the city, streets that begin by being merely raffish grow gradually villainous until the intruder, without having marked the dividing line, will suddenly feel that he has passed from a world of disorder into one of menace. Only a block or so back he was strolling along, a confident observer, amused by the antics of a street vendor, eyeing a girl's invitation from a doorway or meeting with a blank look a tourist shark's speculative grin. But his pleasure in the exploration of the city evaporates as he abruptly becomes aware that the scene is no longer merely strange to him, but that he is now provocatively strange to it. The gutters may be dirtier and the houses more patched and raddled, but the important difference is less in the appearance of the street than in the composition of the crowd on its pavements. The moderately well-to-do elements, present in large numbers a few minutes earlier, have vanished, and the poor, who in the Paseo walked with bowed heads, here, fortified by their numerical ascendancy and resentful of any stray from a more prosperous quarter, eye him with hard stares which, if met, become aggressive. To add to his unease the people are no longer thrusting in one direction or the other, for now the street is their personal territory, a scarcely less private extension of the packed rooming-houses and tenements which provide the backdrop against which they loiter. With little else to occupy their attention their gaze tends to linger and pursue. The tables have been turned. On the Paseo it was the poor who blenched under the scorn of the rich, while here it is the rich who shrink under the contemptuous, calculating eyes of the poor.

If he has the nerve to continue his exploration the stranger is sure before long to pass what often appears as no more than a cleft in a stretch of blank wall, the entrance to a *vecindad*. There are scores of *vecindados* in the city, slum colonies shut away from the streets and centred on an alley or courtyard. They may be single-storied and are rarely higher than three floors. At a glance they resemble prisons but they are shabbier and more crowded and the people come and go as they please. The foreigner would have to be exceptionally intrepid or thick-skinned to enter uninvited into one of these formidable lairs. Even if chance should make him a guest he may still find his visit a disturbing experience. In general the living quarters consist of single windowless cells, each normally occupied by a family group in which there are almost as many adults as children. The dense physical congestion, the overflow, animated and otherwise, cluttering stairs, courts and alleyways, and the excremental seepings from under the doors of clogged latrines produce a pestiferous atmosphere, made only a degree more tolerable by the dry antiseptic quality of the city's climate. The brutalizing effects of such conditions are compensated for by certain corporate virtues such as close communal loyalty and habits of sharing and helping out which do not extend elsewhere in the capital beyond the tight knot of family relationships.

To learn what good can come out of lives so lived, an outsider would require to gain the confidence of the community as a whole, and this could only be achieved by an approach of great tact and dedication.* To learn what is bad it is only necessary to turn to the crime pages of the city's newspapers. A gang of boys, the youngest twelve and the eldest sixteen, drag an old woman into a narrow lane, rape her in turn and leave her dead. Another gang shouting 'Sangre! Sangre!'† stab a girl to death in the back of a bus. Two lacerated youths and a man's severed head are found in the closed bin of an abandoned refuse lorry. These three items are only a haphazard selection from a file of clippings taken from the press over several months. The incidents occurred in the poorest quarters of the city and the two gangs and the youths in the lorry all came from local *casas de vecindad*. Another report illustrates with a macabre twist one of the slum-dwellers' major virtues, their entrenched communal solidarity in the face of intervention from the outside world.

A man working in a tailor's shop is bitten by a dog. The

---

* Oscar Lewis has magnificently succeeded in his book *The Children of Sanchez*.
† Blood.

tailor, suspecting that the dog has hydrophobia, takes the man to hospital. He escapes from the hospital to his *vecindad*, where he becomes rabid and begins to claw and bite his neighbours. Thinking that he is drunk they shut him up in a room by himself. The police come to look for him, but they refuse to say where he is. Only when the people whom he has attacked also become rabid, do they begin to realize that his earlier behaviour was abnormal. They panic and send for the police. By now the man is dead and half a dozen of his neighbours are too far gone to be saved.

Before reacting with outraged horror to such stories it is as well to remember that much the same conditions existed in London less than a hundred years ago, and although England was then the richest country in the world little enough was done to improve them. Modern Mexico, though far from wealthy, faced with the less pleasant consequences of her spectacular leap from the mid-nineteenth into the mid-twentieth century, has been spurred by a vigorous social conscience into a courageous attempt to tackle the problem of the welfare and education of her slum-dwellers. Inevitably the struggle between the thrust of progress and the pull of the past remains unresolved. A comparison of the horror columns already referred to with items on the front pages of the same newspaper will often illustrate the character of the opposing forces.

Almost every day the front-page headlines are bold with the announcement of yet another forward step. The foundation stone of a hospital is laid, a new school put into service, an improvement in social security enacted or a recently completed section of a worker's 'city' declared open. In the pictures which accompany such headlines the mayor is shown with trowel in hand, a minister inspects work in progress or the President of the Republic slashes through a swath of white ribbon.

On the horror pages, which are usually at the back, every item deals with a crime of violence: the straight, brutal murder, the passionate or drunken killing, the cold-blooded pay-off by the police or, most typical of all, the impulsive plugging of one of his fellows by, to use the journalist's favourite terminology, 'an irascible citizen'. While many such crimes and their motives are common to every large city in the world some have a specially Mexican character, for example those instigated or executed by such traditional figures as the witch or *curandera*, the boss with a gun, the *pistolero* or his legal counterpart, the police agent, and the *macho*, the fanatic of the *machismo* cult.

In the capital witchcraft is officially frowned upon and professional magicians are liable to prosecution. Nevertheless in one market there is a section given over to witches where they are allowed to sell their wares openly. This is the more surprising since one of the proudest achievements of the progressive municipal government of recent years has been the tearing down of the old rat-infested markets and their replacement by hygienic, hangar-like constructions with concrete floors and tiled counters.

Situated in a single short alley, the witch's market is made up of not more than a dozen booths from which the *curanderas* peer out surrounded by a collection of objects as fascinating as they are decorative. Above the heads of the proprietors, some of whom are young and attractive, float puffer- and devil-fish, racoon tails, squirrel pelts, stuffed alligators and strings of emerald humming-birds. On shelves behind are jars containing anything from herbs and flower petals to the corpses of toads and axolotls preserved in alcohol. The counter is loaded with trays of polished beans, peyotl cactus, sea-shells, starfish and an assortment of amulets. In front the municipal tiles are hidden by tortoise-shells, swags of herbs, strings of beads and the skins of boa and rattlesnake. From holes in violently activated sacks at the foot of each counter project the tails of iguanas or the snouts of armadillos.

These are the chemist shops of the poor who still retain their faith in the medicine of their native villages. Some go to them knowing what they want to buy. Others describe their symptoms and accept the preparations recommended. These same people, instead of calling on a doctor in case of illness, will consult the *curandera* of their neighbourhood. If she fails, they may take their trouble to a 'spiritualist'. The 'spiritualist' deals in magic rather than medicine. Her patients must have faith, and Catholic prayers will be included in her ritual. She will be a medium with power to communicate with the dead. She will know how to manipulate 'magnetic fluids' and to perform

116

psychic operations, puncturing the body and drawing off putrid matter without shedding blood or leaving a scar.

It is not only among the poor nor even among the Mexican-born that devotees of the supernatural are so numerous. Foreign residents are notable dabblers in the occult and the North American, European and Asiatic followers of a wide range of esoteric beliefs have established thriving but not always harmonious colonies in the city. However, according to the newspaper records under consideration, it is only the practice of traditional witchcraft which encourages crimes of violence.

There are accounts of three murders so instigated. All are variations on a single theme. A wife stabs her husband's mistress in the belief that she has used witchcraft to gain her husband's affection. A *curandera* is murdered for the activities by which she is alleged to have brought about the separation of two lovers. A man shoots his wife because he believes that out of jealousy she has had a spell cast on him which has made him impotent.

In the city, though not in the country, murders arising out of witchcraft are comparatively rare; but those in the 'boss with the gun' category, if stretched to include the police, who have the boss mentality, and the *pistoleros*, who work for gun-minded bosses, account for a high percentage of the daily killings.

The tradition of the gun-toting boss goes back to colonial history. The first bosses were the handful of Spanish settlers who found themselves surrounded by a native population which frequently rebelled against the slavery imposed on them. Naturally the Spaniards were quick to enforce their will with their weapons. For their own safety they gathered round them armed retainers who were equally ruthless. It was, perhaps, from the role of these retainers that the country-wide profession of gunman or *pistolero* developed. The army and police force, in order to deal with them, adopted their mentality and surpassed them in their methods. Such traditions, once established, were reinforced during the struggle for independence, the anarchy which followed it, and the later periods of dictatorship and revolution. In the growing order of the last decade they have begun to wane, but one report from the file of cuttings will show that only recently they were not dead.

The owner of a small factory, like many of his kind, refuses to pay his workers the minimum wage laid down by the government. One of the workers rebels and demands the correct wage for himself and his comrades. On being refused he threatens to report the matter to the authorities. The owner invites the man to his office for a discussion. Sitting at his desk with his foreman beside him, he tries first by cajolery and then by bullying to persuade the man to accept an increase which is still below the legal minimum. The man refuses and after an argument turns to leave the office. The owner signals to the foreman who pulls out a revolver and shoots the worker in the back. Some of his comrades, who have been listening at the door, rush in. They seize the foreman, but the boss escapes through the window, jumps into his car and drives away.

Killings by the police and the armed watchmen who patrol the streets at night are common. By law the police are allowed to fire at any suspect who runs away from them. It follows that, in the absence of witnesses bold enough to speak the truth, private scores can be paid off with impunity. There is one newspaper report, however, of a case in which the policeman is unable to cite this law in his defence as the killing was provoked not by his victim's flight but by his refusal to go away. The policeman, drinking in a tavern, becomes annoyed by a young man at a neighbouring table who keeps singing the same song. He orders him to stop and get out. When the man refuses and goes on singing, the policeman shoots him.

The Mexican police agent thinks of himself as a boss and takes any challenge to his authority as a personal insult. Usually a fanatic of the *machismo* cult, he would be outraged if asked to consider himself a public servant. But it is not necessary to be a boss, a *pistolero*, or a policeman to be a *macho*. The majority of Mexicans still believe that the cult represents an ideal to be lived up to and many conduct their lives accordingly. These people become imbued with such an explosive need to demonstrate their virility that their first instinct is to outrage or annihilate any man, woman or child who happens, however innocently, to exacerbate their hypersensitive condition. They want, if not literally, at least in its colloquial sense, to 'fuck everyone', and in such a context the pistol becomes a handy adjunct to the penis. By far the largest number of murders recorded in the file can be attributed to the *machismo* reflex. The three reports given below, though not the most dramatic, are typical examples of the reflex at work.

A twenty-year-old student, the son of a wealthy *politico*, is sitting in his car with his arms round his girl-friend. Another car draws up a short distance behind him. The driver, also a student, hoots his horn to attract the attention of a friend in a near-by house. The first student thinks that the hooting is directed at himself. He turns with a threatening gesture, but the hooting continues. Infuriated by the supposed insult, made the more intolerable by the presence of his girl-friend, he jumps out of his car, walks up to the offending driver, sticks his gun through the open window and shoots him. He returns to his own car and drives home. When the police arrive he has vanished. His father denies any knowledge of his whereabouts.

A man is driving down a residential street (cars feature frequently in *machismo* killings) in which there is little traffic. Some boys are playing baseball on the pavement. One of them unintentionally strikes the ball into the windscreen of the car and smashes it. The driver gets out, goes up to the boys and shouts at them. The boy responsible for the damage begins to laugh. The man pulls out a gun and kills him.

Two men, sworn *compadres*,* inseparable since childhood, are sitting together in a *cantina*. They have been drinking but they are not drunk. Suddenly one of them points his gun over the top of the table and fires. His comrade falls forward with a bullet in his chest. The murderer throws his arms round him, weeping. When asked why he has killed his friend, he replies that he did not like the expression on his face.

In spite of the large number of violent crimes in the capital the ordinary visitor, unless he looks for trouble, will be unlucky if he witnesses a murder or even the drawing of a gun. Foreign residents of long standing, although they cannot help being aware of this darker side of the Mexican temperament, usually have no knowledge of it other than what they have learnt by hearsay or from the newspapers. During a stay of five years, I

---

* Godfather. The relationship between the godfather and the father of the child. Close friends are often called *compadres*.

encountered only one case of witchcraft and one corpse. I had many brushes with the police, but I was never shot at. Once when an agent, reacting to my reluctance to obey his orders, moved his hand towards his holster I capitulated and was put in prison.

Augustina came from a small town a few miles from the capital. She was twenty-four, a year younger than Maria, the cook. Unusually self-possessed, she was calm and deliberate in her movements. Her eyes were large, black and watchful. Her plump body moved with a provocative awareness of its own attractions. She was a cousin of Maria and to begin with the two girls seemed to get along well together. If their conversation, as it was carried from time to time through the swing of the kitchen door, sounded one-sided, it was because Maria's voice was low and husky while Augustina's had a higher pitch and was frequently punctuated by laughter. After the first fortnight their relationship began to deteriorate. Augustina took up with the dissolute *mozo** of a neighbouring household. Maria disapproved largely because she was jealous. Her father had forbidden her to have a *novio* and she found the prohibition irksome. She remonstrated with Augustina and even complained to her family, but to no effect.

As the tension between them deepened, Augustina became silent and watchful. She continued to take every opportunity to meet her lover. When she was absent, the atmosphere perceptibly lightened. After a few weeks Maria, who had lost all her habitual cheerfulness, began to complain of headaches and pains in her stomach. There was no longer any sound of voices from the kitchen.

The crisis broke when we left the two girls alone together at a weekend. On our return we found Augustina prostrate on the lawn at the back of the house sobbing hysterically. She refused to tell us what was the matter. Inside the house we found Maria lying unconscious on the kitchen floor. When our efforts to revive her failed, we sent for an ambulance and she was taken to hospital. The doctor described her condition as a deep coma. On returning to the house we found that Augustina had disappeared. She

---

* House boy.

had taken her belongings with her. We never saw her again.

The next day Maria recovered, but she could not give any explanation of what had happened to her. At one moment she was with Augustina in the kitchen and at the next, as it seemed, she awoke to find herself in hospital. She had no recollection of feeling ill before losing consciousness. The doctors examined her again but could find nothing wrong with her. In the afternoon they allowed her to come home.

When we questioned her, she was either unable or unwilling to add anything to what she had told the doctor. She had eaten her midday meal with Augustina, but nothing unusual had passed between them. It was shortly afterwards that she had been taken ill. Although frightened by what had happened, she did not seem to find it surprising. When we suggested possible explanations such as the food she had eaten, she only shrugged her shoulders. She was clearly convinced that she knew the cause of her illness but was unwilling to tell us what it was. She had no recurrence of the headaches or stomach pains from which she had previously suffered. With a new maid to help her she was soon as healthy and cheerful as she had been in the past.

From time to time she received news of Augustina from her family. As we had supposed, she had gone off with the *mozo*. He had promised to marry her, but had later confessed that he was already married. After a few weeks he deserted her and went back to his wife. When Maria gave us this last piece of news she added that she was sorry for the wife because Augustina would be sure to try to harm her.

'In the same way as she tried to harm you?' I asked.

For a moment she was startled, then she nodded. 'Yes. In Augustina's village the women are all *curanderas*. They know about such things.'

Sunday was a strange day in the capital. In our district it started off in a carefree atmosphere with a promise of gaiety. From the early hours cars flashed along the near-by Paseo on family outings. Under the trees which divided the two lanes of traffic, *charros** wearing embroidered hats and silver-studded

---

* Horsemen who wear the costume described on page 37 (footnote). In Mexico City and other towns there are *charro* clubs which hold steer-throwing contests.

pants and jackets paraded their horses at a dashing trot. Along the pavement at the entrance to the park, street-vendors teetered under pyramids of celluloid propellers or clouds of painted gas balloons. By ten o'clock the people had begun to pour in from all directions, on foot or by car or ejected from tightly packed buses, to enjoy for a few hours the open pleasures of the park. Towards midday picnicking started and soon hardly a patch of ground was left unoccupied. But in spite of the thousands gathered, including hordes of young children, just at what should have been the climax of the day the festivities gradually subsided. The pleasures of eating and drinking were taken quietly and the promise of gaiety remained unfulfilled. As the afternoon progressed torpor descended on the picnickers and spread outwards to the whole city. Only the bullring came to life as the bands played and the crowds assembled.

It was at this curiously hushed and lethargic hour, when the sun was already low enough to have turned the dust in the dry air to gold and the cries of children in the playground at the end of the street, so jubilant in the early morning, had become as melancholy as the last bird-calls at sunset, while the metal swings and see-saws on which they played gave out doleful clangs like cracked funeral bells, I encountered my corpse stretched out on the grass verge beside the pavement at the roots of a jacaranda tree.

As I left the house the sight of the sprawling white-shirted figure did not strike me as remarkable. At almost any hour, and often in far less enticing spots, the streets of Mexico are littered with slack, abandoned bodies sweating out fumes of pulque or tequila. I hoped that this particular drunkard would not revive as I passed and, as sometimes happens, turn aggressive. Coming closer, I was struck by an awkwardness in the arrangement of his limbs. He was lying on his stomach with one hand bent round his head and the other stretched out on the grass beside him. His legs were close together, but his right foot was sharply twisted. As I came level with him I stopped and looked down into his face. From what I could see of it he must have been handsome—a young man of not more than twenty—but now he had a bullet hole in his left temple and his eyes and forehead were masked with blood.

I knew that to have anything to do with a corpse was dangerous and that even to report my discovery was to risk imprisonment.* Although I was certain that he was dead I felt that I must do something. I looked round. The street was deserted but voices came from beyond the garden door outside which he was lying. I walked up to it and rang the bell. Almost at once the door opened, but only a few inches. A middle-aged woman, elegantly dressed, looked out, hard-eyed and suspicious. I had a glimpse of a garden behind and children romping.

'There's a wounded man here,' I said. 'Could you telephone for a doctor?'

'He's not wounded, he's dead. Someone shot him. It's nothing to do with us.'

The door slammed. I hesitated a moment, then hurried back to my house. I telephoned to the Red Cross and told them there had been an accident in the street and asked them to send an ambulance. They wanted me to give my name but I rang off. Then I went to the gate and waited. The door at which I had rung the bell opened and a dozen children came tumbling out on to the pavement. They were followed by their parents, who stood grouped in the doorway saying good-bye to their hosts. Meanwhile the children, in their frilly frocks and Sunday suits, swarmed round the dead man, and after squatting to get a closer look, began running backwards and forwards, skipping over the body until their parents, impatient to be off, petulantly called them away.

Just as the last car had left, a wailing ambulance, trailed by a police jeep, swung into the street. At the first glimpse of the jeep I stepped back into the garden and closed the gate.

He stood thumbing through my papers. 'Two blocks back you drove the wrong way down a one-way street.'

'Nonsense!'

'It's not nonsense!' You're drunk. Get into your car and follow us.'

---

* A man who reports a murder in Mexico is kept under arrest until he can prove that he did not commit it himself.

'But it isn't safe for me to drive if I'm drunk.'

I did not move. It was then that his hand began to slide over the ample curve of his belt towards his holster. I glanced left and right along the shadowy street. It was midnight and a cold breeze was blowing. The street was empty.

'All right. I'll follow you.'

They pulled up a hundred yards from the police station. I stopped behind them and got out. Two of the policemen were already on the pavement. Now they were smiling and friendly. 'It'll be a big fine, you know.'

This was the cue for me to pull out my wallet and make an offer, but I was too angry to play it their way. I shrugged my shoulders. They stopped smiling.

'Come on then.'

Inside the station an officer sat behind a desk. The bare hall was lit by two naked bulbs which gave a yellowish light, leaving the walls murky and the corners black. The two traffic agents took me over to the desk.

'Picked him up driving the wrong way in a one-way street. Dead drunk, but he's sobered a bit now.'

'They made me drive here in my own car. If I'd been drunk . . .'

'Silence!' The officer glanced over my shoulder. There was a movement behind me. A hand caught my arm and pulled me back into the centre of the hall and held me there under the yellow lights.

The agents went on talking, giving particulars of time and place. The officer wrote laboriously on a sheet of paper. When they had finished they touched their caps, lounged across the hall and went out through the door into the street.

The officer took down details from my driving licence and passport. At last he looked up. 'So you weren't drunk, is that it?'

'If I had been, why did they make me drive the car myself? I might have killed someone.'

'Doctor!'

A sound of snoring from the darkest corner broke off with a snort.

'What is it?'

'We've got a customer for you.'

A little yellow-faced man, unshaven and wearing a filthy white tunic, came yawning out of the shadows.

'This gentleman says he's not drunk. What do you say, Doctor?'

The doctor gave me a drugged stare and remained speechless. He was at least four yards away, but he made no move to come closer.

'Well, if he says he wasn't drunk and the others say he was, you'd better split the difference. Half-drunk. Come on, write it down.'

Bending over the desk the doctor wrote very slowly on the sheet of paper. When he had finished, the officer nudged him away and he shuffled back into his corner.

'How much is the fine?'

'You'll have to settle that with the *transito** in the morning.'

'I don't mind so long as I can go home to bed.'

'You can't; you'll have to stay here.'

'Why shouldn't I go to the *transito* now?'

'It wouldn't be regular.' He gave me a steady look. 'It'll be a heavy fine, you know.'

This was the same cue again.

'I don't care, I'll pay it.'

'It's up to you.' He beckoned to the policeman, who had been standing behind me, and handed him the charge sheet. 'This man'll take you.'

I followed the policeman into the street. We got into my car and I started the engine. 'Which way do we go?'

He sat there grinning. Escaped from the musty air and murky light, I had the nerve to be outraged again.

'Well, we're going to the *transito*, aren't we?'

All the way I had to prompt him for directions and up to the last moment, as we crossed the pavement to the barred gate of the building to which he had brought me, he kept up his devious angling for a bribe. As I watched him despondently ringing the bell beside the gate, I laughed to myself imagining the officer's rage when his henchman returned empty-handed.

In response to the bell a man in shirt-sleeves came out from the lodge, unlocked the gate and opened it. I walked in, but my

---

* Traffic-police headquarters.

125

escort stayed outside. He handed over the charge sheet and the man, after glancing at it briefly, clanged the gate to and turned the key.

'I've got to pay a fine,' I said. 'Where do I go now?'

He gave me a cold, bleary look. 'This way!'

I followed him across a yard into a passage, where he stopped outside an iron door and unlocked it. I glimpsed in the dismal light figures hunched in tiered bunks and huddled in a tight pack on the floor. I turned and ran to the gate with the gaoler calling after me. The policeman was still in sight. I yelled at him through the bars until he looked round and came hurrying back.

'You said you were bringing me here to pay a fine, but that bastard wants to lock me up.'

He fixed me with sad, sympathetic eyes. 'Yes, señor, but now it's too late.'

I heard footsteps behind me. 'I'll give you all the cash I've got if you can get me out.'

'How much?'

I pulled out my wallet and counted the notes. He nodded, and called to the gaoler, but after a mumbled conversation, turned with a shrug. 'It's no good, he won't play.' Gloomily he wished me good night and slouched off across the pavement.

I turned to the gaoler. 'They told me I had got to pay a fine.' I waved my wallet. 'Can I pay it now?'

He shook his head and grasping my arm began to pull me away.

'You've got forty-eight hours inside, then you'll have to find someone to pay up for you.'

'To pay up? But can't I pay it myself?'

'It's against the law.'

'How can I get hold of anyone? None of my friends know I'm here.'

'There's the telephone. You can make one call.'

'I'd like to make it now.'

In the lodge a telephone was fixed to the wall. I glanced at my watch. It was two o'clock. I was alone in Mexico. I had been there less than three months. The only people I could ring up at such an hour were the friends with whom I had spent the evening. They at least would know that I was not drunk when

I had left them. I was going to pick up the telephone when I realized that I had forgotten the number. 'Can I have a directory?'

'No, there isn't one.'

I stood gaping at the instrument while the gaoler jangled his keys behind me. A card pinned to the wall had some addresses and numbers typed on it. There were two or three police stations and hospitals, the fire brigade, and the Red Cross. I dialled this last number. It rang for half a minute before a voice grunted, 'Red Cross, emergency section.'

'Will you help me, please? I'm in trouble.'

'What do you want?'

The voice was testy and suspicious. 'I'm in gaol and I've got to ring someone to get me out. There's no directory here and I don't know the number. If I give you the name, will you look it up for me?'

'Go ahead, what is it?' The voice had become warm and friendly. I gave the name and address. 'Hold on.' The gaoler grumbled behind me, 'Can't wait all night, you know!' The voice came back. 'Is this it?' It gave my friend's name, address and number. I thanked him and rang off.

As I moved to dial again, the gaoler caught my arm. 'You've had your call, come along now!'

I shook free and went on dialling. I had just finished when he grabbed me again and started pulling hard. I held on to the receiver with my free hand until the cord was stretched tight. I could hear the number ringing, but I was afraid that if he pulled any harder the whole apparatus would come off the wall. He must have realized the danger himself, for he slackened his grip and swore. Suddenly I heard L's voice at the other end. Doing all I could to sound calm, I told her what had happened. Her response was immediate. 'Don't worry, I'll come at once! José's still here. I'll bring him with me. He's good with the police. If anyone can get you out, he can.' She rang off and I put the receiver back on its hook. With a firm grip on my arm the gaoler led me across the yard, unlocked the cell door, pushed me inside and locked it behind me.

The cell, about fifteen feet square and eight feet high, was crowded. There were triple-tiered bunks round the walls, all of which at a glance appeared to be occupied. The row of sleepers on the floor stretched without a gap from one end to the other. The few prisoners who were awake sat crouched on the edge of their bunks, their haunches pressed against the recumbent figures behind them. An opening in one wall led into a small court where a naked prisoner was soaping himself while another, stripped to the waist, was washing his shirt under a tap. My entry caused a stir and I was stared at by alert, inquisitive eyes. No one spoke, but clearly they thought me an odd fish to have landed in such a net.

Unnerved by so much attention, I looked round for a refuge, and was surprised to see behind me a tier of vacant bunks. I backed towards them and staked a claim to the lowest by balancing on its edge. The metal frame cut into my thighs and my body was doubled up with my shoulders against the bunk above. As I settled myself as comfortably as I could there was a murmur from all sides which became so excited when I swivelled round and lifted my feet on to the bunk, that I quickly dropped them to the floor again. I sat wondering what was the matter until a wide-boy type, soon to reveal himself as the cell's principal spokesman and wag, sat up on his bunk and asked me if I was a Christian. Not wishing to make myself out any more of an oddity than I evidently already appeared, I replied that I was.

'You believe in the Virgin and the Saints?'

'Yes, but I'm not a Catholic.'

'Then you're a Communist.' He spoke the words with a flourish as if he had explained something in my appearance or behaviour which up till that moment had been incomprehensible. Before I could disillusion him, he prodded a sleeping prisoner at his side. 'This fellow's a Communist, too.'

The man rolled over and stared at me.

'He's got me wrong,' I said. 'I'm not a Communist.'

'Of course you're not. Anyone can see that! You're a *gringo*!' He turned his back on me with a scornful grunt.

'I'm not a *gringo* either. I'm from Europe. I'm an Englishman.'

'Aren't the English Christians?' It was the wide-boy again. 'Don't they believe in the Virgin and the Saints?'

We were back where we had started. 'Yes, most of them are Christians.'

'You're not a Christian though.'

'I told you that I was.'

'But you don't believe in the Virgin.'

'Why are you so sure?'

He looked away over my head as if the proof of my disbelief was lodged somewhere above me. 'You wouldn't be sitting in Her place if you did.'

For a moment I wondered if we were talking about the same virgin. By now nearly all the prisoners were awake and listening. As they, too, kept on glancing above my head, I decided to stand up and see what it was that drew their attention. I unfolded myself and looked round. On the top bunk stood a small statue of the Virgin with a candle-stump burning at her feet. Now I realized why the tier had been left vacant. But it was not only this much-needed space which had been sacrificed, for beside the candle was a saucer heaped with centavos.

I hurriedly felt in my pockets for an offering but found that I had no coins. Faced with the prospect of further cross-questioning on my beliefs, I took a five-peso note from my wallet and placed it in the saucer.

I had hoped that after this gesture I would be left alone, but the sight of the five pesos caused a far greater stir than my occupation of the Virgin's bunk. In a minute five or six prisoners, the wide-boy among them, were pressing round me peering into my wallet.

'You're a Christian all right. How about giving us something for a smoke?'

'How much?'

The wide-boy's nimble fingers pecked out twenty pesos. Waving them triumphantly, he scrambled up the bunks to the one minute window of the cell. In response to a whistle through the bars, footsteps approached and stopped below. He handed down the note with hissed instructions. The footsteps rang out again, and gradually died away.

A heavy silence closed in on their retreat as if the sound of a human being free to come and go had brought back to the prisoners, in the middle of the diversion I had created, the tyranny of the walls which enclosed them. Even my wallet lost its allure, and the men who had collected round me wandered listlessly back to their bunks or stretched out again on the floor. Their faces, with all the spirit gone out of them, in the stark prison light—the mestizo skins sallow, pock-marked, blackened with stubble, the Indians' the colour of dark mud—appeared degraded and brutalized. Struck fully for the first time by the realization of my own trapped state, my morale dropped. I remembered stories of people who had spent months shut up on the mere suspicion of a crime before their friends had been able to extricate them. L's talk of José's prowess with the police was probably no more than a hastily thought-up tranquillizer. The gaoler had threatened me with forty-eight hours, but when I thought of how I had got into my predicament, it seemed just as likely that it would be that number of days before I got out of it.

It was now three o'clock. Since my clash with the Virgin I had been standing propped against one of the uprights which divided Her bunks from a neighbouring tier. Soon I began to feel so tired that nothing in my doubtful future seemed so important as my immediate need to sit or lie down. Every few minutes the prisoners took turns, two at a time, to go out and wash in the yard. From the first I had been struck by the obsessional vigour with which they scrubbed themselves. Now I began to wait for each change-over, hoping that it might result in a space being left vacant. I had no luck until the routine was broken by one of the men lying on the floor. After scratching violently he caught and burst a blood-filled bug on his leg. Immediately he got up and without waiting his turn went out into the yard. Thinking he had gone to wash, I was just nerving myself to take his place when he returned with a bucket and started scrubbing the floor. As he came to each sleeper he tapped him with the brush. The man got up and as soon as his piece of floor had been scrubbed lay down again without waiting for it to dry. I now resigned myself to standing up all night, but at that moment the key rattled in the lock and the gaoler came in. He nodded in my direction. 'You've got some friends to see you.'

I followed him into the passage. Half a dozen prisoners including the wide-boy came crowding after me. L and José were standing at the prison gate. I hurried towards them and we held a brief conference through the bars. José had tried all his tricks on the gaoler without success, but before leaving the house they had rung up a lawyer who had promised to come early in the morning to see what he could do. Carlos had gone off to buy me some food and would be along in a few minutes. Was there anything else I wanted?

I was deeply touched by their kindness, but they looked at me so tragically that I began to feel that I was inside, not as a result of a ridiculous if sinister farce, but for some serious crime which might carry with it a formidable sentence.

Back in the cell I found my stock had soared. The unexpected outing and glimpse of L at the gate had roused the prisoners who had followed me into a state of friendly exuberance. Whatever their previous reservations after the affair of the Virgin, the fact that I had been able to call on someone as beautiful as L to come to my rescue at three o'clock in the morning had won for me not only their respect but a space beside the wide-boy on his bunk.

In my absence the cigarettes bought with my money had been delivered and with them a small packet the contents of which was being methodically kneaded in with the tobacco. My companion explained as he prepared a cigarette for me that the police always kept a proportion of any drugs they confiscated, to trade among prisoners. Just as we were lighting up, the cell door opened again and Carlos, with the gaoler behind him, came in carrying a large paper bag full of food. Before leaving he promised that if I did not get out, he would bring me fresh supplies at midday.

I opened the bag and distributed its contents, cold chicken, ham, cheese, rolls and chocolate, among my comrades. As we smoked and ate, the atmosphere became mildly festive. I was asked the usual questions about England and produced the usual answers. But my prestige dropped sharply when they found that I could not give a first-hand account of the inside of an English prison. I tried to make good with a description of what it was like to be locked up by the Turks, but they were not impressed. Clearly they thought it was an experience which a man should be able to record of his own country.

'What d'you want to travel for?' the wide-boy asked. 'What d'you get out of it?'

'I like seeing different countries and getting to know the people.'

The young man in the next bunk sat up. 'I'm a traveller too,' he said. 'I've got around so much they call me "*El Vagabundo*". I have to keep going, I can't help it.'

'Why not?'

'It's this bastard!' Leaning forward, he grasped a fistful through the fork of his pants. 'Started me off when I was a kid and never let up since. Even when I've got it really good for him, after a couple of goes he gets the idea he can make it some other place even better. He's taken me all over Mexico and up into the States and down south into Guatemala. It's the hell of a life! The stories he could tell you!' Glaring down at his crotch, he burst into a frenzy of obscenities and only broke off to give himself such a punishing cuff that he rolled over doubled up on his bunk.

'He's crazy,' the wide-boy said. 'What's he want to go trekking all over the place just for that? Why, I've got half a dozen waiting for me not a mile from here when I get out.'

'You've got to get out first.'

'The hell I have!' He turned over on to his stomach and, butting into the palliasse, he began groaning hoarsely. The others snarled at him to shut up. In the silence that followed, the last dregs of festivity drained away. One by one they lay back yawning and stretched themselves for sleep.

Crouched on the bunk edge which the wide-boy had made over to me, I had begun to doze when I felt a touch on my arm. A prisoner who had been lying on the floor was standing beside me.

'What do you want?'

'Please, will you get up a moment.' Now that he was on his feet I saw that although he must have been the youngest inmate of the cell he was also the tallest.

Wearily I stood up. He placed himself beside me so that our shoulders touched. 'Look, we're exactly the same height.'

'So we are.'

'Like brothers.'

'You're certainly tall for a Mexican.'

'That's true. And the funny thing is my mother's only so high.' He held out his hand well below his chin. 'And my father's even shorter.' His hand dropped six inches. Suddenly he became thoughtful. 'But perhaps it isn't so funny when you come to think of it. You see my father isn't really my father.'

Caught out for a suitable comment, I sat down again.

'You can't sleep like that. Lie there.' He pointed to the gap he had left in the row of sleepers.

I thanked him but protested. 'No, that's your place. I'll be all right.'

'But I want you to take it. Don't you understand, we're like brothers?'

He looked so ready to be hurt that I gave in. Where he had been lying, the floor had dried out. I lay on my side so as to make sure of keeping on the dry patch, but the cement was too hard on my hip. I turned over on to my back and was almost asleep when I remembered the interest which had been taken in my wallet. As I still believed its contents to be my best hope of getting out I slipped my hand inside my coat to cover it. I had not realized that the man on my right was awake and watching.

'Do you think someone's going to steal your money?' When I did not answer he took my hand and pulled it away. 'Don't worry. In here you're one of us. No one'll take anything from you.'

I slept for a couple of hours and might have done so for longer had I not been wakened by a jab in the ribs. The floor was being scrubbed again and I had to surrender my patch.

At ten o'clock the gaoler appeared and ordered me to follow him. As we came out of the passage, I saw Carlos, José and the lawyer standing at the gate. I was led into a small room where a plain-clothes official sat behind a desk. He looked at me with amused astonishment. 'However did you get in here?'

I told him my story.

'Most unfortunate. No doubt it was all a misunderstanding.' He glanced at the papers in front of him. 'Let me see, forty-eight hours and a fine of two hundred pesos.'

'I've friends outside who'll pay the fine.'

'That's good. The trouble is you've only done eight hours out of the forty-eight. But perhaps we can arrange something. Supposing we make the fine up to seven hundred, then you can go right away?'

Without waiting for a reply he nodded to the gaoler and

waved me towards the door. But I hesitated. Although he had called the extra five hundred pesos an increase in the fine, I knew, of course, that it was a bribe destined for his own pocket. My morale was again high enough to allow me to be angry. Now I had come to know my fellow prisoners, a couple of days in the crowded cell was no longer an intolerable prospect. It seemed even shameful to buy my way out when, for all I knew, the crimes for which they had been shut up might be just as nebulous as my own. But the official misjudged the reason for my hesitation.

'You needn't worry about the money. Your friends have already paid.'

Outside in the yard the gaoler nudged my arm. 'I let you make two telephone calls, you know. And by rights you shouldn't have had all those visitors.'

I took out my wallet and gave him a note. 'You'd've saved a lot of trouble if you'd have accepted this in the first place.'

'No, señor, it wouldn't've been correct. The law's the law. Things have to be done in the proper way.' He led me to the gate where my friends were waiting, unlocked it and let me out.

One of the attractions of the glass-fronted luxury hotels on the Avenida Juarez is the view over the Alameda. Above the tree-tops the domes and towers of colonial churches stand out against the flat roofs of the modern city and lift the eye easily to the hills at its outskirts, beyond which serene clouds adrift in the blue sky draw slips of shadow over a backdrop of pink moun-tains. In the park itself the people patterning the sunlit paths and open spaces shift languidly. Now there is nothing in their behaviour, observed at least from the height of the sealed windows of an air-conditioned bedroom, to shock the suscept-ible. Even to a delicate social conscience poverty at this range looks reassuringly picturesque. If the boot-blacks, plying from bench to bench, have the words 'justicia social' painted on their shirts, their light-hearted antics make the message, only to be picked out by a sharp eye, read like a joke. But whatever the boot-blacks may think, the concept of social justice, despite the cynicism aroused by the lip service paid to it by electioneering politicos, has provided the mainspring of the drive which has kept the country moving since the revolution. It has even helped to transform the physical appearance of the capital, for among its most dynamic champions have been the city planners, who have adopted as their first principle the slogan: 'Only the best is good enough for the poor'.

While the speculators throw up luxury hotels and office and apartment blocks, the planners, aided by some of the most adventurous architects in the world, concentrate on hospitals, social centres and housing estates destined for the use of the working class. In scale, beauty of design and lavishness of equipment these buildings frequently outclass the flashy hives created for the opulent.

The ideas behind the policy of the planners are not merely quixotic nor are they inspired by the profits to be gained from needless extravagance. They do derive in part, however, from the Mexicans' natural inclination towards superlatives and the grand scale. They also embody one of the principles by which, in recent times, the country has made some of its most spectacular forward leaps. It is the principle not simply of putting the cart before the horse but of building a fine new cart when there is not even a horse in sight to pull it. The Mexicans believe, and usually they are proved right, that, providing the cart is a really splendid one, the horse is bound to turn up.

They decide, for example, on the need for a highly specialized research laboratory. Regardless of the lack of qualified technicians to staff it they go ahead with this building. Then they decorate it with frescoes and mosaics and fill it with the most expensive and up-to-date equipment. Critics may grumble about pretentious extravagance but, incredibly, when the building is complete, the technicians materialize. They may be so few and inexperienced that at first the laboratory can only function on a limited scale, but the very fact of its impressive existence will set a whole batch of young men studying, as no mere government promises or blueprints would have done, to qualify for the work which it has to offer. Naturally in some instances the challenge set by the architectural shell takes a considerable time to be met. A doctor who set up a hospital in a waterless village in the belief that the scandal of a hospital without water would force the authorities to lay a pipeline from a not too distant reservoir, had to work for two years with pulque as the only liquid available in large quantities. The staff and patients spent most of their time mercifully intoxicated. But in the end water was brought to the village.

When the planners say that only the best is good enough for the poor they do not, of course, imagine that by building a social security centre or a workers' apartment block they will make the poor any richer. What they do believe is that the evidence that they are being given the best will encourage them to acquire the dignity and self-respect without which they will never slough off the slum mentality inseparable from the life of the tenement houses and shack settlements.

Largely as the result of the planners' achievements the modernization of the city has not been confined to the wealthier commercial and residential areas. Often even the drabbest districts are relieved by impressive examples of the genius of contemporary native architecture. Where one good building goes up, others tend to follow. If the present impetus of reconstruction is maintained, within a few years Mexico City will have an aesthetic claim, besides a statistical one, to be ranked among the first of the great cities of the world.

In the meantime the capital strikes the observer as a place of spectacular contrasts. Here, in and around the Alameda, they are obvious enough: the glittering steel and glass of the new hotels beside the decaying stonework of the colonial churches; trees heavy with summer foliage jostling stark branches stripped as for winter; in the open the flat scorching gold of the sunlight, and in the shade the sharp alpine nip; the roar and surge of the traffic surrounding the relaxed indolence of the park; sleek American automobiles wing to wing with shambling tin buses; on the pavement the elegant business man strolling to his club, and on the grass the pregnant mother surrounded by her ragged children.

Such a list, even if confined to so small an area, could be expanded indefinitely. But this particular quality of the capital remains epitomized, in my experience, by one brief incident.

The day must have been the anniversary of the birth of Juarez, for I was attracted to the park by the sight of some Indian dancers performing behind the heroes' monument. I placed myself on the fringe of the crowd which had collected to watch them. They wore feather head-dresses and their plump coppery bodies were scantily decked out in tawdry pseudo-Aztec trappings. Picturesque as such troops appear from a distance, at a closer view they are disappointing and the monotonous rhythm in which they dance quickly tires the spectator. My attention wandered and was caught by the figure of an old woman standing isolated on the pavement. There was nothing remarkable about her general appearance. A drab *rebozo* was drawn round her wrinkled face. She wore a patched blouse and a skirt which reached almost to the ground. Her feet were bare. It was only her eyes which fascinated me, for they were fixed with the absorbed gaze of a visionary on something far away above my head. I glanced round, but the blue sky above the tower of San Juan de Dios was empty. When I turned again, the woman's expression had not altered, but now a glitter at her feet drew my attention. A little gilded puddle was spreading out from under the hem of her skirt. Suddenly she lowered her eyes and shuffled away. The pool she had left behind her covered only a foot or two of the pavement, but it reflected on its surface one of the city's proudest symbols, the soaring shaft of its tallest skyscraper.

Although centred on one of the busiest areas, the Alameda is not at the heart of the city. Indeed until the late nineteenth century it lay almost on its fringe. The real heart lies a few hundred yards beyond the skyscraper, where the bottleneck of Avenida Madero, prolonging the axis of Avenida Juarez, opens into the Plaza de la Constitución.

To the left of this great square, half squatting, half reeling, stands the gigantic basalt and sandstone mass of the cathedral, while directly opposite, as impressive in its length as the cathedral is in its bulk, stretches the seven-hundred-and-fifty-foot façade of the palace of Cortés. The vast central area claimed by the square itself is a desert little frequented at any hour and then only by postcard vendors and tourists. Confronted by this formidable concrete waste, the stranger may ask himself, especially if from his first impressions he has begun to suspect its inhabitants of heartlessness, whether in fact it has a heart at all. He will be wrong. For this is the city's heart, but a heart which beats only once a year, when, on the night of September the fifteenth, the anniversary of National Independence is celebrated by the President of the Republic echoing from a balcony of the palace the '*Grito*', Hidalgo's call for justice which roused his followers to strike the first blow against Spanish rule. This cry, taken up by the thousands of spectators who cram the plaza, is a convincing demonstration that the people not only have hearts but that, on this occasion, at least, they can beat as one.

7

Kilometre Eighty-One

The September ritual of the *Grito* in the great square is symbolic of that wider and more mysterious cohesive force which ensures the unity of the republic as a whole. This force is not centrifugal although the capital exercises the pull of a great city. Certainly one factor to it is the presence of such a powerful and, in earlier times, aggressive neighbour as the United States. But whatever its origins, the foreigner who has travelled widely and can compare such northern state capitals as Chihuahua and Monterrey, both very different in character, with those of the south such as Campeche and Tuxtla Gutiérrez, which have little in common but belong to another world, racially and climatically, from their counterparts in the north, cannot fail to be impressed by the unanimity with which the inhabitants of all these places regard themselves first and foremost as Mexicans. This is less true of the country than the towns. There are even a few remote tribal communities—the Seri of Puerto Cueca and some of the Maya Indians, for example— which remain hostile to the concept of the nation and resist the altruistic attempts of the authorities to integrate them. But apart from isolated tribal revolts, since the declaration of independence there has been only one serious separatist movement. This occurred early in the nineteenth century when Yucatan cut away from the central government and joined Guatemala in an independent alliance.

The remoteness of the Yucatan peninsula from the capital and its economic independence, based on the sisal crop, might have resulted in a permanent break but for an Indian uprising, known as the War of the Castes, which pressed the creole and mestizo rulers so hard that after attempted flirtations with the United States, England and Spain, they were forced to accept the intervention of the Mexican army. The separatist movement expired, but the Indian rebels, driven into the eastern forests of the peninsula, set up their own independent community. Every few years expeditions were sent out to subdue them, but they all failed. In 1901 the war was unofficially liquidated and the Indians were left to govern themselves in their remote jungle settlements. The eastern area of the peninsula was separated from the state of Yucatan and proclaimed a 'territory' under the direct administration of the federal government. It was given the name, Quintana Roo, after a writer and intellectual of the period of the War of Independence against the Spaniards.

The name, Quintana Roo, fascinated me the first time I saw it on the map. I soon learned that, except for the islands of Cozumel and Mujeres and the adjacent mainland site of Tulum, it was rarely visited even by the Mexicans. The road from Merida to its capital, Chetumal, had not yet been completed and its main link with the world beyond its frontiers was the dirt track which led across the Hondo river to Belize in British Honduras. The territory was almost entirely covered in jungle, from low scrub in the north to valuable timber forests in the south. Apart from the dissident Mayas, who until recently had killed all Mexicans on sight,* and the citizens of Chetumal, many of whom were said to be the descendants of British pirates, the area was largely uninhabited. In the early years after its separation from the state of Yucatan it had suffered from a succession of racketeering governors. More recently the town of Chetumal had been wrecked by a hurricane. The accounts I was given of existing conditions there—none of them were first-hand—left me with a picture of a shamble of ruined houses and stick-huts, half submerged by the jungle, where a handful of cut-throat officials ruled over a sleazy population of degenerate buccaneers.

Together with the remoteness of the area and its dramatic history, this picture had its attractions; but it was not for these alone that I decided to visit Chetumal. About seventy miles to the west of the town there was an ancient Maya site known to archaeologists as Rio Bec. The buildings were remarkable

---

* This practice ended in 1935 with the signing of the agreement, known locally as the Great Peace, between the dissident tribes (the *sublevados*) and the Mexican government.

because the architects had carried the Maya custom of making the steps of their pyramids so steep as to be almost unclimbable to its extreme. The steps at Rio Bec were not only steep but too narrow to give a foothold. They were surmounted by dummy temples with false doorways, intended, it might be supposed, solely for supernatural visitations. Other characteristics of the architecture included stone mosaics, elaborate stucco masks and dragon-mouth portals. The ruins, buried deep in the jungle, had been rarely visited and only superficially explored. They offered a rewarding objective but a difficult one. I had little hope of success but thought the attempt worth trying, for I had seen marked on a recent map of the area what appeared to be a new road striking across the peninsula due west from Chetumal. If it existed, I calculated that it should pass within a few miles of the ruins.

By the time I was able to leave Mexico City for Yucatan it was already late autumn, but still too early in the season for winter tourists. I stopped at Villahermosa to visit Palenque, which I had all to myself, and even at Uxmal and Chichén-Itzá the ruins were mostly deserted. I stayed longer than I had intended in each of these places and found myself left with less than a week for my expedition to Quintana Roo. At the office of the local airline in Merida I was told that I had been wrongly informed about the time-table and that the flight I had planned to take in a few hours did not leave until the following day. Worse still, the entire plane had been reserved for the governor of the territory who was flying down from Mexico with a party of officials. On the advice of the booking clerk I decided to go out to the airport at the time it was supposed to leave and beg for a vacant seat if one was available. Although I now realized that my chances of reaching Rio Bec were very slim I thought that if my friends in Mexico had been accurately informed, the scene of human dereliction and tropical decay provided by the city of Chetumal would prove of itself ample justification for the journey. I left the booking office with the agreeable prospect of an unpremeditated stay of twenty-four hours in Merida.

At that time, especially in an off season, the town still preserved an atmosphere of drugged isolation as though it persisted in living on the memory of its brief period as the capital of an independent state. According to contemporary accounts this was an idyllic epoch when paternal, pleasure-loving *hacenderos** enjoyed the favours of mestizo beauties and the service of indolent peons with smiling, submissive ways. In the opinion of the great American traveller, John Lloyd Stephens,† the principal charms of the place were its feeling of being cut off from the rest of the world and its air of universal contentment.

Even after the exposure of these myths by the Maya revolt and the abrupt surrender of independencies, the wealthy families of the region continued to regard Mexico as too uncivilized for their tastes. They preferred, when they travelled, to go to Europe, where they also sent their sons—usually to France or England—to be educated. The women followed—with a time-lag of a few months—the Paris fashions without discarding the Spanish mantilla. Every winter a company of Italian singers performed in the opera house, adding lustre to a season which otherwise consisted of elegant balls, gambling parties and riotous bull fights. It was a city of baroque churches and Moorish houses, of barred windows and flower-filled courtyards and, above all, of the hammock. Alone of European refinements, the bed was universally despised, the inhabitants preferring their finely spun, multi-coloured nets, distinguished for their size and strength, and, at that time, as celebrated a native product of the place as hats were of Panama.

Inevitably much of the old life disappeared with the revolution. The large estates were broken up and the sisal plantations farmed on a collective system. The opera house ceased to function as such and was in due course converted into a cinema. The old families who managed to salvage part of their fortunes were careful not to flaunt their affluence. There were no more balls or other manifestations of an elegant society. When competitors in Africa and other parts of the world claimed a share of the sisal market, the economy as a whole began to decline. Fewer ships called at the near-by port of Progreso, and with a five-day rail journey as the only overland

---

* The owners of large estates.
† Author of *Incidents of Travel in Central America, Chiapas and Yucatan* (1841) and *Incidents of Travel in Yucatan* (1842). He made the first extensive survey of ruins in the Maya territory. He was accompanied by an English artist, Frederick Catherwood, who made a superb collection of drawings to illustrate his books.

link with the capital, the town subsided into a state of isolation, lethargy and neglect.

In recent years all this has begun to change. The road from Mexico has been completed, new industries have been set up and new hotels built to accommodate the rising flood of tourists. But at the time of this, my first visit, Merida looked much as it must have done since the beginning of the century. As I walked about the narrow streets and in and out of the colonial churches, or sat in the square watching the women sauntering by in embroidered shifts while the men lounged on iron benches wearing straw hats and white cotton smocks and trousers, the age of the *hacenderos* did not seem remote. If the air of universal contentment remarked by Stephens had been replaced by one of torpor, the town still retained the charm of a place cut off from the world and securely islanded in its past.

That evening there was a full moon which enticed me to stay out late. After wandering for an hour or so I ended up in the great square where a few white figures still lingered in pools of shadow under the trees. I paused for a moment to look up at the façade of the cathedral with the moon sailing over it, then reluctantly turned back towards the hotel. I had only walked a dozen yards when a man lurched out of a side street so suddenly that I almost collided with him. He was youthfully plump, fair-skinned and blue-eyed. He stood there in the moonlight swaying a little and smiling. In his right hand he held dangling from his fingers a small glittering object which he thrust towards me.

'Take it!' he said speaking English in a voice which, though halting and slurred, had only the faintest trace of an accent. 'Take it! It's yours. You can go wherever you want to.'

Experience had taught me to be wary of drunk Mexicans but I was curious to know what it was he was offering me. I bent forward and looked more closely. I had expected some kind of talisman, but the object he held between his fingers was a key.

'Take it! I give it to you!' As he spoke he swung round with a grand expansive gesture, and I saw behind him, drawn up against the pavement in the side street, a slim, silver convertible. 'Go on! I mean it! It's yours!'

Two companion figures now loomed out of the shadows. They were a rough-looking couple, the one middle-aged, the other a boy. The boy was reeling and waving his arms to keep his balance. The man stepped solemnly towards me. 'Don't take any notice of him, señor. He's drunk. He doesn't know what he's saying.'

'Shut up, Pepe! I know perfectly well what I'm saying. This gentleman's a friend of mine. Everything I have is yours; my car, my horses, my house.'

'It's very kind of you, but it's late and I'm going to bed.'

'Nonsense! The night's only just begun. You could spend a couple of hours in the brothels, drive down to Progreso for a swim and be back before daylight.'

'I'm tired and I have a plane to catch tomorrow.'

He appeared deeply offended. His eyes became moist and for a moment I was afraid that he was going to cry. He let his hand drop to his side and the key fell ringing on the pavement. Pepe stooped and picked it up.

'Of course if you don't want my car, I can't force you to take it.' Suddenly he brightened up. 'Oh well, it doesn't matter. Come then, at least you won't refuse a drink.' Clutching my arm he began to pull me along the pavement. I had no desire to go with him, but it seemed churlish to resist.

We turned in through the door outside which the car was drawn up, and entered a room lit by crimson-shaded lamps. There was a dance floor in the centre with small tables grouped round it. At one end a bar gleamed with bottles. Some stools stood in front of it and to one side there were low, comfortable-looking wicker chairs. Four or five girls sat bunched at a table in the darkest corner. Momentarily alerted, their black eyes peered at us out of dusky faces, but they quickly turned away and their mouths pouted in evident disappointment. The only other occupants of the room were a waiter and a barman. We crossed to a table on the opposite side from the girls and sat down. After ordering drinks, two whiskies and two beers, my host introduced himself and his companions. He told me that his own name was Octavio. I told him mine, and we both rose, shook hands and sat down again.

'And this fellow here,' he went on, 'is my chauffeur, Pepe.' I clasped Pepe's hand across the table. 'And this is Juanito, my jockey.'

Juanito was far too drunk for hand-shaking. His head kept

rolling from side to side. Twice Pepe had to catch hold of him to prevent him from falling off his chair.

'I tell you, my friend, although you might not think it to look at him, Pepe's the handiest man with a car in Yucatan. And as for Juanito,' he tweaked the boy's ear, 'he's the best jockey in the whole of Mexico!'

Juanito jerked his head away and looked at his master through eyes which he had difficulty in keeping open. 'And you, Don Octavio, everybody knows what you are. You're a goddam son-of-a-bitch!'

Octavio pushed back his chair and stood up, swaying but dignified.

'Juanito, if you don't apologize I'll . . .'

The boy looked at me, grinning. 'It's true, he's just a goddam son-of-a-bitch.'

'Shut up, Juanito!' Pepe cuffed him sharply. 'You know he doesn't mean it, Don Octavio. It's all your own fault, you let him drink too much.'

'Even if he's drunk he's got no right to speak to me like that. I'm not going to sit here to be insulted by one of my own stable boys.'

Staggering a little, he crossed the dance floor and sat down at a table on the other side with his back towards us.

'Go on, Juanito! Go over and tell him you're sorry.'

The boy shook his head, still grinning.

'You can't do anything with him when he's like that. Don Octavio's the kindest master a man could wish for—and generous! Why, if he wasn't so rich he'd be in rags with all the money he's given away. Now look what's happened! Those girls're after him already. If I don't get rid of them, they'll be helping themselves from his pocket.'

Three of the girls had collected round Octavio's table. One of them was trying to put her arms round his neck and he was warding her off feebly. Pepe jumped up, hurried across the room and hustled away the girls who withdrew to their corner hissing obscenities. Bending over his master, he coaxed and caressed him like a child, but Octavio refused even to turn his head in our direction. After a few minutes Pepe gave up and came back to Juanito. 'You ungrateful little bastard!' He seized him by the shoulder and began beating him over the head. 'Come now or I'll knock your brains out!'

'Hey, leave me alone! . . . All right . . . I'll come . . .' The boy rose, caught his foot against the table-leg and fell back on to his chair. Pepe took hold of his arm and tried to lift him, but he sagged sideways. I got up and took his other arm. Together we steered him across the floor to Octavio's table. I stuck an elbow into his ribs.

'But I tell you, señor, it's true, he's just a . . .'

'Shut up!' Pepe raised a threatening fist.

'Oh well, then . . . Don Octavio, I'm sorry.'

Octavio did not seem to hear. He stared at the wall in front of him. Suddenly he turned to me. 'Phew! Those girls! I've had them all so often, I simply can't face them any more. But why don't you have a go? I'll pay. They've all got clap. That little one in the middle's the best of them.'

I declined his offer.

'I don't blame you.' He got up and we returned to our table.

As we sat down there was a stir at the entrance. The barman put a record on the pick-up. Octavio looked round hopefully. A middle-aged couple came in, walked to the edge of the dance floor and walked out again.

'Christ!' Octavio heaved his arms in disgust. 'They're the only sort of people who come to Merida these days. If I didn't get away to Paris every year for a couple of months I'd go off my head with boredom.'

He rolled his blue eyes wildly. I tried to be sympathetic. 'It's an attractive town to visit, but I suppose it must be rather dull to live in.'

'Oh no, it's not so bad as that, in fact, I wouldn't dream of living anywhere else. It's free and easy. One can do what one likes. It's just that I need a change sometimes.' He glanced across the room at the dark corner. 'Of course it's quite different for you. How long've you been here?'

'Only a few hours.'

'Ah well, you've got plenty to look forward to. There're some marvellous girls although you wouldn't think so from that lot. Beautiful figures and all sorts of interesting little tricks. Oh, you'll enjoy yourself all right. By the way, have you ever made love in a hammock?'

'No, I shouldn't have thought it was very comfortable.'

'You're completely wrong! A bed's all very well, but a hammock! Believe it or not, I always take mine with me when I go to Paris. You've no idea! It adds such variety! Of course I'm not talking about these wretched things you hang up in your English gardens. We have real hammocks. There's no end to what you can do in them. After all with a bed it's nothing but bounce, but with a hammock there's rhythm and swing. Ours are so broad you can use them sideways if you feel like it. Woosh! Up you go, and down.' He swung his arms in the air as he spoke. 'And woosh! Down and up! It's terrific!'

Three young Mexicans lounged in, picked themselves partners from the girls in the corner and started dancing. Octavio watched them enviously. 'There you are! They've grabbed the best of the bunch. Pepe, you old fool, it's all your fault! Why can't you leave me alone? But still, I know just what they're in for. Couldn't be bothered to go through with it myself.' He broke off and clutched my arm. 'Look! Look what's coming! Ah, that's more like it!'

The new arrivals were American. The girl had a home-spun appearance, but she was young and blonde. She might have been a schoolteacher. Her companion was a tall, hulking red-head with a crew-cut. They ordered drinks and settled in the wicker chairs by the bar.

'Come on,' Octavio said, 'let's go and talk to them.'

'But perhaps they won't want to talk to us.'

'Nonsense! They'll be delighted. Just look at that hair! You don't know what it does to me. I haven't had a girl with hair like that since I was last in Paris.'

'I'm sorry, I'm not coming.'

'Oh well then, I'll have to go by myself.'

He had not touched his whisky and was much steadier than when we had first arrived. Even so he cannoned against the tables as he crossed the room. When he reached the Americans, he stopped and bowed. The man stared at him blankly but, undeterred, he pulled up a chair and sat close to the girl.

Pepe shook his head. 'You shouldn't have let him go by himself, señor, there's sure to be trouble.'

Octavio was talking and the girl smiling, but the man remained sullen. When she began to giggle, he leant forward until his face was close to Octavio's and said loudly and deliberately: 'Get out! Scram! Go away!'

Without even turning, Octavio made a vague brushing-off gesture with his hand and edged his chair closer to the girl.

'Please, señor! Please go to him and persuade him to come back.'

Reluctantly I got up and crossed the room. I nodded to the American and bent down over Octavio. 'I'm your guest, you know. You invited me for a drink. You can't just go off and leave me.'

'Of course not, my dear fellow; I'm so sorry. But why don't you join us?' He pulled up another chair. 'Let me introduce you. This charming young lady's come all the way from Illinois, and this gentleman . . .'

'He's Donovan. You can call him Don. We got acquainted out at the ruins.'

'Waiter,' Octavio shouted, 'bring us another whisky.'

The girl smiled at me. She had a shiny, eager face and freckles. 'Pleased to meet you,' she said. 'Won't you sit down?'

I hesitated, looking at the man. He gave a resigned grunt. 'Well, if you can't get your friend to go away, you might try and control his conversation.'

Already Octavio was off again. I couldn't hear what he was saying, but the girl looked as if she was enjoying it. I sat down and asked Donovan what he'd thought of the ruins. He said he hadn't thought anything of them at all. His boorishness irritated me. He was sitting forward trying to listen to Octavio.

I decided to make it difficult for him, so I started off, in as loud a voice as possible, on a long rambling gabble about Chichén-Itzá. I kept it up for ten minutes without a break; then I collapsed. In the silence I heard Octavio end an excited interrogation with the word 'hammock'. Hurriedly I started off again, but had only got a few sentences out when the girl screamed. I looked round. Her face was crimson and she had jerked herself away over the side of her chair as if she were afraid that Octavio was going to bite her. 'Oh, he's disgusting!' she gasped.

Donovan heaved himself to his feet and stood glowering. 'That's enough now! Come on, you little grease spot, we'll settle this outside.'

I jumped up. Pepe, the barman and the waiter came crowding round.

'Can't you see he's drunk?' I said. 'He doesn't know what he's saying.'

'For Chrissake, you keep out of this!' The man took a step towards me, but Pepe moved in between us. 'Hell! What d'you expect in a lousy dump like this! Come on, honey,' he took the girl's arm, 'let's get out of here.'

Pushing the girl in front of him, he made for the door. As they went out she turned and fixed Octavio with a bewildered, fascinated stare.

We went back to our table. Juanito had passed out, his head angled awkwardly on his folded arms. Octavio slumped into his chair with a groan. 'The bitch! Just like a *gringuita*! They're all the same. Lead you on till you're getting really excited and, then ...' He broke off and started hammering with his fists on the table. 'Pepe!' he shouted. 'A woman! Pepe, get me a woman!'

But it was too late. The dark corner was empty. While we had been with the Americans, all the girls had gone.

He was silent for a moment, then he seized his glass and drank the whisky at a gulp. 'Well, it's no good staying here. We'd better go. Come, Juanito, it's time for bed.'

He lifted the boy's chin and, after looking into his vacant face, let it fall with a thump. 'You know,' he said turning to me with a sheepish grin, 'what he said about me is true. I am a son-of-a-bitch—just a goddam son-of-a-bitch.'

They carried Juanito out to the car, Pepe taking his head and Octavio his heels, and stuffed him doubled up into the back. 'Next time you visit us,' Octavio said as we shook hands, 'you must come to my house and meet my wife.'

He jumped in beside Pepe and the silver convertible slid off into the shadows between the peeling walls and high-grilled windows of the street.

I had been told that the plane for Chetumal would leave at three o'clock, but the governor and his party did not arrive at the airfield until four. About fifty friends and officials came to see him off. From the moment he got out of his car they milled round him, elbowing and shoving, as they plied him with last-minute advice and requests. I saw there was no hope of getting near him, so I joined the mob round his secretary. When I at last succeeded in breaking through to his side, he eyed me with testy impatience, but as soon as he learned that I was English he shook my hand and told me that the governor would be delighted to hear that I was travelling on the plane. I thanked him but was careful to edge well to the front as the crowd started to move across the airfield. There was plenty of room inside the cabin, however, and I settled with a couple of seats to myself at the back. It was after five o'clock and the sun was already beginning to set by the time we took off.

Although they had travelled all the way from Mexico City together the members of the party had still so much to discuss that, once free of their safety belts, they spent the rest of the flight in a constant state of agitation, either huddling into volatile groups or making such concentrated rushes on the governor that they threatened the stability of the plane. They were a mixed collection. When I was not looking out of the window at the monotonous folds of green jungle beneath us, I distracted myself by trying to guess their identities. A few were obviously minor officials, harassed-looking creatures who were perpetually called upon to produce files and documents. Others I took for local business men, but there were two or three wearing smart tropical suits and accompanied by elegantly dressed wives whom I found difficult to place. They were more composed than the rest and were distinguished by their intellectual air. Though they were often the centre of excited huddles they remained in their seats throughout the journey. I decided that they must be high-ranking advisers, university professors, perhaps; but I could not imagine what they were going to advise about in Chetumal.

Of the whole plane-load, there were two who totally mystified me. Ignored by the rest of the party, they sat side by side, silent and immobile. One was fat and the other thin. Both were elderly and wore almost identical clothes: black suits of a material far too heavy for the tropics, black ties and soiled white shirts. This is the garb usually adopted by priests in Mexico, since the wearing of soutanes, except when taking part in a service, is forbidden by law. The appearance of the Mexican clergy is often unimpressive, but this couple looked too humble and innocuous to have any connection with the church. I tried all sorts of professions on them from school-master to sanitary inspector, but none seemed to fit.

By the time we began to descend towards Chetumal dusk had already fallen. Some lights glimmered ahead of us, but the strip on which we landed was surrounded by unbroken jungle. As the governor stepped off the plane, a crowd, three times the size of the one which had seen him off at Merida, surged forward to welcome him. In the airfield waiting-room the mêlée was so dense that I had difficulty in forcing my way to the exit. The parking area on the other side of the building was jammed with cars and taxis but when I tried to engage one of the latter, I was told that they were all reserved for the governor's party. Although it was a clear night and the air was surprisingly cool I did not feel like walking several miles through the jungle in the dark carrying my suitcase. I was still standing by the door when the governor came out and, shaking off his followers, plunged into the large black saloon which was waiting for him. His secretary followed and noticing me just as he was about to get in, apologized that there was no room in the car and promised to send it back for me.

When they saw the governor drive off, the people who had come to meet him made a rush for their own cars. There was a violent revving of engines as they ruthlessly manoeuvred for precedence in the official *cortège*. Soon I found myself alone watching the trail of red tail lamps disappearing into the darkness. As the sound of the engines died, the tropical night closed in with the clamour of frogs and crickets.

Well disposed as the secretary had shown himself, I had little faith in his promise. I went back to the waiting-room. The only occupant was an old man who had settled himself for the night on a bench. I roused him and asked if it would be possible to telephone for a taxi. He shook his head. The office was closed and the officials had left. I wandered out on to the airfield and at once my hopes rose. A truck had been backed against the aeroplane and was being loaded, under the super-vision of the black-suited couple who had so mystified me on the journey, with a vast assortment of crates and packages. The two men, now in shirt-sleeves and braces, were jumping about nervously shouting at the porters. Sometimes they even lifted packages themselves as though they were too precious to be entrusted to other hands. I walked over to them and managed to distract the fat one from his work. His face had come out in crimson blotches and his sweat-soaked shirt stuck to his chest and shoulders. I asked him if I could have a lift on the truck. He flung up his hands. It would be quite impossible. Five of them had to squeeze into the front as it was. I told him I would be very happy to sit in the back, but he was horrified. 'Out of the question! I'm sorry, señor, but half of it's going to be ruined as it is.'

'What've you got there that's so precious?'

'Why, the banquet! The governor's banquet! Plates, glasses, the food, the wine, everything!'

The mystery of his own and his companion's profession was now solved, but I was no nearer getting to Chetumal.

I went back to the waiting-room. The old man had covered his face with a newspaper. I could not decide whether to follow his example and spend the night on a bench or set out for the town on foot. As I hesitated I heard the sound of an engine. I grabbed my suitcase and ran to the door. A pair of headlights swept over the parking space and a moment later the governor's car drew up beside me. The chauffeur, a casual young man wearing an elegant white shirt and sharply pressed slacks, got out and asked me in English if I was the gentleman who had travelled on the governor's plane. When I replied that I was, he picked up my suitcase, opened the door and invited me to get in. As we swung off down the smooth tarmac road into the jungle I asked him where he had learned to speak English so well.

'I had an English education. I went to St John's college in Belize.'

'Do a lot of people go there from Chetumal?'

'They used to but now we have better schools of our own. Are you on your way there yourself?'

'No, I'm stopping here.'

'But you're an Englishman, you ought to go and see it.'

'I haven't got time. What's it like?'

'Oh it's nothing. Just a large brothel. The women aren't bad. There's no other reason for going there. It isn't civilized.'

His tone made me feel personally responsible. 'I'm sorry to hear that.'

'What d'you expect? It's a colony.'

I was silenced, but he had not finished with me. Leaning forward he turned a knob on the dashboard and a harsh blast of music ricocheted round my ears. I was stupefied, then realized with a shock that I recognized the tune. It was 'Little Brown Jug' played by a military band.

'That's Belize for you!' he shouted.

'For God's sake turn it off!'

Whether he heard me or not he took no notice. For the rest of the journey we swept through the jungle darkness to the accompaniment of the Grenadier Guards.

As we came to the top of a hill lights appeared below us. They were far more numerous and widespread than I had expected, but I had only a glimpse of them before we turned off into a side road and stopped outside a large motel. It was quite new and of its kind as impressive as anything I had seen in Mexico. The chauffeur switched off the Grenadiers. 'There's a room booked,' he said as he opened the door for me to get out. I gave him an enormous tip which he hardly acknowledged. But when I clinched my gratitude by shaking his hand, he thawed and pulling out his wallet, presented me with his card. 'That's my name. If you want to go anywhere, let me know and I'll take you.'

'In the governor's car?'

'Of course, why not? It's as good as mine really. Anyhow he can always walk.'

The inside of the motel fulfilled the promise of its exterior. The hall and dining-room were spacious and well furnished. The main block must have contained at least thirty bedrooms, and the bungalows in the garden as many more. The manager had been warned of my arrival, but there had been no need to book a room, for only three were occupied in the whole building. The other guests, as I found when I entered the dining-room, were the intellectuals of the governor's party. Their meal finished, they were sitting with their wives drinking coffee. I now realized that I had met one of the men in Mexico City, but could not recollect on what occasion. By the time I had finished my own dinner, the wives had gone to bed. As I got up from my chair, the man I had recognized rose and came towards me with outstretched hand.

'I saw you on the plane. I think we met once at dinner with Señor X.'

'Yes, of course, I remember very well.' It was true. I did remember; but I still could not place him. 'What're you doing in Chetumal?'

'My firm's responsible for most of the reconstruction here. We've got two or three schools in hand and some new government buildings—I suppose you're on your way to Belize.'

'No, I'm hoping to go to Rio Bec.'

'Where's that?'

'I'm not too sure, but it should be about sixty miles west from here. It's the site of some interesting Maya ruins.'

'Never heard of it myself. I'll ask the others.'

Both his friends knew the name, Rio Bec, and remembered the characteristics of its architecture, but they had no idea that it was in the region of Chetumal. They asked me how I proposed to reach the place.

'I've got a map which marks a road running west to the Campeche-Tenosique railway. If it exists it should pass close to the ruins.'

'That's the road they've just started, but it only goes for a few miles. There may be a track leading on, but you wouldn't get through even in a jeep at this time of year.'

I was beginning to feel the effects of my evening with Don Octavio, so I left the architects and pondering their unwelcome information, went out through the garden to my bungalow. The curtains were undrawn and I stood for a few minutes at the window. The motel was built on a hill overlooking the town. The lights below covered an area about a mile deep by two miles wide. Lines of neon lamps marked the principal thoroughfares. Ever since my arrival at the airfield I had begun to suspect that Chetumal was not going to prove the kind of place I had imagined. Now as my gaze traced the neon geometry of its streets, I realized that the descriptions I had been given in Mexico City belonged to the past. I decided to put my romantic picture of it out of my mind, and to concentrate, despite any initial discouragement, on the ruins as my main target. After all, the architects were outsiders like myself. For reliable information I would have to talk to local people with first-hand knowledge of the country. As I got into bed I determined to wake early and begin the day by continuing my inquiries in the town.

I slept longer than I had intended. It was eight o'clock by the time I left the bungalow and walked through the garden to the main block of the motel. I had already questioned the breakfast waiter, but he turned out to be a recent arrival from Coatzalcoalcos. Now I tackled the manager, whom I found standing at the reception desk in the hall. He wanted to be helpful, but the name Rio Bec meant nothing to him and he knew of no ruins in the neighbourhood. He could not even suggest anyone who might be able to give me information. As I turned away from his shaking head I felt a touch on my arm. It was the governor's chauffeur. He had come with an invitation for me to attend the end-of-term celebrations at the high school. My first instinct was to refuse, then it occurred to me that schoolmasters were likely to be better informed than any-one else on the subject of ruins, so I accepted and followed him to the car.

The road outside the motel was unpaved, but after fifty yards we turned into a fine tarred boulevard which sloped through the centre of the town to the sea-front. The houses on either side were mostly battered wooden bungalows with verandahs and tin roofs, but there were a few new buildings in contemporary Mexican style. The high school which was only a short way down the hill was one of these. Its handsome L-shaped block faced on to an extensive playground where a dozen rows of chairs had been placed along the touch-line of a netball pitch. Most of these were already occupied but the front row remained empty. The officials and notables for whom they were reserved stood about in groups awaiting the arrival of the governor. Teams of girls and boys wearing shorts and T-shirts were limbering up on the other side of the pitch. As I approached, an official came forward and introduced himself as the director of education. He made a short speech of welcome and ended by announcing, with an air of triumph, that he had found a piano.

Though mystified, I congratulated him. It was now obvious that there had been some mistake about my identity, but I was determined to make the most of the situation before I was found out. After admiring the school buildings and parrying a suggestion that I might like to visit the other schools in the town, I turned to the subject of ancient Maya sites and asked him if he had heard of Rio Bec.

'No, I'm afraid I haven't. But I'm not from this part of the world. Like most of the other officials and schoolmasters I came here with the governor when he was appointed. I've hardly been outside the town and I've never heard any mention of ruins.'

I asked him if he could introduce me to some local personality who might be better informed, but after a brief glance round he shook his head. Then the governor's car drove up, and he hurried away to join in the official welcome. As I was watching the governor's slow hand-shaking progress, his secretary came up to me and presented me with an envelope.

'It's your invitation to the banquet,' he explained. 'Two o'clock tomorrow at the plywood factory. I'll arrange for a car to take you.' He darted off to join the other officials as they scrambled for the seats closest to the governor's.

When they had all settled themselves, I took one of the remaining empty chairs at the end of the front row. I drew out the card from its envelope and read it. The banquet was being held to commemorate the anniversary of the governor's appointment. Failure to accept would undoubtedly cause offence and diminish my chance, for this was a plan I had come to rely upon, of borrowing an official jeep for my expedition. But acceptance meant another wasted day in Chetumal which I could not afford when I had so little time available. While I was trying to think of an excuse for refusing, which might also provide a favourable approach to a request for transport, I became aware of someone hovering at my side. I looked round to find myself confronted by an obvious Englishman. Realizing that he must be the expected guest for whom I had been mistaken, I decided it would be wise to find out who he was, so I waved him into the vacant chair next to mine.

While the director of education launched on a speech of welcome, we whispered furtively. Everything was quickly but astonishingly explained. A small English opera company touring the Caribbean had been persuaded by the Mexican consul in Belize to visit Chetumal to take part in the governor's celebrations. My neighbour had been sent down from Mexico City to find out the conditions under which the company was to perform and, if necessary, to help with the arrangements. Less fortunate than I, he had missed the governor's plane and had been forced to come on from Merida by bus. He had travelled all night. The bus had stuck in the mud where the road was still under construction and had only arrived half an hour before.

The director of education was followed by several other speech-makers including the governor, who appealed to the youth of Chetumal to uphold the principles of the Mexican revolution and to ensure by their industry the speedy promotion of Quintana Roo from a 'territory' into a state.

The children responded with a beflagged march round the playground and the singing of a paean, composed by a local poet, in praise of the President of the Republic then in office. When this was over, the director of physical education announced the play-off of the senior boys' and girls' netball competitions. The boys formed up on the pitch. The teams carried their respective names, '*Equipo Juarez*' and '*Equipo Cuauhtémoc*', embroidered on their shirts. The governor started the game by punching the ball deftly into the centre of the pitch. The boys ran after it without enthusiasm. They were a wretched, undersized lot with nothing about them to suggest that they might be the descendants of British pirates. Their play was not only feeble, but they kept so strictly to the rules that the director of physical education, who acted as referee, had scarcely any need to blow his whistle. The spectators soon lost interest in the game and began to talk. When the *Equipo Juarez* scored the only goal of the match, the director himself had to clap in order to encourage some half-hearted applause.

As soon as the girls' teams came out on to the pitch the spectators stopped talking and the males among them craned forward in their seats. If the boys had appeared small and puny for their age, the girls gave the opposite impression. As they pranced about waiting for the game to begin, plump breasts bobbed under tight T-shirts and brief shorts wrinkled up over splendidly developed thighs. Even their choice of team names, '*Equipo Venus*' and '*Rebeldes sin Causa*', seemed to promise a more exciting contest than the one which had just ended.

The director of education presented the ball to a local dignitary in the front row. Perhaps wishing to outdo the governor, he gave it a tremendous punch. It soared high, but off-centre. The wind took it in a wide arc and plumped it into the *Rebeldes'* net. The *Venus* girls screamed their triumph while the *Rebeldes*, riled in a just cause, flung themselves on the referee. With a whistle blast and a panicky cry he gave out the goal as disallowed. Yelling with fury, the *Venus* team made a dash towards him, but he skipped aside and flung the ball into the centre. Both teams raced after it and clashed in a fierce scrimmage. The referee danced round them shouting and blowing. Suddenly a *rebelde*, her shirt half ripped from her back, elbowed herself free and scooted with the ball down the pitch. The whistle shrilled again, but a *Venus* girl had already caught her by the waist-band of her shorts. As the elastics gave, the crowd gasped, then the attacker stumbled. Released, the band retracted with a stinging slap. The *rebelde* dropped the ball and the referee grabbed it. He managed to calm the girls and make them listen to him. If they did not pay attention to his whistle he would stop the game. But the director of education had had enough. He hastily reminded the governor of another appointment and hurried him off to his car. The rest of the officials followed reluctantly, glancing over their shoulders as the game was resumed. The referee was taking no chances. The whistle blew while the ball was still in the air. I was watching, fascinated, when my neighbour nudged my arm. 'I'll have to go,' he said. 'D'you mind coming with me and putting things straight?'

I protested. 'But we can't go now, we'll miss the game.'

'I'm sorry, but we'll have to. If you don't come, they'll think I'm an impostor.'

I followed him as he chased after the governor's party. By the time we caught up with it the governor was already in his car and the director of education was about to get into his. I stopped him, introduced my compatriot and explained the mistake about my identity. He was not in the least ruffled. 'Delighted to have you both. Come on, get in. We're just off to look at another new school. I'm sure you'll find it interesting.'

As the car drove away, I glanced back towards the pitch, but the view was blocked by the spectators who were all on their feet while some had even climbed on to their chairs. The director of physical education's whistle was shrilling in a sustained blast.

When we arrived at the new school, the governor was being shown round by the architects. I went up to his secretary, told him of the misunderstanding and handed back the invitation to the banquet. He pushed it away. 'No, no, of course you must come! I'll send another invitation for your friend.'

Dismayed, I confessed my plan to go to Rio Bec.

'Never heard of the place, but even if it exists, how're you going to get there?'

'I hoped the governor might lend me a jeep.'

'I don't know about that. You'll have to ask him yourself. But you won't get one tomorrow. We'll be needing everything on wheels for the banquet.'

Following the governor and the architects, the party now trailed upstairs to inspect the upper floor of the building. I hung behind and managed to slip off unnoticed. Back in the main boulevard I sat down at a table in a crowded café. When the waiter brought me my drink, I asked him about Rio Bec, but he, too, was a stranger who had only lately arrived from Veracruz. My neighbours at the next table had overheard my inquiry. One of them told me that there was a mound with a few stones on the other side of the bay. I explained that the ruins I wanted to visit were at least a hundred kilometres inland. By now everybody in the café was listening, but though they all began discussing my problem, not one of them was able to offer any information or advice. I inquired in five other cafés without success. After eating in a restaurant on the sea front, I gave up and started to walk back to the motel.

It was the siesta hour and shops were closed and cafés empty. The tarmac of the deserted boulevard tapered in a blue ribbon up the slope of the hill. The neon lamp-stands rose tall and elegant on either side. New buildings, scattered among the wooden bungalows, caught the sunlight on their flat planes of concrete. The place in its small way had a pleasant thriving appearance. Certainly the governor's achievement in making such rapid progress with its reconstruction was remarkable.

For this reason alone I was glad I had seen it, but once seen, it had little else of interest to offer. The sun was hot and the road longer and steeper than I had realized. I began to feel tired and dispirited. A couple of days in Chetumal would be more than enough; perhaps it would be best to abandon my attempt on Rio Bec and take the first bus or plane back to Merida.

I had almost reached the top of the hill when the governor's car nosed into the pavement beside me. The chauffeur's head poked out of the window. 'Care for a swim?'

The idea had not occurred to me, but now I felt it was what I needed. I thanked him and got inside. As we swept over the hill and out of the town, he switched on the radio. It was woman's hour in Belize. An English female voice told us to take an onion and chop it fine. With a shrug of disgust, he cut her off.

We were heading inland. Though the trees were not high, the jungle was dense and lush. The sea lay well behind us.

'I thought we were going to swim?'

'Yes, that's right, at Bacalár.'

We came to a fork. As the car swung to the right, I glimpsed the other road cutting away to the west through the jungle.

'Where does that go to?'

'It's the new road. They've only been at work on it for a year.'

'Where will it go when it's finished?'

'God knows!'

'Have you been along it yourself?'

'No, I wouldn't risk wrecking my car.'

'I'd like to try it. There're some ruins I want to see which lie somewhere in that direction.'

'If it's ruins you want, there's one where we're going. You'll see it in a minute.'

Soon the country became more open. A bare hill rose above the trees crowned by a ruined fort. We turned off the road on to the track which led up to it and stopped under its walls. The chauffeur told me that it had been built by the Spaniards. During the War of the Castes the settlers had made their last stand there, but they had all been massacred. Later the army had come and the Indians had withdrawn to the north. Since then this part of the territory had been almost uninhabited.

The fort was a rectangular stone building, picturesque, but of no architectural interest. Its walls were twenty feet high and it had a squat crumbling tower. I looked back at the country behind us. The forest rolled without a break to low hills on the horizon. I began to walk round the ruin to find an entrance, but as soon as I had turned the first corner I stopped. The hill fell sharply from the walls to a broad serpentine stretch of water which coiled away for miles through the jungle. The colour of its surface varied from light sapphire over sandy shallows, through intermediate viridians, to a deep sky-reflecting blue. When I had recovered from my surprise, for I had expected another monotonous expanse of forest, I started to scramble down the hill. The chauffeur followed and guided me to a beach of hard white sand shaded by an enormous tree. He left me there while he went to visit friends in the village of Bacalár which lay farther on out of sight. I undressed and dived into the lagoon. The water was clear and fresh. Warm breezes broke its peacock surface into bright ripples which glittered against the dark rim of the jungle. The fort from its hill threw down a quivering streak of gold among the blues and greens. I spent the next couple of hours alternately swimming and resting on the sand. Then the chauffeur came back. I put on my clothes and we walked up the hill to the car.

It was sunset by the time he dropped me at the motel. There was no sign of the architects and I ate alone in the empty dining-room. When I had finished, I decided to go into the town and make another round of the cafés. I visited them all and even stopped the more intelligent-looking people I passed in the streets, but I was no more successful with my inquiries than I had been in the morning. More dispirited than ever, I strolled out along the sea-front and sat down on a bench. My bathe in the lagoon of Bacalár and my solitary meal in the empty dining-room of the motel had given me ideas for an argument with which to prise a jeep from the governor, but what I needed most was to be able to tell him that I had had confirmation of the whereabouts and accessibility of Rio Bec.

The sea-front, unlit and deserted, looked the last place where I would be likely to change my luck. I was about to get up and go back to the town when I saw three figures approaching. Thinking that I might just as well question them as anyone else, I waited on the bench. But when they came close enough for me to speak, I hesitated, for their appearance fulfilled all too faithfully my original conception of the inhabitants of Chetumal. Ragged and unshaven, one pock-marked, another squint-eyed, the third greasy and gross with a look of animal cunning, it was not difficult to imagine the trio as descendants of buccaneers. As soon as they saw me, they stopped talking and stared at me furtively. I kept silent and let them pass, but a few yards on they halted and turned round. I could hear them whispering. Then the fat one detached himself from his companions and lounged up to me. He asked me if I was from Belize. I explained that I was English but that I had come from Mexico City. He said that Belize was a good place: Chetumal was no good. I did not say anything.

'You can't even get a drink here, it's against the law.' He spat on the ground. 'But if you want a bottle, I've got a friend who makes it. It's good stuff. Five pesos, that's all.'

While he was speaking his companions had come closer. They were grinning hopefully.

'I'll buy you a bottle if you can help me.'

They leered in expectation. 'A woman?'

It seemed hardly worth it, but wearily I came out with my piece about Rio Bec. Their faces went blank until I mentioned the road going west. Then at once they became interested. They had a friend from Kilometre Eighty-One. They'd just been drinking with him. It was out on the new road. They'd find him for me if I liked.

I jumped up. 'All right. Let's go.'

They didn't move. 'What about the drink?'

I said that I wanted to meet their friend first and would buy the bottle afterwards. But they had other ideas. It was not safe to drink in the town. I was to stay where I was. The fat man would get the bottle and bring it back to me. The others would fetch the friend. It sounded like a confidence trick. I argued with them but in the end gave in. After all, it was only five pesos. I handed over the money and they went off. I decided to wait for twenty minutes and if they did not return, to start walking back to the motel.

To my astonishment, the fat man reappeared almost at once, his hand resting on a bulging trouser pocket.

'Come on,' he said. 'We can't drink here.'

'What about the others?'

'They'll know where we are.'

We walked farther along the sea-front and out on to a deserted mole. Timber barges were tied up alongside. The fat man jumped down into one of them and I followed. When we had settled ourselves on a stack of planks, he pulled out the bottle, drank from it and handed it to me. I tilted it cautiously. It contained an explosive brew with a venomous back taste. I let him do most of the drinking only pretending now and then to take a gulp. Soon I saw the others coming towards us along the mole with a third man between them. They jumped down into the barge and presented him to me as Don Tomás from Kilometre Eighty-One, adding triumphantly that he knew everything about the ruins. The man nodded. He had bleary bloodshot eyes and looked as if he would be prepared to tell any lie for the sake of a drink. The bottle was passed from hand to hand and quickly emptied. I produced five pesos for another, and the fat man went off to fetch it. I decided it was time to question Don Tomás.

His answers were more promising than I had expected. He kept a store at Kilometre Eighty-One and had come to town to stock up. It was not much of a place, a small jungle settlement started under a government scheme two years before. Only twelve families lived there, but people came in to buy at his store from remoter settlements. Sometimes they offered him *muñecos** which they had dug up. He had bought a few and sold them in Chetumal to a man from Merida. The jungle was full of ruins. He had only seen one himself, a mound with a tree on top of it, but there were others he had heard about which were not far from the settlement. If I went to Kilometre Eighty-One, he would find me a guide.

I asked him how I could get there. He said the new road went as far as Kilometre Seventy-One. After that only the big trucks could get through. 'There's one leaving the day after tomorrow. The driver's a friend of mine. We can go on it together.'

---

* Dolls. This word is often used by country people to describe terracotta figures found on ancient sites.

I agreed to take it if I could not find other transport which would get me there sooner. He gave me the name of the doss-house where he was staying so that I could get in touch with him. His information had been slight enough, but its very meagreness was convincing. Although he would probably have liked to make it sound more spectacular he lacked the imagination to invent. At least he had confirmed my expectation that the new road headed into an area where ruins were plentiful. Beyond this, there was clearly nothing to be learnt from him. With the next bottle he and his companions would be too drunk to talk sense. When the fat man returned, I got up to go. They clamoured in protest but I bought my freedom with another five pesos and left.

I called on the governor at nine o'clock the next morning, but had to wait two hours for an interview. I started by congratulating him on the achievements of his administration. He responded with an outline of his programme for the development of the territory as a whole. His ideas were confined to education and natural resources. My own gambit was tourism. He gave me an opening by asking what I thought of the new motel. I praised it enthusiastically but regretted that so few people were staying in it. Why shouldn't Chetumal be brought into a tourist circuit with Merida, Cozumel and Campeche?

'Yes, but there are no tourist attractions.'

What about the lagoon of Bacalár? It was one of the loveliest in Mexico and the swimming was perfect. The fort could be rebuilt as a hotel. There was a marvellous beach just below it. I gave him a picture complete with umbrellas and sailing boats.

'Do you think we'd get people to come just for that? It's the ruins which bring them to Merida.'

'But there are ruins here too.'

He had not heard of them. Where were they?

I told him about Kilometre Eighty-One and the splendours of Rio Bec. Of course I did not know exactly where they lay in relation to the new road, but if I could have a jeep I would go there to find out.

'When do you want to go?'

'As soon as possible.'

He rang for his secretary and arranged that a jeep with an experienced driver should pick me up at the motel at five o'clock the next morning. I thanked him and we shook hands. As I left the office he called after me: 'Don't get lost! You must be back in time for the opera!'

At the motel I found the architects preparing to leave for the banquet. They offered me a lift in their car. We drove out of the town on a fine road which ran south to the frontier. It only took us a few minutes to reach the plywood factory where the banquet was to be held. We were among the first guests to arrive. As I was about to follow the architects into the building, the governor's car drove up with a party of officials. The chauffeur beckoned to me. 'Do you want to have a look at your colony?' he asked. 'It's only a couple of kilometres down the road.'

I got in and we drove off fast on the smooth surface. He turned on the radio. Belize was back on military bands. To the blare and thump of 'Colonel Bogey' we pulled up at the frontier post. Helmeted Mexican soldiers stood on guard. Beyond the barrier a ramshackle bridge crossed the Hondo river to a narrow mud track, humped and pitted, which trailed uncertainly into the jungle.

'That's it. Does it make you feel at home?' He left me gazing for a few minutes down the dismal track, then he turned the car round and we swept back without a bump to the banquet.

Twirling a tray aloft on one hand and with the other prodding a fork into a ham-handed, locally recruited acolyte, the fat waiter lunged past me as I walked out to join the guests gathered on the terrace to one side of the factory. The governor's arrival, delayed by my frontier trip, prolonged the generous circulation of his whisky and tequila. When he did appear, another half-hour passed before he led the way into the banquet. By that time the male élite of Chetumal, three hundred strong, had become relaxed and voluble. Jostled along in the scramble for seats, I was grabbed by the director of education who pulled me into a chair between himself and the Englishman from Mexico City. As the guests seethed and settled, massed *marimbas** burst into jangling melody and a horde of dishevelled waiters, each balancing four or five plates of lobster mayon-

---

* A kind of xylophone, popular from Veracruz southwards. It can be played by four or five men at the same time.

naise, launched out among the tables. They were directed by the flailing arms of the thin maestro and goaded from behind by the jabbing fork of his fat colleague. With the lobster came wine, not poured by the glass but distributed liberally by the bottle. After some general conversation with my neighbours, I asked the Englishman how he had progressed with preparations for the opera.

He had had a bad time. Some passable furniture for the set, borrowed from a merchant's house, had proved, when inspected on the stage, to be holed by termites. The singers would have to be warned, especially if they were heavyweights. But it was the piano which had been the real problem. Most of the keys were stuck and one of the pedals was out of action. When he had asked for help, they had sent him a drunken carpenter who claimed that he had spent the night drinking with an Englishman; doubtless some down-and-out from Belize. 'Anyway, we got it into some sort of shape in the end, but I'm sorry for the chap who's going to play it.'

'When does the company get here?'

'Tomorrow morning. They're in for a shock.'

'Are they flying?'

'No, they're coming by car. They'll be lucky to get through.'

'I've just been down to the frontier. The road looks terrible. It doesn't compare very well with the one on this side.'

'The Mexicans don't want it to. They're out to show that they can do better than we can. They've got their eye on Belize. They don't mind so long as we stay there, and they'll stand for it being independent, but they're not going to sit quiet if Guatemala tries to take it over.'

The director of education had been listening. He understood English better than I had realized. Leaning forward, he broke in: 'Of course we wouldn't let them. How could we? They're fascists. Look how they treat their own people. They won't even let the Indians learn to read and write. They're frightened that they might come up in the world, then there'd be no slave labour to pick their coffee.'

The waiters were now launched in a second wave. Our empty plates were whisked away and replaced by munificent helpings of cold turkey, ham, hot peppers and salad.

'You can see for yourself that we Mexicans do things

differently. This factory was built by the state to give a decent living to the workers. We try to give everyone an opportunity. Our schools are for the people, not just for the rich. I thought twice about it when the governor asked me to take this job. I was very comfortable where I was and it meant leaving my family; but I've never regretted it for a moment. He's a wonderful man to work with. You've seen for yourselves how much he's done for the place already. It was a wreck after the hurricane. But we've got to admit that things were bad before that. It was cut off from the rest of the country, and the revolution hardly touched it. There was a lot of corruption. A few people made fortunes out of the timber, but as for the rest . . .'

A plump, swarthy man seated farther up the table had been glaring at the director. Suddenly he exploded through a mouthful of turkey.

'Yes, but what're you trying to do with them now? Turn them into a lot of Marxists?'

The director swung away from us to counter the attack.

'Now they're off,' said the Englishman. 'How long do you think this is going on for?' The waiters were swirling round the table with plates of ice-cream and bottles of champagne. 'I've fixed up to meet the electrician at four.'

It was already four o'clock when a loud knocking warned us that the speeches were about to begin. They lasted for a long time. Two local dignitaries spoke first. They were followed by the manager of the factory and finally by the governor. As in each speech references to the revolution and the rights of the working man came rolling out with resounding eloquence, the applause from the guests, other than those surrounding the governor or such imported officials as the director of education, became progressively feebler and less frequent. The coldness on the part of those seated at the tables was compensated for by the warmth of the applause from the factory workers themselves who, fresh from their own fiesta in some other part of the building, had crowded into the back of the hall. When the governor sat down, they gave him a massive ovation, while the élite, as they reluctantly clapped, grumbled to each other and shook their heads.

When all was over, the director of education offered to drive me back to the town. I accepted gratefully. He had drunk nothing during the banquet and I was thankful for his sober caution as the cars of our fellow guests roared past us on the road. He stopped outside a café on the main boulevard and invited me to take coffee with him on the terrace. We had hardly sat down when a large black sedan, far bigger than the governor's car, rolled past. Its sole occupant, apart from the uniformed chauffeur, sat huddled in a corner at the back, his face half-hidden behind dark glasses. I asked the director who he was.

'Oh that's our only consul. You can guess what country he represents.'

'I didn't see him at the banquet.'

'I don't suppose he was asked, but he probably went all the same. We never have anything to do with him. Why should we? We have no trade with his country and we don't want to have any other relations either. Everybody knows he's really a spy.'

A spectacular storm broke later that evening. The thunder clapped down on my bungalow with a force which made the walls shudder. Through the window I saw the town lit up for a few minutes at a stretch in the violet flare of the lightning. The rainfall was massive. It was still rumbling on the roof when, with fears of flooded roads and swollen rivers, I fell asleep.

The next morning as I left the bungalow, the green dawn spread into a sky washed so clear that the stars still shone as in full nocturnal brilliance. Out on the road the jeep was already waiting. The governor's secretary had promised an experienced driver, but the boy hunched drowsily at the wheel looked scarcely above school age.

As I got in beside him, he sat up and started the engine. We set off with a jerk which scraped skid marks on the wet gravel. In a few minutes we were out of the town and heading at a tremendous pace in the direction of Bacalár. My hat blew away but when I asked him to stop, he refused. We were being followed by spies and it was necessary to drive fast to throw them off. I looked round. Although the road was straight for a couple of kilometres, no other car was in sight.

When we reached the junction I had noticed on the way out to the lagoon, we swung off to the left on to the new road which was banked about twelve feet above the jungle. Its hard but uneven surface made the vehicle weave and bounce. To the danger of being catapulted off the embankment was added the discomfort of the cold, for at the speed we were travelling the keen air cut through my cotton shirt and trousers. I implored the boy to go slower, adding as an excuse that I wanted to look out for wild animals. He replied that the only animals we were likely to see were tapir. The faster we drove, the better our chance of coming up with them before they could run away. He had hardly spoken when the jeep struck a rain-filled pot-hole which slammed a sheet of muddy water over the windscreen. Blinded, he braked sharply and the tyres ripped sideways into a skid. We stopped with one wheel over the embankment. When we got going again it was at a speed little faster than a walking pace.

Relaxing, I looked round at the landscape. It was quite flat and the vegetation rose hardly to the level of the road. In all directions the dark, dome-shaped foliage was pierced by sentinel trunks, peeled and splintered, the remnants of high timber decapitated in the hurricane. Bleached to a stark white and topped by singly perched hawks or vultures, they looked like a forest of totem-poles.

After a few miles we passed out of this stricken area and the road began to lift and fall in a gentle switchback. The sun rose, and from high points there were views over green rolling country which sparkled with the gloss of the night's rainfall. As we drove deeper into the hills, the road surface became more treacherous. It was no longer banked up and in the hollows there were pools of flood water. His confidence now fully regained, the boy plunged the jeep through them, laughing at the wings of spray thrown up by the wheels. I asked him if the road became worse farther on. He replied that he did not know as he had never been so far along it before. He had been told that it was impassable, but I need not worry; he would get me through.

We had been driving about three hours and had covered seventy kilometres without seeing either people or dwellings. We had passed no vehicles, although in the softer patches the mud had been deeply rutted by trucks. With only ten kilometres to go, I was beginning to feel hopeful, when the track entered a broad depression. Its surface, after continuing for a hundred yards on the downward slope, disintegrated. At the bottom of the hollow and on the rise beyond, the full width of the strip cut through the jungle had been churned into a rich brown sludge. It was just stiff enough to have retained the form of the trenches gouged by the recent passage of a large truck. I shouted to the boy to stop, but he accelerated and plunged in.

At first we kept going with two wheels in a rut which was not quite deep enough to tip us over. Soon it became deeper. He stopped and changed into four-wheel drive. I urged him to back while there was still a chance of getting out, but he refused. We lunged on for a yard or two as he tried to swing the wheels out of the rut. He succeeded, but the jeep only slewed sideways and stuck with its nose bedded in a wall of mud. Now, too late, he put the gears into reverse. The tyres whined under us and we sank, toppling perilously. I kicked his foot off the accelerator and the engine stalled. In the silence the mud squeaked and gurgled.

I pulled myself up by the roof struts and climbed on to the bonnet. The sludge rose ahead of us in choppy waves like a congealed cataract. The ruts behind had caved in. I had already decided to abandon the jeep and continue the journey on foot when I noticed a movement on the skyline where the cleared strip topped the rise on the far side of the depression. Twin objects, tossing up and down, emerged as the heads of white buffalo. Gradually their bodies lurched into view pulling a cart in which the driver stood upright prodding the beasts with a goad. The boy climbed on to the bonnet beside me and, when the cart was close enough, exchanged shouts with the driver. The man agreed to help. When he reached us, he unharnessed the buffalo and attached them to the rear of the jeep. Slowly they lugged us out on to firm ground. Before going back for his cart, the man showed us a footpath which, he told us, rejoined the road beyond the depression. He thought it might be just wide enough for the jeep to get through.

The path started at right angles to the road, but turned so often that I lost my bearings. The ground rose for half a mile, then levelled out. We were clear of the depression but the undergrowth was so dense that there was no possibility of sighting the road before we reached it. Soon the path began to split up and the boy swung off to left or right, apparently at random, although he always claimed that we were heading for the road. So far, despite some difficult passages, we had encountered nothing solid enough to hold us up, but now the path we had taken wound through a thicket of young trees, too stout to be bent aside. We scraped between them, ripping out hunks of bark, but jammed finally with wheels spinning.

The boy got out, took an axe from the back of the jeep and began to chop at one of the trees which held us. Before, when we had been stuck in the mud, I had at least known in which direction we had to go, but now we were not only stuck but lost. Leaving the boy to chop, I walked on. The path became narrower, the undergrowth denser and the trees more numerous. Then suddenly I came out on to the road. The surface, though of earth, was firm. Once we could get the jeep on to it, we would be within a few minutes of our destination. I hurried back and, while the boy chopped, plotted our course and cleared the undergrowth with a *machete*. In half an hour we were through. A few minutes later we sighted a nest of stick huts and wooden shacks in a clearing at the crown of a broad plateau.

We drove into the centre of the settlement and stopped. I got out, but the boy, after glancing round scornfully, lit a cigarette and settled in his seat. I had expected our arrival to cause a stir, but not even a child came out to gaze at us. The huts and shacks stood back in a loose circle round a grass-covered space criss-crossed by paths. Beyond, in the outer clearing, young trees had already sprung up. Their foliage glittered from the rain. On all sides the land sloped away so that the village, rimmed by low horizons, lay open to a vast expanse of sky. The air was still fresh enough to take the heat out of the sun.

I walked towards the nearest shack and had almost reached it when a man appeared in the doorway. He was tall and lean and as dark as a Negro. His unbuttoned shirt hung loose, exposing a purple weal which ran from his shoulder half-way across his chest. His face was deeply furrowed and he stared at me with eyes narrowed to slits. It was too late to change course. I stopped in front of him and held out my hand. He hesitated before taking it in a brief cold-fingered clasp. I explained the reason why I had come and asked for his advice. His expression did not change but, when I had finished speaking, he turned and nodded to me to follow him. We crossed the single room of the shack and out through another door into a fenced enclosure screened from the sun by a cane awning. In the centre stood a rough table and some chairs. Three naked, dome-bellied children were playing in the dirt. In one corner a woman crouched over cooking pots at a charcoal fire. Her brown, firm-waisted back was bare. The band of her skirt drew a sagging curve across the hollow between her haunches. She did not look round as we entered. The man offered me a chair and we both sat down at the table. The children stopped playing and stood beside their father staring at me with round black eyes.

Still frowning, he told me that it was lucky that I had come to him because none of the other people in the village were to be trusted. He knew the jungle better than any of them. He had never heard of a place called Rio Bec, but there were some ruins, which covered a wide area, a day's journey to the west.

'Have you seen them yourself?'

'Yes. There are many of them—a whole city.'

'What do they look like?'

'They're mostly covered by the jungle, but there are buildings with carved stones and high mounds with little houses on top of them.'

'Could you climb up to the houses?'

'I did not try, but it would be difficult. The mounds are very steep.'

'How can I get there? Can you take me?'

'Impossible. There's a big river to cross. It'll be swollen by the rains.'

'Are you sure?'

'Quite sure. You'll have to wait and come back in the dry season. There're some ruins much closer but they're only small ones. Do you want to see them?'

'Yes, if it's impossible to see the others.'

'I can't take you myself, but I'll try to find someone to go with you.'

He turned to his eldest child and gave him instructions. The boy ran off round the corner of the shack.

'Would you like something to eat?'

I had not thought of food, but now I realized that I was hungry. I accepted his offer of coffee and eggs, and went out through the shack to ask the driver to join me. He was sitting in the jeep and declined to move. He did not eat village food, he said.

When I got back to the enclosure, the man had gone. I sat down at the table and the children stood on the opposite side and stared at me. Their mother still squatted by the fire. Only her arms were active. She held the rest of her body so firmly poised that it would have been difficult to see that it moved at all, but for a coin of sunlight which fell from a chink in the awning to rest now in the hollow between her haunches and now, a centimetre further down, on the waistband of her skirt. To the alarm of the children, I leant across the table and addressed their mother's back over the top of their heads. The señora, I said, need only cook two eggs as my companion did not want any. As I spoke, the coin jumped an inch or two up the depression of her spine, then slid slowly down again to the hollow. It was the only indication that she had heard me. One of the children was so startled that I thought it was going to cry. It occurred to me that if it did, its mother would turn round. Then I saw that the man had come back and was standing in the doorway watching.

He came forward carrying a knife and fork and a saucer of green chilis which he put down on the table. His silent presence loomed oppressively under the low awning. I asked him where he had lived before he came to the settlement. He told me he was a native of Campeche. He had had a good job there, but had been attracted to Kilometre Eighty-One by the government's offer of land. He was among the first of the settlers to arrive. The others were mostly riff-raff from Veracruz on the run from the police. They were a rough lot. Recently two men had been knifed in a brawl. As a result, a squad of soldiers had been sent from Chetumal to keep order.

He noticed my gaze drop to the scar on his chest. Glancing down, he pulled his shirt aside to show where the blade of the *machete* had cut deep into the flesh of his arm below the shoulder. He smiled grimly but offered no explanation. As I was about to ask how he had got it, the woman called to him. The coin of sunlight slid down her skirt as she rose with a plate of eggs in

173

one hand and a mug of coffee in the other. For a moment the curve of her breast filled the angle under her raised arm. Before she could turn, he stepped forward and took the mug and plate from her hands. Relieved of them, she sank back on her haunches.

I had just finished eating when the child who had been sent to find a guide for me returned. He was followed by a young man who stopped in the doorway and propped himself against it. The child said that the neighbour whom he had been sent to fetch was out, but that Manolito had offered to go with me. His father glared at the young man, then jerked his head at him as if ordering him to leave. But he stayed where he was, grinning. A pock-marked, yellow-skinned mestizo, with jet eyes, quick-moving and crafty, and a thin moustache which curled round the corners of his mouth, he looked a likely product of one of the seedier quarters of Veracruz. His ragged shirt and trousers hung on him precariously. A long *machete* dangled in a sheath from his belt.

I looked at my watch. It was eleven o'clock.

'It's getting late,' I said. 'It might be best for me to spend the night here. You could arrange with your neighbour, when he comes back, to take me out early tomorrow. I would have the whole day to look at the ruins.'

The man was silent for a moment, then glanced at his wife. 'You'd be wasting your time. It'll only take you a couple of hours. This fellow knows the way.'

Manolito moved forward from the door. 'Yes, I know the ruins. We can leave at once if you like.'

I got up from the table, paid the man for the coffee and eggs, and thanked him for his help. He came with me as I followed Manolito through the shack. In the doorway he caught my arm. 'That's a government jeep you came in.'

'The governor lent it to me.'

'Are you a friend of his?'

'Yes, he's interested in the ruins.'

Letting go of my arm, he turned to Manolito. 'Wait here. Don't leave till I come back.' He walked away and disappeared among the huts. Manolito shrugged his shoulders. 'Come on,' he said. 'Let's go.'

Without answering, I strolled over to the jeep. The boy was

dozing at the wheel. I woke him up and told him I was going for a walk in the jungle and that he was to wait until I returned. I took my haversack from beside my seat, opened it and removed some of its contents which I did not need. I closed it again carefully, adjusted the strap and slung it over my shoulder. I was still standing by the jeep when I saw two young men coming towards me. They wore khaki caps on the back of their heads and carried rifles on their shoulders. They explained that they had been ordered by their sergeant to go with me to the ruins. The four of us set out with Manolito in front and the soldiers behind. Beyond the clearing, which circled the village, the country was unexpectedly open, a patchwork of low thickets scattered with rare groups of taller trees. Over the tops of the foliage I caught glimpses of wooded hills. To the south clouds were mounting on the horizon.

Manolito loped along with lithe animal ease. I found myself almost running to keep up. The soldiers shouted at him to go slower, but, though he complied briefly, he was soon moving even faster than before. As the path twisted, the soldiers dropped behind until they were out of sight. We had covered about a mile when we came to an open space veined with shallow runnels of loose red earth. Pausing at the edge of it, Manolito shouted a warning, which I did not understand, and sprinted forward. I followed, also running, but more slowly. As I caught up with him, he stooped and brushed his sandals with his fingers. Watching him, I felt a paralysing stab in my ankle. I hitched up my trousers and discovered two red ants crawling on my shin. I flicked them off and removed several more from my socks and boots. I had just satisfied myself that I was free of them when I heard shrill cries behind me. I looked round and saw the soldiers racing back from the centre of the clearing beating their legs as they ran. They stopped on the far side and pulled their trousers up to their knees, but the attack had already probed higher. The next moment they were ripping open their belts and buttons. Tumbling about like clowns, they yelped and rummaged, doubled up in ridiculous postures. We watched, chuckling heartlessly, but after a moment Manolito was pressing to push on. We had only a short distance to go, he said. They could catch us up at the ruins.

The shared comedy had brought us together. I agreed

without hesitation and we set off again at the same gruelling pace. Glancing round as we reached a bend in the track, I had a final glimpse of my bodyguard, stark naked, shaking out their clothes and beating them with sticks.

Half a mile on we turned down a narrow path. A green mound, about thirty feet high, rose out of the jungle ahead of us. Manolito pointed to it, smiling. I beamed back with an enthusiasm I did not feel. It was not an impressive ruin and since it was so close to the village, all our hurrying appeared to have been unnecessary. When I reached the base of the mound, my disappointment deepened. It was entirely covered with bushes and although I walked round it slowly, poking with a stick, I could find no trace of stone steps or facing. It was only when I had completed the circuit that I noticed a block of masonry jutting out from the high foliage. I climbed up to it with Manolito following. The bushes at the summit grew taller than those at the base and concealed a circular tower-like structure of rough stone. Its crumbling walls were at no point more than ten feet high. If it had ever possessed a roof, all trace of it had disappeared. The masonry above the original entrance had collapsed and I had to climb over the rubble to get inside. The stonework was rough and featureless but plentifully festooned with snake skins. Hung from holes and crevices they scraped against the stone with faint whispers as the wind stirred them. Discouraged from further exploration, I backed out hurriedly and scrambled down through the bushes. When we reached the bottom, Manolito told me that there was a larger and more interesting ruin farther on. It had pictures and carvings on the walls. We would have to start at once if I wished to see it. There was still no sign of the soldiers, but he scoffed at my suggestion that we should wait for them. They were town boys, he said, who did not like the jungle. By now they would have returned to the village.

We walked to the main track, followed it for a short distance, then branched off on a path which led us into deep undergrowth. It formed walls on either side which shut out the breeze but gave little protection from the sun which was now directly overhead. I took out my handkerchief and knotted it into a turban, but the heat struck through and I began to sweat. Manolito walked faster than ever. I protested, but it made no difference. He was either unable or unwilling to check his effortless stride. The paths divided frequently and we changed direction every few minutes. I soon realized that if I failed to keep up with him, I would have little chance of getting back to the village by myself.

Suddenly he stopped and threw out his arms in a showman's gesture. I had lagged some way behind, blinded by the sweat which poured from my forehead. As I came up to him, I took off the handkerchief and wiped my face and eyes. Beyond the point where he was standing, the jungle opened to an area covered with low bushes. In the centre, on the summit of a steep slope, a long range of light grey masonry imposed the relics of man-created order on the green tangle of the wilderness. After my recent visits to the great Maya cities of Uxmal and Chichén-Itzá, the excitement that I felt at coming on this lone, jungle-bedded ruin was like that of an encounter on its native terrain with a rare wild animal, albeit an inferior specimen, only seen previously in a zoo. Here and there surviving patches of stone mosaic, its rectilinear pattern accentuated by the vertical rays of the sun, laced with a fine tracery the horizontal planes of the façade, which were further broken by the sprouting of tufted trees and spiked agaves rooted in the walls and vault. The slow, unimpeded transformation of architectural form into formless rubble had reached the point at which the resistance of stone to the onslaught of vegetation had produced a transient masterpiece, doomed by the process which had created it—in ten, twenty, thirty years' time—to total annihilation.

Elated and marvelling, like a hunter I began to circle slowly through the bushes intent on a preliminary inspection of my prize before I moved in to possess it. But I soon realized that possession would not be easy, for there was no sign of an entrance in the whole length of the building. I now saw that what I had taken for the slope of its earth platform was, in fact, a shrub-covered accumulation of stone fallen from its superstructure. At either end the façade rose a few feet higher than in the central section and the rubble mounds below were more substantial. It seemed likely that these were the remains of dummy, tower-like temples similar to those at Rio Bec.

I walked to the end of the building and found that it was

about twenty feet wide. Its back proved to be less impressive than the front. Much of it was overgrown by bushes and no mosaics were visible. At one point the wall had partially collapsed, leaving a cavernous gap below the vault. It was too high for me to reach unaided, but I noted it as a possible means of entry.

When I came round to the front again, Manolito was on the slope below the ruins hacking a path through the bushes. He had taken off his shirt and a gloss of sweat was forming on his shoulders as his *machete* flashed and whined. When he reached the top, he turned and beckoned to me to join him. I climbed the path and stopped with my face at the level of his feet. His *machete* had uncovered a small triangular opening in the masonry. Its sides were formed by stone slabs leaning towards each other and wedged by a keystone. This was the usual device of a Maya arch. I realized that it must be the top of one of the original entrances. The base of the triangle was a large slab which had fallen from above and lay half-buried in the rubble. I calculated that it would be just possible to wriggle over it into the tunnel beyond. Deep inside, diffused light spread from an invisible opening. It was bright enough to indicate a possible exit. I took a torch from my knapsack and flashed it into the tunnel. The vaulting of the arch continued for about six feet through the thickness of the wall. For the same distance the packed silt, which formed the floor of the tunnel, maintained the level of the slab at the entrance. Where the wall ended, it appeared to fall away sharply. Beyond, across the width of the chamber, the torch beam moved over the interior wall. There were cracks and holes in it but no snake skins.

I switched off the torch and looked up at Manolito. The sun struck fiercely on my bare head and its glare, after the darkness of the tunnel, dazzled me. I started to sway and Manolito appeared to sway with me. I clenched my hands and, steadying myself, managed to hold us both to a fixed position. He looked down at me with a grin which mocked my discomfort. I would have liked to climb up to his level, but the space he had cleared was only sufficient for one person. To keep my eyes on his, I had to force my head painfully back. I asked him if he had ever been inside the building himself.

'Many times.'

'Is there anything to see?'

'Yes, the carvings and pictures I told you about.'

'I'd like to have a look at them.'

I waited for him to lead the way but he neither spoke nor moved. The vertical sunlight shadowed his narrow eyes and the hollows below his blunt cheek-bones. The pock marks on his face were like craters. He had an ugly Mongol look with his thin moustache curling round his mouth. As I had followed him through the jungle, his figure had seemed slight and wiry; but stripped of his shirt, his ivory-yellow torso, silhouetted against the blue sky—for our confrontation was at an angle to the building—was unexpectedly broad and there were deep crescents of shadow below his muscles.

'What about snakes?' I asked.

'There aren't any.'

'But there were in the other ruins.'

'Yes, but not here.' He waved his *machete* so that the blade flashed over the dark opening. 'It's quite safe. You can go in. Nothing will happen to you.'

'I'd like to be sure first.' I pointed to a tall sapling which grew on the slope several yards away. 'If you'll cut that for me, I'll poke it down inside.'

He nodded and pushed towards it through the bushes. I switched on the torch again, grabbed a handful of loose stones and flung them into the tunnel. They rattled against the far wall. There was no other sound or movement. I heard the *machete* whine as it sliced through the sapling. Ducking my head and shoulders into the hole, I wriggled forward on my elbows. It was a close fit but I worked fast. Once my feet were inside I gave a kick and jerked myself forward head first over the edge of the silt on to the floor. I got up and began to explore with my torch. The chamber was about seven feet wide and eight feet high from floor to keystone. It extended ten feet to the right of the tunnel but to the left the vault had collapsed and a ramp of stone and silt sloped up to the opening through which the daylight entered. I searched the walls inch by inch but could find no trace of fresco or carving.

When I had finished, I looked back along the tunnel. The building threw a strip of shade across the entrance, but the leaves glittered in the sunlight beyond. I turned away and began to scramble up the rubble slope. When I reached the top, I found that the vault-slab on the right had caved in, leaving an eight-inch gap netted with vegetation. The keystone looked as if it might fall at a touch, bringing the other half of the vault with it. The gap could only be widened by levering the fallen slab lower down the slope. The earth and stones beneath it were loose. With a little burrowing I managed to topple it down at an angle which left a wedge-shaped space just big enough for me to crawl through. The foliage held me but I tore it aside and broke out, dishevelled and scratched, on to the roof. For several minutes I lay on my stomach panting, then I got up and walked to the edge above the entrance of the tunnel. Clutching the trunk of a young tree, I leaned forward. Manolito was directly below, standing in the shadow with his back to the wall. The cut sapling lay on the ground beside him and his *machete* was still in his hand. My shadow must have betrayed me, for he turned, stepping out into the sunlight, and looked up.

'No snakes?' he asked.

'No snakes—and no pictures or carvings either.'

'Someone must have taken them.'

'Very likely,' I said and kept looking at him. Then we both laughed. Still laughing, he slid his *machete* into its sheath.

I spent an hour exploring the building. Much of it was densely overgrown and there were awkward blocks of masonry to scale. The superstructure had totally collapsed, but it had clearly consisted of something more massive than the ordinary Maya roof comb. At one end there was a rectangle of stone which could have formed the base of a tower or temple. I tried to find openings into the other sections of the vault. There were two or three places where the slabs had fallen, but the gaps they had left were choked with rubble. The hole in the wall which I had seen from the ground was impossible to reach from above. It opened to a straight drop of ten feet and even if I had been able to lower myself into it I would have found it difficult to get out.

My survey completed, I sat down in a patch of shade to enjoy for a few minutes longer my brief possession of this un-touched fragment of the Maya past. Mounted high on its arched back and surrounded by the green flood of the jungle over which the clouds drew undulating strips of shadow, I felt as though I was being carried along on the shoulders of a huge animal. At my first sight of the ruin I had been struck by how the coupling of architecture and vegetation had given it the look of being alive. If the building could produce the illusion of movement through space, it was tempting to imagine that it could give the same effect in relation to time. The creation of a people obsessed by a celestial chronology, it had become subject, during a thousand years of neglect, to a vegetable calendar in which its dissolution had been minutely recorded by the seasonal out-thrust of roots and sprouting of suckers. A voyage into past or future seemed equally appropriate; but the sun moving round began to burn my arm. Tied firmly to the present, I was reminded that I must leave at once if I wished to reach Chetumal before dark.

I lowered myself from the roof into the branches of a young tree which grew close to the back wall. When I reached the end of the building, without looking round, I made straight for the point from which I had seen it as I came out of the jungle. I wanted to revive in my memory the startling impact of my first sight of it, but when I turned, I found that its appearance had changed. The sun was now lower and a broad band of shadow, draping the length of the façade, obscured its mouldings and mosaics. Even the main outlines of the building were almost lost, relegated to the background by the triumphant vegetation which, with its upper leaves still catching the sunlight, appeared to have taken a leap forward towards final conquest. The trick in time, which I had imagined possible a few minutes earlier, might now actually have occurred, for it would have been easy to believe that not just an hour, but a whole decade had passed since I had first glimpsed the sunlit ruin as I stood beside Manolito on the track.

Suddenly I realized that Manolito had disappeared. I shouted his name but there was no answer. The jungle was silent. I thought he might have gone round to the other side of the ruin to look for me. I walked back through the bushes but when I reached the corner I could not see him. I shouted several times, turning in different directions and making a trumpet with my hands. There was still no answer. I came back to the front of the building and ran up to the top of the slope. I was about to start shouting again when I saw him a few yards away lying asleep under a bush. He had put on his shirt. His belt and sheathed *machete* lay on the ground beside him. I walked over and roused him by shaking his arm. He sat up smiling drowsily as he buckled on his belt.

It took us only twenty minutes to walk back to the settlement.

After festivities which had included such outstanding events as the *Venus-Rebeldes* match and the governor's banquet, it was inevitable that the opera should have come as an anticlimax. However effective in establishing the cultural pre-eminence of Chetumal, a programme of English pieces was hardly likely to prove a popular hit. Nothing short of a full-scale production of Aïda in Maya gold and feathers would have met the occasion. It was, perhaps, just such an entertainment that the architects and their wives anticipated, as, at the moment of my return, they stood grouped in elegant evening outfits in the hall of the motel.

Dusty and mud-caked, I avoided the entrance and walked through the garden to my bungalow. I took a bath and changed into a clean shirt and trousers. I had no jacket with me, but borrowed one from the manager. I tried to get a taxi but was told that I would have to wait half an hour, so I set out for the opera on foot.

As I walked down the main boulevard, a line of cars moved slowly past me. The élite of Chetumal were assembling once again, this time for the grand finale of the governor's celebrations. Outside the cinema a ragged crowd of less privileged citizens had collected to watch the arrival of the guests. Pressing my way through them, I felt my arm grabbed. I turned to find myself face to face with the carpenter. He clapped me in an *abrazo* which made me gasp. The air I gulped in was sour with alcohol. Still hugging, he pounded me with questions. Had I been to Kilometre Eighty-One? Was it true what Don Tomás had said? Had I found the ruins? Didn't I want a drink? Hadn't I five pesos to buy a bottle?

I heaved him away and thrust some money at him. He took it with a hideous wink and made off. I moved on with the crowd. The Englishman from Mexico City, looking worn and harassed, stood by the door. He had had a terrible day. Everything had gone wrong. The conditions backstage were appalling. The curtain pole had collapsed and could not be repaired. The carpenter had left a bag of nails in the piano.

'But at least the company managed to get here,' I said, trying to console him.

'Oh yes, and they've taken it very well. They say it's civilized compared to Belize. God knows what that must be like!'

Our conversation was interrupted by the arrival of the governor. He was surrounded by the usual huddle of hangers-on. When he saw me, he stopped and asked if I had had any luck with my ruins. I told him I had found some, but that I had not been able to reach the place for which I had set out.

'What were they like? As big as those at Chichén-Itzá?'

I had to admit that they were not.

'That's no good. You'll have to do better next time.'

I sat down near the back of the hall in a seat next to the gangway. From the outside the cinema looked like a derelict hangar. The interior was no less forbidding. Its original roof of wood had been blown off in the hurricane and had been replaced by corrugated metal sheets, some of which had worked loose and, vibrating in the wind, set up a syncopated chatter. The bare bleak walls still showed the high-water mark of the tidal wave which had followed the hurricane. The seats both looked and felt as if they had been submerged for a considerable time. A few naked bulbs, dangling on worn flex from the roof, partially lit the vast, cavern-like stage. It was set with some pots of flowers, a few bamboo chairs and a settee, each object standing several yards apart in sinister isolation. The atmosphere in the body of the hall was stifling. The residue of innumerable sweat-soaked cinema sessions had left a powerful odour.

Forced to their seats by the governor's arrival, the audience sat wide-eyed as though they anticipated an outrage on their persons. The hush had become alarmingly tense when, to a trill on the piano, a bewigged lady and gentleman in eighteenth-century costume glided on to the centre of the stage and, stationing themselves among the bamboo furniture, burst (the rarest of birds that ever let fly in Chetumal) superbly, but, alas, almost inaudibly, into song. True and clear and finely balanced their voices rose, flailing into the cotton-wool density of the trapped, tropical air, to descend, at least in that part of the hall where I was sitting, in ghost-notes, as eerie and disembodied

183

as sounds picked up by chance from the other side of the world on a low-powered radio. For the next two hours, to the accompaniment of the cracked piano and the rattling roof, arias, duets, trios and recitatives, airily elegant, plaintive or gay, climbed, sank, or mingled with near faultless execution to reach the baffled ears of the citizens of Chetumal as the merest tuneful pipings. Of the whole audience, only the carpenter and his friends, who had crept into the back row, remained alert right through to the final chorus, sitting with their mouths agape as they passed their fiery bottle to and fro between them.

Once the show was over, after brief clapping, there was a mass bolt for the door. Swept along in the crowd, I found myself once again in the carpenter's embrace and was forced to buy him off with another five pesos. As I crossed the pavement I saw the consul getting into his car. The upper half of his face was screened by his dark glasses but from the curl of his lips he looked as if he had enjoyed the entertainment.

8

Maya

For Guatemala Mexico is, as for Mexico the United States, the too massive northerly neighbour with a record of territorial and political encroachment. Their independence gained, Mexico lost Texas, and Guatemala, Chiapas. Today the conservatives in both countries are in power, but Mexico's revolutionary past is still mistrusted by the government of Guatemala.

Guatemala's history since the conquest has paralleled, with brief time lags but contrary results, that of Mexico. In some respects it has been even more dramatic. The kingdom hacked out by Alvarado, the red-faced *conquistador*, for himself, Charles V and God, with a butchery excessive even by Hispano-Catholic standards, stretched from Mexico to Panama. Not content, he bid for a stake in Peru but, bought off by Pizarro, turned north to California to be killed in a casual skirmish.

When the news of his death reached the capital, injudiciously sited between two volcanoes, his widow, Beatrix, had the palace hung with funeral draperies and the walls plastered black inside and out. The devout dubbed this display impious, and prophesied disaster. Once the period of mourning was up, Beatrix abandoned grief and set about getting herself elected governor in her husband's place. During the three days in which the high council debated the succession and finally voted in her favour, there were continuous thunderstorms. They were still rumbling overhead as she signed the declaration which made her the first and, to the present, only woman to have become a national ruler in either of the Americas. With a foreboding, shortly to prove justified, she added to her signature the words '*la sin ventura*',* then, as an afterthought, struck out her name and left the ill-omened phrase to stand alone.

---

* The unfortunate one.

The storm raged on. Struck buildings flamed and streets turned into torrents. Earthquakes added to the horror. Finally, at midnight, a mountain cliff retaining a volcanic lake burst open and a vast weight of water crashed on to the town. Only the palace survived intact, poised over the ruins like a gigantic coffin in the lurid glow from the volcanoes. But Beatrix had already fled to her chapel. A less solid construction, it collapsed and buried her as she clung to the altar cross.

This catastrophe, which occurred within twenty years of the conquest, left only a hundred Spanish knights and ecclesiastics alive. For the Indians it offered an excellent opportunity for revolt. That they did not take it indicates the extent to which they were already cowed.

A new capital was founded two years later in 1645 close to the volcanoes but far enough off, it was supposed, to be safe from eruptions of either fire or water. It was christened like its predecessor, Santiago de los Caballeros, and its history, though longer, was equally disastrous. For the two hundred and thirty years of its existence pestilence followed earthquake and earthquake pestilence without a break. The volcanoes flamed for months at a time, flinging up such clouds of ash that the sky was darkened and candles had to be lit in the city at midday. The end came in 1773. On July 29th violent convulsions levelled almost all the remaining buildings. The few that survived were finally toppled on December 17th by a single catastrophic shock.

Throughout this period the Spaniards in Guatemala were being subjected on a smaller scale to the same kind of ordeal from destructive natural forces as the early Indian settlers in the valley of Mexico. The horrors experienced by the Aztecs in that volcanic cauldron may well have encouraged their belief that the gods of the place were such monsters that they could only be placated by a diet of human hearts.

At the height of the 1773 disaster the effect on the Spaniards was scarcely less traumatic. They even grovelled in the dirt to beg forgiveness of the Indian slaves whom they had maltreated through a lifetime. They had good reason to feel guilty. With Alvarado's example to incite them, their brutality had far excelled that of their compatriots in Mexico. The English Jesuit

Thomas Gage,* who travelled in both countries in the first half of the seventeenth century, was appalled by the conditions of the Indians in Guatemala. 'I have known myself some of them that have come home from toiling and moiling with Spaniards after many blows, some wounds and little or no wages, who have sullenly and stubbornly lain down upon their beds, resolving to die rather than to live longer a life so slavish and having refused to take either meat or drink . . . that by so pining and starving they might consume themselves. Some I have by good persuasion encouraged to life rather than a voluntary and wilful death; others there have been that would not be persuaded, but in that wilful way have died.'

Independence brought the break-up of the kingdom and for Guatemala itself a brief spell of liberal government. Ironically, the liberals were overthrown by the Indians. A cholera epidemic, blamed on medical measures taken by the government, led to the city's infestation by a horde of half-naked wretches, headed by Rafael Carrera, an illiterate outlaw who acknowledged no authority but that of the church.

J. L. Stevenson,† the American traveller, was given an eyewitness account of the event when he arrived in the capital a few months afterwards. 'Among his [Carrera's] leaders were Monreal and other known criminals, robbers and murderers. He himself was on horseback with a green bush in his hat which was hung round with pieces of dirty cotton cloth covered with pictures of saints. A gentleman who saw them from the roof of his house and who was familiar with scenes of terror which had taken place in that unhappy city, told me that he never felt such consternation and horror as when he saw the entry of this immense mass of barbarians. Choking up the streets, all with green bushes in their hats, they seemed to him at a distance like a moving forest. They were armed with rusty muskets, old pistols, fowling pieces, some with locks and some without; they carried sticks formed into the shape of muskets with tin-plate locks, and clubs, *machetes*, and knives tied to the ends of long poles. And swelling the multitude were two or

---

* Author of *The English American, his Travail by Sea and Land.*
† Author of *Incidents of Travel in Central America, Chiapas and Yucatan.*

three thousand women, with sacks and *alforjas** for carrying away the plunder. Many who had never left their village before, looked wild at the sight of the houses and churches, and the magnificence of the city. They entered the plaza, vociferating *Viva la religion, y muerte a los estranjeros!*† Carrera himself, amazed at the immense ball he had set in motion, was so embarrassed that he could not guide his horse . . .'

For three days the whites awaited the revenge they believed inevitable, but the wheedling clerics persuaded Carrera to hold his followers back. At last, in exchange for eleven thousand silver dollars, a thousand muskets and a lieutenant-colonel's commission, he agreed to withdraw his hordes from the city, leaving the inhabitants unharmed and their property virtually untouched. Within a few years, fawned on by the conservatives and the church, he returned to become the country's first dictator. While his contemporary in Mexico, the great Indian leader, Juarez, was the champion of liberal reform, Carrera, accepting the authority of the priests, bolstered reaction. Under his rule barbarous Spanish practices abolished by the liberals were restored and new whipping-posts were erected throughout the country. Stevens, after describing the horrors of a village flogging, records another even more fiendish punishment.

'Among the onlookers were several criminals, whom we had noticed walking in chains about the plaza; and among those were a man and woman in rags, bareheaded with long hair streaming over their eyes, chained together by the hand and foot, with long bars between them to keep them out of each other's reach. They were a husband and wife who had shocked the moral sense of the community by not living together.'

After Carrera's betrayal the Indians sank back into the murk of serfdom. It was not until 1945, more than a hundred years later, that laws were passed guaranteeing their basic liberties. In Mexico, the policy of Juarez was exactly the opposite of Carrera's. He attacked the power of the church and established the Indian's right to equal citizenship. The influence of these two leaders, despite later periods of chaos alternating with

---

* Large sacks.
† 'Long live religion [the Catholic Faith] and death to foreigners!'

188

variously coloured dictatorships, has been mainly responsible for the different social and political characteristics which their respective countries have developed. The shut-out, benighted world of the Guatemala Indians, however picturesque, creates an atmosphere of intolerable gloom. In Mexico if the Indians remain apart it is of their own choosing. They resist well-meaning attempts to assimilate them because they prefer their own way of life and are jealous of their independence. This is illustrated by the difference in character between the Maya Indians of the Chiapas village of San Cristóbal de las Casas in Mexico, and those of Chichicastenango,* a hundred and fifty miles to the south in Guatemala.

At San Cristóbal the Chemulas and Zinacatecans who file in from the country carrying their merchandise on their backs have the remote wary look of travellers from another world. Though persecuted by the Spaniards in the past and still callously exploited by the *ladinos*,† they have the reserve and dignity of the untamed. They are extremely poor but the men are very clean and carefully dressed. The wearing of rags is reserved for the women. Male costumes are gay and elegant. Tribe and status are denoted by different types of flat-brimmed, brightly beribboned hat. A short black or white tunic is worn above brief cotton shorts. Legs are left bare and feet shod in sandals with high heel-guards.

San Cristóbal is *ladino* dominated, but its market is an Indian enclave where the intrusion of whites is tolerated. Contacts are kept mainly to the business of buying and selling which is conducted with deceptive gentleness in speech and gesture. The spectacle is an attraction for tourists, but the Indians, though proud of their appearance (they carry fragments of mirror in which they constantly preen themselves), are reluctant to be photographed. Sometimes young men in need of money dress in their best clothes and, with their brown mountaineer's legs lightly oiled, pose provocatively in the Plaza. They turn away or hide their faces as soon as a camera is raised but will concede a single snap on payment of five pesos in advance.

---

* The Indians of Chiapas and Guatemala are all of Maya stock.
† Whites or mestizos. The word carries implications of sharp practice and villainy.

No such attitude would be thinkable among the Indians of Chichicastenango. The clothes of both men and women are more remarkable than any to be seen at San Cristóbal, but it would never occur to them to question the right of tourists to turn their cameras on them as they please. They have the air of having emerged from another century rather than another world and, zombie-like, to have left their minds behind them. Fantastically decked out in the kerchiefs, embroidered jackets and knee breeches of early buccaneers, they fill the plaza on market days with the muted murmur of their voices, their sandals' shuffling and their garb's pervading crimson gloom. Subhumanly permissive, though not to the abject depth of the Peruvian Incas, they allow the tourist to click, stare and gape, not only on the square but even inside the church,* as crouching on the floor over clumps of candles they rave and rail at God's infinite neglect.

Despite the work of the Mexican Instituto Nacional Indigenista, which sets out to integrate the Indian tribes into contemporary life through a programme of education, medical care and resettlement, Chiapas, while comparing favourably with any state in Guatemala, remains one of the most backward in Mexico. Travelling east from San Cristóbal towards the border, conditions become increasingly primitive and pass from pre-revolution in the cattle country round Ocosingo to pre-Columbian among the pagan Caribs or Lacandóns in the rain forests of the Usumacinta. Most of the area is mountainous and densely wooded. The lush valleys plunge perilously to streams and rivers which in the wet season are impassable. Land communications are precarious. Under favourable conditions it takes twelve hours to travel by truck from Comitán to Ocosingo, a distance, as the crow flies, of about fifty miles. Sometimes it takes much longer, and if the rivers are in flood, the journey cannot be attempted. In recent years light aeroplanes have brought some of the most inaccessible districts to within an hour's journey of Comitán, San Cristóbal or Tenosique, the three outlying towns with permanent road or rail links with neighbouring states. Today most of the coffee crop harvested in central Chiapas and the pigs reared in the

---

* There are two churches. One of them can be entered only by Indians.

Usumacinta valley are flown to whichever of the three towns happens to be nearest.

But with the arrival of air transport, land communications have deteriorated. The old mule-tracks are no longer kept open, and only the footpaths used by the Indians survive. These last, cleared to Indian head level, are impassable on horse-back and fatiguing for anyone over five foot six to follow on foot. Thus the civilizing range of the air-strips is limited and they have left some districts in greater isolation than before. The strips themselves are usually short and narrow and often perilously sited. The hazards of using them can be judged from the amount of wreckage with which they are littered. Flying into Ocosingo from Comitán on Christmas Eve, I could see two crashed planes at the end of the runway, an off-course American five-seater which had overshot into a stone wall, and a local plane which had hit the top of the church tower when, to celebrate his engagement, the pilot had looped the loop too low.

At the time of my visit, apart from the increased ease and speed with which the richer inhabitants could get themselves and their belongings in and out of the place, the introduction of aeroplanes had brought little change to life in Ocosingo compared to their effect on villages which had not previously possessed even a truck route to one of the outlying towns. But despite its accessibility by both land and air Ocosingo's trafficless plaza, with its white church and colonnaded houses has a leisured tranquillity which encourages the illusion that it is not only two or three times its actual distance from Comitán or San Cristóbal, but that it is divided from their relative sophistication by not less than half a century.

Such sudden-seeming plunges from one age to another, so frequently experienced by travellers in Mexico, like the abrupt changes in scenery and climate, can have the disconcerting impact of hallucinations. Switched back at one moment, the traveller may be as miraculously pitched forward again at the next. In either direction the experience can come as a shock.

Seated in a window of the one restaurant of the plaza watching the files of silent soft-footed Indians coming in from the neighbouring villages, drawn, as they must have been every Christmas for the last three hundred years, by the seasonal celebrations and the midnight mass, I felt that I had rarely moved deeper into the past. Most of the Indians had produce to sell, chickens, turkeys, clutches of eggs or piles of rough-baked pottery carried on their backs in baskets supported by bands around their foreheads. Soft-voiced and gently persistent they passed from door to door. Bargaining on the *ladino* side, tough and scoffing, was aimed at undermining their stubborn patience, but both participants generally knew the eventual outcome from the first exchange of words or gestures.

These leisured negotiations were set against a fitting background. The grass flourished on the spacious square in the absence of any promenading sufficiently resolute to beat it into paths or confine it into patches. The tree-shaded benches at one end were all occupied by prostrate sleepers. On the pavements under the colonnades scores of Indians, who had either succeeded in selling their wares or had abandoned the attempt, sat grouped in drowsy huddles. Behind them *ladinos* lazed in doorways or could be glimpsed through open windows lying at ease in their sagging hammocks. The tepid sunless atmosphere was heavy and damp. Above the white houses, steep hillsides, toppling with vegetation, were truncated by a ceiling of unbroken cloud. Influenced by the timeless somnolence of the place, I was beginning to drowse over my coffee when the wrench came. With a shattering roar an amplifier, situated somewhere beyond the houses on the far side of the plaza, bellowed a trumpeted tango. The raucous mid-twentieth-century din crashed over the tiled roofs of the village and ricocheted in criss-cross echoes among the enclosing hills. After two minutes it broke off and was succeeded by a voice as loud and omniscient-sounding as a major prophet's. Its message, however, was mundane. Don Rafael Rodriguez had slaughtered a magnificent porker and was offering its flesh and innards for sale at his house on the corner of Juarez street. The tango bashed out again briefly. When it stopped, another announcement followed.

An hour later the alternating bouts of voice and brass were still succeeding each other as we climbed the crest of a hill high above the village and descended into the welcome silence of the valley beyond. The sun came out and the dense vegetation on either side of our path began to steam. Soon we were climbing again, following a steep cleft overhung by pine trees. In another half-hour we reached our destination, a cone-shaped hill covered by scrub and ringed by terraces of hewn stone. It was an ancient Maya site. We had hardly begun to explore the ruins when my companion stooped and picked up a green jadeite chisel from the rubble at his feet. He passed it to me and I held it in the palm of my hand. A miniature Stone Age axe-head, it was smooth, plump and perfectly symmetrical. Spurred by this discovery, I scrambled all over the hillside prodding with a stick but found nothing. Only as we were about to leave, I noticed that, blundering among the bushes, I had become infested with jungle ticks, minute creatures smaller than pin-heads, which were already burrowing their way through the seams of my shirt and trousers. When I had brushed off as many of them as I could see, we set off again by another track for Ocosingo.

Half-way down we came out on to a sloping pasture where some cattle grazed round a whitewashed farmhouse. The farmer called out from the doorway to offer us a drink. He was one of the personalities of the district. An officer of the revolutionary army, he had stayed behind in Ocosingo to become the village schoolmaster. Even now in retirement his wisdom was so respected that his former pupils frequently came to him for advice. He had the reputation of being an accomplished sorcerer and had a number of remarkable cures of human beings and domestic animals to his credit. When he had arrived with the army, he had brought with him the virus of an influenza epidemic. As soon as he had recovered from the sickness himself, he had set about nursing the villagers whom he had infected. This had brought him into contact with local *curanderas*, and when the epidemic was over he had made a study of their herbal remedies. It was by the intelligent application of these and additional discoveries of his own that his fame as a sorcerer had been established.

His house stood on the lip of the Ocosingo valley. As we gathered round the door drinking his 'authentic *Comiteca*',*

---

* A raw cane spirit manufactured in Comitán and drunk, often with disastrous effect, by the Indians.

the sound of the amplifier reached us in faint raspings from below. He was about to leave for the village and his Indian servant was saddling his pony. He showed us a red circular wound on its rump where it had been attacked the night before by a vampire bat. It was then that I noticed the odd clumsiness of the servant's movements, but it was only when he bent forward and adjusted a strap with his teeth that I realized that he had no hands. The farmer explained that he had lost them when he was three years old. His father had had the reputation of being a sorcerer and when a cow belonging to neighbours with whom he was on bad terms had died they had held him responsible. Other misfortunes had followed and confirmed their suspicions. One night, after a ritual drinking bout, they broke into his house and attacked him with *machetes* as he lay in bed. When they had finished chopping him up, the child, who had been hiding, crawled out from under the blankets with both arms severed at the wrists.

By the time we reached the village it was already dusk. The amplifier had been silenced, but soon after our arrival a generator started up with a resonant thump, and lights flickered on round the square and in some of the shops and houses. But the houses most brightly lit, sending wide beams flooding out through their open doorways, were those in which Christmas Eve was being celebrated round moss- and tinsel-covered grottos in which the Infant Christ, illuminated by a thicket of candles, lay in his manger surrounded by clay models of all the characters, animal, human and divine, of the Christmas story. The main event of the evening was the recital of the rosary by the family and their friends kneeling in a circle round the crèche. The recitals took place in each house at different times so that relatives and neighbours could slip away from their own 'nativities' to attend.

My companions were foreigners, but it was their second winter at Ocosingo and they were so liked in the village that we were drawn into one house after another to join the circle kneeling in the candle-light at the Christmas shrine. The faces which surrounded us, smooth or wrinkled, varying in shade from pale olive to rich copper, were all so gently smiling and devout that it was difficult to believe that they belonged (least of all the doe-eyed Indians) to a community in which violent killings, such as the one in which the farmer's servant had been mutilated, were so common that they were the cause of almost as many deaths as accidents or disease.

The recital of each rosary took at least twenty minutes and after sessions at half a dozen shrines my unpractised knees began to ache. At eleven-thirty the thump of the generator, which had served to remind us that we were still in the machine age, stopped, and the lights all over the village waned to orange points and went out. By now the last of the 'nativities' was over and the people were leaving their houses to go to church. Although the clouds had not lifted, the night was fine. The whole valley was washed in the radiance of a full but hidden moon, so that even the surrounding hills were clearly visible. Across the grey waste of the plaza the church appeared taller than by day. Its pale, blank façade looked insubstantial, a cardboard cut-out to frame the glowing interior revealed through its open doors. From all sides the people flocked towards it, the white-clothed Indians, silent and spectral, like droves of homing spirits.

Late-comers, we found the nave already crammed with kneeling worshippers. We bobbed down in the nearest vacant space on the stone paving. Huge candles flamed on the high altar and scores of lesser ones ringed the shrines and images along the walls. Despite their warming glow here in the church nothing survived of the genial atmosphere of the 'nativities'. The influx from the countryside had put the *ladinos* in a minority. The mass of the congregation was Indian, and it was the feverish pitch of their devotion, brooding and querulous, which prevailed. A few feet away from us an effigy of Christ in torment rose above the ranks of bowed backs. Its emaciated corpse-white body was lacerated with horrific wounds, each one a nodal point for a network of gory runnels. It seemed a more appropriate object of worship for the dark fervour of the Indians than the divine innocent whose birth they had come to celebrate.

Looking round, I met from all directions furtive but hostile glances. The man next to me was swaying from side to side. Soon he was bumping against my shoulder. When he turned towards me, I was so overwhelmed by the stench of alcohol that I drew away. He must have been counting on me to maintain his equilibrium for he heeled over knocking against me so violently that I almost fell. I at once returned to my former position. The bumping continued but soon I hardly noticed it. Nothing was any longer important except the pain in my knees. The bones felt as if they had been turned into sharp blades. Shifting my weight from one to the other, I kept looking round in the hope that fellow sufferers might succumb and by sitting or squatting offer an example which I could follow. I noticed that the church floor had been spread with pine branches and that the people were using them as kneelers. Unfortunately there were none within reach. I managed to hold out until the sermon; then, to my relief, my neighbour flopped over and stretched out full length, resting on one arm like a Roman at a banquet. Furtively I raised myself from my knees and sat back on my haunches. At once I felt a prod and, looking down, saw that from his reclining position the man was nudging me with his toe. He gave me such a ferocious stare that I jerked forward on to my knees again. The pain returned and was soon even sharper than before. Other people close by began to grow restive but as soon as they changed to more comfortable positions, my neighbour growled at them and if they did not obey, crawled over and forced them back on to their knees.

Suddenly an Indian staggered up in the centre of the nave and stood swaying and shouting. Gently persuasive, his friends plucked at his clothes and tried to coax him back on to the floor. When this had no effect, the village guard intervened and the man, still shouting, was removed from the church. Taking advantage of the diversion, I had slipped into a sitting position. Now I received another prod, but this time the man showed more mercy. Pulling a pine branch away from one of his companions, he thrust it under my knees. But my Christmas penance was not yet over. With one torment mitigated, another began. I had not been as successful as I had thought in getting rid of the ticks which I had picked up in the ruins. Now their bites began to itch. As soon as I clawed in one place the irritation raged in another.

The sermon had already lasted half an hour but the priest showed no sign of ending it. Even the fervour of the Indians had begun to sag and the congregation was becoming restless.

There were several more disturbances when worshippers, raving from drink or boredom, had to be dragged out by the guards. The length of the ordeal had the effect of breaking the reserve between my neighbour and myself. For the last twenty minutes we were on the friendliest terms, and he even began to scratch himself, either out of sympathy or because some of my ticks had strayed. When at last the sermon was over and the service ended, I helped him to get up. Swaying and scratching, we supported each other into the square.

If the people of Ocosingo tend to linger in the colonial past (riding out to the ruins of Tonelá, a site littered with massive Maya sculptures to be had for the cost of their transportation,* we passed on the outskirts of the village a strip of pasture land which had been designated for common use under the agrarian reform of the nineteen thirties, but was still held, despite government pressure and local protest, by the original owner, a *ladino* millionaire ranching three thousand head of cattle), further south, where the Chiapas highlands sink into the rain forests of the Usumacinta valley, there are tribal Indians whose way of life has hardly changed since before the conquest. These pre-Columbian survivors still worship the Maya gods and have only recently begun to abandon the stone-age weapons of their ancestors.

The last stronghold of the pagan Maya to resist the Spaniards was at Tayasál on lake Petén-Itzá deep in the rain forest on the Guatemala side of the Usumacinta. Cortés stopped there in 1525 on his great march to Honduras and was hospitably received. He left a lame horse behind him, intending to return

---

* Unless the local inhabitants were to object.

The village of X, north of Coatzacoalcos, is close to an Olmec site. Beside the track leading to it, a gigantic stone head lies face downwards in the bushes. There are similar heads in the museums at Villahermosa and Jalapa and in the National University. They are generally considered to be among the finest achievements of ancient Mexican art. It was intended that the head at X should also be placed in a museum. Because of local objections to its removal the officials decided to take it away during the night, but the villagers intervened and pushed it off the lorry on which it was being transported. It still lies where it fell. A man who kept a shop in the village showed me boxes full of pottery and figurines which had been picked up on or near the site. I asked him if he sold them to visitors. He replied that they were not his to sell as they belonged to the village.

for it later. The people were so impressed by this unfamiliar creature that they treated it as a god. When it died they erected its stone effigy in one of their temples. A Franciscan father visiting Tayasál in 1618 destroyed the idol. But for the intervention of his more diplomatic colleagues, he would have been killed by the outraged inhabitants. Later missionaries received rough treatment and at least one was sacrificed. But it was the destruction of a small expeditionary force which provoked the Spaniards into making a full-scale attack. The city was finally taken in 1697 with the help of a galley constructed on the spot. The temples were destroyed and most of the inhabitants were either massacred or drowned.

After the fall of Tayasál only a few pagan nomads survived in remote areas of the forest where they could not easily be reached by Spanish soldiers or missionaries. They lived by cultivating patches of maize and by hunting pigs, monkeys and deer with bows and arrows. They made regular visits to the abandoned temples of Yaxchilán where they worshipped the Maya gods and burnt copal in front of the carved stelae.

In early times *ladino* settlers who pushed east from the Chiapas highlands occasionally came into touch with them, but it is only within the last hundred years that intruders from the outside world have begun to penetrate their terrain. First came the woodcutters with their ox teams in search of mahogany, setting up permanent camps or settlements known as '*monteros*'.

They were followed in the nineteen twenties by the *chicleros* or *chicle* gatherers. *Chicle* is the sap of the sapodilla tree and high prices were paid for it as the raw basis of chewing-gum. To begin with the *chicleros* worked in Campeche, Quintana Roo and the Petén, but as the demand for *chicle* increased, their activities spread to north-east Chiapas and the Usumacinta valley.

It was a tough and unhealthy profession. In the forest through which they had to cut their way, the trees grow a hundred and fifty feet high and their foliage is so dense that when a storm breaks, although the rain can be heard roaring overhead, it may take twenty minutes for the drops to percolate through the leaves and fall to the ground. The undergrowth is sparse under the high trees, but elsewhere thick and thorn-covered and frequently poisonous to the touch. Venomous snakes are common and there are myriads of insects which burrow, bite or sting. Malaria and yellow fever, the latter in recurring waves (one of these had reached the Petén from the south when I visited Tikál; but as the mosquitoes kept to the tree-tops only the monkeys suffered, both spiders and howlers falling dead out of the branches to plop like over-ripe fruit on the jungle floor) are prevalent with other tropical diseases which, if not actually lethal, can so weaken a man as to minimize his chances of getting out of the forest alive. Apart from the toll taken by these natural hazards, the *chicleros* frequently fell victim to each other's violence. It was inevitable that a profession which offered quick returns for a life of extreme hardship should have attracted a tough and unscrupulous riff-raff ready to cut throats at the smallest provocation.

After the Second World War the replacement of *chicle* in the manufacture of chewing-gum by a synthetic product reduced the *chicleros'* activities. Their unused tracks and air-strips were quickly overgrown. But both woodcutters and *chicle* gatherers had been responsible for the discovery of jungle-buried cities abandoned centuries before by the ancient Maya. This resulted in a third invasion, that of the archaeologists, professional and amateur, and their more recent followers, the romantic enthusiasts for the ruins of lost civilizations in outlandish places.

All these intruders have contributed to the decline of the pagan Maya nomad, since they brought with them diseases unknown to the jungle against which the Indians had little resistance. Today there are only about two hundred survivors living in two groups, one to the north at El Cedro and the other further south in the region of Lake Miramár. Ethnically there is no difference between them. They look alike, speak the same Maya dialect, practise their religion at Yaxchalán, wear the same kind of clothes and have the same customs. They are usually known to outsiders as Lacandons but prefer to be called Caribs. They have no connection, however, with the people of that name who inhabit the Gulf islands off the Guatemala coast.

It is possible that in spite of having so much in common the two groups differ in temperament; for it appears that from early times the El Cedro clan have been more flirtatious in their attitude to intruders. During his visit to Palenque in 1840 Stephens was told that fifty years earlier some Caribs had been partially converted by the local priest. On his death they had vanished into the forest never to be seen again. At the end of the century Maler, the German archaeologist, visited an Indian camp on lake Petja, half way between Palenque and El Cedro. The inhabitants were presumably Carib. Although the chief was hostile, the rest of the clan received him as warmly as they dared. They were evidently on good terms with the neighbouring *monteros* as several of them spoke Spanish. They accepted his presents with enthusiasm. A man who thought himself neglected did not hesitate to demand a necklace for his wife.

An aspect of their relationship with the *chicleros* forty years later is revealed by Carlos Frey's experience in their camp at El Cedro as recorded by Pablo Montañes in his book, *Lacandonia*. Frey was an American adventurer who claimed to be the first white man to have discovered the ruins and frescos at Bonampak. While searching for the ruins he stayed with the Caribs at El Cedro. One morning soon after his arrival he was left alone with the women and children while the men went out hunting. They had hardly left the camp when some *chicleros* appeared and started to molest the women. Frey shouted for help and held the *chicleros* off until the men came running back and drove them from the huts. No one appeared grateful for his intervention, least of all the women who refused to speak to him for the rest of the day. It did not take him long to realize why his action had been received with so little enthusiasm. Each of the Carib men had four or five wives whose combined passions they were unable to satisfy. The *chicleros*, unlike the *monteros* who had women in their camps, were avid for any sexual outlet they could find. Their visits to the Carib huts were occasions which gave relief to all, since they brought the husbands the respite and the women and their lovers the satisfaction they required.

The invention of synthetic chewing-gum and the decline of the *chicleros* left the Caribs once more to their own resources. No doubt the men welcomed any opportunity for a break, and I need not have been surprised at encountering my first male of the tribe taking a holiday from the jungle in a hotel in Tenosique.

Of the three peripheral towns of the Chiapas area Tenosique, just over the border in the state of Tabasco, is outwardly the most sophisticated. It has always had more regular communications with other towns than either Comitán or San Cristóbal. Sited below the last rapids of the Usumacinta, it can be reached by boat from Villahermosa, the state capital, and has direct access to the Laguna de Terminos and the Gulf. The railway line, constructed at the turn of the century between Merida and Veracruz, passes close beside it. Although the time-table is irregular, a train leaves every day in one direction or the other. In the nineteen forties, when the demand for *chicle* was at its height, it became a base for the *chicleros* who by this time had taken to air transport. As a result it developed into a small but important aviation centre.

Owing to the uncertainty of local weather conditions in any season the surest way of reaching the town is by rail. This has the additional advantage of allowing the traveller to make a stop at Palenque, the loveliest of all archaeological sites in Mexico. If part of the journey is undertaken at night, the traveller can enjoy the pyrotechnics of an outsize elater beetle or fire-bug which abounds in that part of the Tabasco jungle. As the train passes, thousands of the bugs whizz up from beside the track with the speed and erratic brilliance of tracer bullets. Terry, the Baedeker of Mexico, was inspired by the performance of these insects to one of his characteristic descriptive passages.

'They are nocturnal creatures, flying only after dusk, and their brilliance is so remarkable that they are said to have saved the lives of travellers temporarily lost in the deep forests . . . To the uninitiated they resemble fiery dragons sweeping through the air with automobile lamps set upon their shoulders . . . The Indians fasten them to their ankles when treading the forest at night: the women wear them in their hair under a thin gauze veil and construct little cages for them, using them for lamps. . . An Indian forest maiden with her hair ablaze with these singular creatures is a somewhat bizarre sight to the uitlander.'

In spite of the town being accessible by air, rail and water,

Tenosique's sophistication is relative. Situated high on the Usumacinta's east bank, where the great river swings in a wide curve, surrounded by barely broken jungle and backed by the dense rain forest in which after a few miles Mexico melts imperceptibly into Guatemala, it has the somnolent air of a remote frontier outpost. Little remains of its wild west period when in the *chicle*-rush its streets were lined with brothels, gambling-halls and brawling cantinas. Now, in outward appearance, it looks respectable enough. It has a pleasant central square set with trees and benches and a few unpretentious modern buildings. One of these last is the principal hotel. By small-town standards it is clean, airy and comfortable. Its restaurant is a narrow room with half a dozen tables on either side. The walls are bare. At one end a door is open on to the street. It was here, on the evening of our arrival, that we met the Carib chief from El Cedro.

Even in so modest a setting, where the normal run of poor Indians would have passed unnoticed, the appearance of Chambor, or Don Benito as he was called in his Christian aspect, was outlandish. He was a little over five feet tall, but his body was broad and powerful. His black hair, chopped in a fringe just above his eyebrows, fell at the back and side to a few inches below his shoulders. His brown leathery face was set with huge, almond-shaped eyes. The lower half was leonine, the broad nose and the swell of his upper lip combining into a muzzle-like protrusion. He wore a voluminous smock tucked into patched and faded cotton trousers. His hands were very large, with square-ended fingers; but his feet, more than matching his muzzle, were so monstrous that they gave him a look not so much of a biological throw-back as of an apparition out of primitive mythology. From wrinkled, column-like ankles their broad insteps spread out to immense prehensile toes. Underneath they were soled and heeled by half-inch layers of horn-hard human hide.

It was explained to us that the chief had flown in from El Cedro to attend a service at the Baptist mission. Like his ancestors at Palenque his conversion was not complete, for back in the forest he still burnt copal to his pagan *santos*.* He

* Saints or sacred images.

was returning to his camp the next morning and promised to have mules ready to take us from the airfield to Bonompak. I tried to talk to him but found that I could not understand his Spanish any better than he could understand mine. I did discover, however, that he was a Carib and not a Lacandón as we had been told. He stayed for about half an hour, maintaining an impressive dignity in spite of the children who crowded at the door to gape at him. Evidently he was still a rare sight, for, when he left, they followed him down the street.

We had supper and went up early to our rooms. As I lay in bed reading I heard a deep droning noise outside. Reverberating like the ground base of an organ, it rose and fell in what I recognized as a remote approximation to a revivalist hymn. I went to the window and looked out. The sound came from a house a little way down the street. Now I could hear feebler voices, valiant but frequently overwhelmed, striving desperately for the correct tune. The door of the house was open and there were children hovering round it. Evidently the mission service was in full swing and Don Benito, esconced among the baptist brethren, was bellowing—great organ-chested creature of the jungle—his respects to the Christian god.

At El Cedro, where we met him three days later, his trousers discarded and his smock revealed as a full-length garment flowing round him to within a few inches of the ground, he had reverted to Chambor, tribal chieftain and priest, worshipper of the Maya *santos* at Yaxchilán. Nevertheless he charged us a good Christian price for the hire of his mules.

We returned from Bonompak the next morning to find that our aeroplane had not yet arrived. Discouraged by the sight of a wrecked machine on the edge of the runway, we sat down to wait under a palm-leaf shelter. There was no sign of Chambor, but members of his tribe, some of whom had appeared the day before, came trickling out of the jungle to gather round us. They were about the same height as their chief and like him wore their hair long, had almond-shaped eyes and were dressed in smocks which reached to their ankles. But there the resemblance ended, for they were all of a younger generation and with few exceptions outstandingly beautiful. Lovely bird-like beings with smooth skins and delicate features, they stood round us laughing in shrill tee-hee-hees, like English maiden aunts, as they plucked at each other's sleeves to draw attention to each newly-noted absurdity in our clothes or physical appearance. We retaliated by imagining ourselves marauding *chicleros*, but found that we all had the same first choice, a pale-skinned creature with a fine arched nose and magnificent eyes turned up at the corners. We tried to speak to them but only one or two had a few words of Spanish. Encouraged, they came close and, lightly touching any of our possessions by which they were attracted, made signs that they would appreciate them as presents. One of them took a liking to my trousers and was not in the least put off when I demonstrated that I had nothing else to wear. To shame us they produced all kinds of clothing and equipment, including a couple of sporting rifles which, they claimed, were the gifts of previous visitors.

As they all had long hair and wore almost identical costume, we had been unable at first to distinguish between the sexes. Now we realized that the girls had their hair parted in the middle. With this discovery came a shock: the pale beauty was revealed as a boy and his three rather plain companions, all of whom looked at least ten years older than he did, were his wives. He had a fourth, he told us, who had stayed behind in the camp. When our plane arrived he was at the forefront of the young men, who, more bird-like than ever with their insistent cries and eagerness to take wing, begged to be allowed to fly with us to Tenosique or New York or anywhere else in the world where we might be going.

Next day as we canoed down the Usumacinta (salvoes of macaws overhead, their crimson tail feathers streaming like rockets) we speculated on the Maya past and the mystery of the abandoned cities. The classic era to which they belonged lasted roughly from A.D. 300 to A.D. 900. Copán, Tikál, Piedras Negras, Yaxchilán, Bonompak and Palenque were among the great centres which flourished during this period. The accurate observation of the seasons, necessary to a maize-growing people, had developed among the Maya into an elaborate ritual whereby the recording of time had acquired vital religious significance. Stelae were erected and ceremonies performed at the end of certain fixed periods of which the ten-year or half-*Katun* was the commonest. This practice died out almost simultaneously throughout the Maya world at the end of the ninth century. It is assumed that the cities were abandoned shortly after the erection of the last calendric monument. By the time the Spaniards arrived, the ruins had already been swamped by the jungle. Sylvanus Morley, the great American archaeologist, gives ten suggested reasons for their desertion,* none of which he finds wholly convincing. One attractive but improbable theory, not included in the list, is that the priests made an error in their chronological or astronomical calculations which so shocked the Maya world that it led to a religious crisis, a revolt against the priesthood and the collapse of the entire social system.

Exploring the site of Yaxchilán, it was tempting to people its sanctuaries with a priestly cast of Chambors and its courts and terraces with flocks of feckless, sky-loving Caribs. That night as we ate our supper by the river below the ruins (frogs as big as footballs bouncing round us in the dark) we saw a man-made satellite riding majestically across the stars and imagined the consternation it would have brought, a thousand years before, to the sacred watch posted in the towers and temples of the city.

Before leaving Chiapas I made an expedition to the southern highlands and spent a day riding round the Montebello lakes, sapphire-coloured, volcanic tarns overhung by pine trees festooned with wax-white orchids and purple air plants. At dusk the weather changed, the rain lashed down and the temperature dropped. I had arranged for a lift to Comitán in a rancher's truck. As we sloshed and skidded through the forest, the clouds drifted in ragged swags among the trees. After a mile or so we met a train of Indians, their mules loaded with wood, heading towards the border. They were Guatematelcos, the driver told me, going home with a clandestine haul from the Mexican forest. Wrapped to their noses in their blankets, they appeared cheerful in spite of the rain and waved to us as we passed. We drove on for an hour, twisting and turning through the trees until we came to a clearing and our head-

---

* *The Ancient Maya*, Stamford University Press. The suggestions listed are: (1) Earthquake activity. (2) Climatic change. (3) Malaria and yellow fever epidemics. (4) Foreign conquest. (5) Civil war. (6) Intellectual and aesthetic exhaustion. (7) Social decay. (8) Governmental disorganization. (9) Economic collapse due to the failure of the Maya agricultural system.

lamps lit up a few ramshackle huts. Their inhabitants were standing in front of them, presumably because conditions were worse inside than out. They looked miserably abject with their sodden clothes clinging to their shaking bodies. They were barefoot and did not appear to possess a single blanket between them. Perhaps because their morale had sunk too low or the wood was too drenched to make it possible, they had not even lit fires to keep themselves warm. As we slowed down, the men rushed to the back of the vehicle and scrambled in. The driver stopped and protested, but they would not move. Jammed together in a dripping huddle, they demanded to be taken to Comitán. We started off again with the truck swinging dangerously under its human load. They were, according to the driver, Indians from western Chiapas who had been induced to settle in the southern highlands as part of a scheme to alleviate the poverty in their overcrowded villages. Even Mexican progress has its victims. Doubtless the officials in charge of the scheme had the best intentions, but these settlers were certainly the most destitute-looking wretches I encountered anywhere on either side of the border.

9
The Last Journey

Every autumn the Indians of the western Sierra Madre gather in the deserts of Central Mexico for the peyotl harvest. Peyotl, a small button-headed cactus, contains the drug mescaline. The Huicholes and Tarahumaras believe it to be a god and worship it with elaborate rites. Unlike the mushroom, which produces all its marvels in the mind but makes reality hideous, the cactus stimulates perception so that trivial objects take on cosmic significance and sounds are heard and colours seen with an absorbing intensity. I had already eaten peyotl bought from a witch in Mexico City but its only effect on me had been a mild headache. I had been told that in October at San Luis Potosí I could be certain of finding the cactus freshly gathered and at full strength.

I arrived in the city late one evening as the tiled domes of its churches reflected the afterglow of the sunset. I took a room in a hotel and made at once for the market. I was directed down a narrow street littered with garbage and lined with barrows of *taco*-vendors. A tunnel-like entrance led into the market itself. The stalls were ranked close together leaving only a narrow passage between them. Their awnings met to form a patchwork roof which sagged so low that I had to stoop to pass beneath it. Oil lamps,* hanging from the rafters, lit the dark faces of the merchants and the wares and produce heaped on the counters in front of them. The tunnel led into a murky labyrinth. As I edged along its crowded passageways, my neck painfully bent, at every step the air had a different smell: the deceptively appetizing scent of guavas, breathtaking acetylene whiffs, spices, sharp and peppery, the female odour of over-ripe, seed-slobbering melons, dried fish stinks, clean calico

---

* A few months after my visit a lamp set fire to an awning and the whole market was burnt down.

wafts from unravelled bales, the reek of freshly cured leather, acrid and animal, luscious fried sizzlings adrift from simmering pots, sour pulque fumes, the musk of captive song-birds, the smoke from maize cobs roasted over charcoal, the aroma of herbs. It was among the herb stalls that I found the peyotl.

They were piled two feet high on the counter, little phallic plants with green knobs on tapering stems. I chose three of the freshest-looking specimens, asked their price and gave the money to the old woman behind the counter. She was hidden to the eyes by her cactus hoard and her hand could hardly reach over the top. I stuffed the peyotl in my pockets and turned back into the crowd.

I tried to leave by the same route as I had come in, but I was soon lost. The people moved at a slow shuffle, pressing, fumbling and nudging. The opposing queues slipped and eddied past each other or came to sudden halts with the leaders wedged face to face. Confused by the maze-like arrangement of the stalls, I kept losing my sense of direction. After twenty minutes, with my neck aching and my mind dazed by the streams of brown, black-eyed faces, I came out into the street.

Back in my bedroom at the hotel, I took out the peyotl and placed them on a table. Choosing the plumpest specimen, I sliced up its button head and, after eating it, lay down on the bed and waited. Half an hour passed but I could not detect any change in my condition. The room and the objects in it looked exactly the same. I stared at the window curtains. It was possible that their crimson stripes appeared more vivid but I could not be sure. The pictures on the walls seemed to tremble, but this could have been due to a draught, the vibrations of a passing vehicle or the intensity with which I was looking at them. Whatever the cause, if this was the only effect the drug was to have on me, it was too insignificant to be of interest. The other plants still lay untouched on the table, but after my experience with the mushrooms I decided against a second helping.

Suddenly the room rocked. Booming and bellowing, the great bell of the cathedral sent rolling down from its tower close by, shock after shock of reverberating sound, gong-like, beating backwards and forwards from wall to wall and from floor to ceiling, blasting and bludgeoning until I felt that I was being lifted like a blown leaf and tossed about the room. The bell stopped. Vague stirrings of nausea made me close my eyes. When the sickness passed, I opened them again. Nothing in the appearance of the room had changed, but every object I looked at seemed to be trembling. I felt restless and had an unpleasant sensation of strain in my head. I walked about until it wore off. Then I lay down again and soon afterwards fell alseep.

When I woke in the morning I could not decide whether the peyotl had worked on the bell or the bell on the peyotl or my imagination on both. I got up, dressed and went downstairs. As I entered the hall, a stout, broad-shouldered man wearing a cowboy hat and hide jacket came up the steps from the street. The porter, standing in the doorway, welcomed him with an *abrazo*. The hugging lasted for several seconds, then the porter was in the air. Legs and arms loosely splayed, he sailed past me high over the furniture and, falling, disappeared behind a table. There was a thud, and a cloud of dust rose to the ceiling. I ran round to the other side of the table and found him sprawled on a sofa, giggling. I asked him if he was hurt but he did not answer. Turning, I saw that the cowboy had vanished. I crossed the hall to the entrance and looked out. The street was empty. In the cathedral square some boot-blacks were playing marbles and an old man lay asleep on a bench. I walked back up the steps. The porter had already returned to his post in the doorway. His hair was unruffled and his black trousers had no trace of dust on them. As I was about to speak to him, he yawned and sauntered away.

The peyotl was my last experience of Mexican drugs. The morning glory of Guerrero, the ubiquitous thorn-apple, the hallucinogenic balche-mix* of Yucatan, each offering a unique passage to unfamiliar territories of the mind, remained untried. Had I realized then (now, of course, it is generally known) the dangers of taking such drugs and their baleful after-effects, it is unlikely that I should have been so foolhardy as to have made the two or three experiments which I did. They were not without reward, however, for they widened the range of my

---

* Not the ordinary Maya bark-beer but a concoction brewed in the neighbourhood of Merida. My informant claimed to have experienced its effects but was hazy about its ingredients.

perceptions so that I became sensitive to the approach of hallucinatory states other than those produced by drugs, and found myself recognizing affinities with them in certain incidents and episodes experienced under normal conditions. Life in Mexico abounded in examples of these. The flying porter of San Luis Potosí was one, others are recorded in previous chapters. While I was never in danger of becoming addicted to the drugs of Mexico, they did help to stimulate my addiction to the country itself. Apart from the beauty of its landscape, the richness of its wild life and the fascination of its people, both the old races and the new, it was what it offered in the way of the strange, the macabre and the unpredictable which attracted me to it as I had been attracted to no other country in which I had previously travelled.

In the Air.

'I have a reservation. Here's my ticket.'

'I'm sorry, señor, the plane's full up.'

'Is that it on the runway?'

'Yes, señor.'

'But it's supposed to leave in a few minutes. Where are the other passengers?'

'All the places have been taken.'

'I booked mine three days ago.'

'They must have made a mistake at the office. We are not allowed to fly overweight.'

'How can it be overweight when there are no other passengers?'

The official shrugged his shoulders. 'All right, if you insist.'

He took my ticket and tore off the counterfoil. I sat down on a bench and waited. The plane was a very old Dakota belonging to a local airline. A sister machine stood on the edge of the airfield being languidly dismantled by an adolescent mechanic. I kept glancing at the road from the town, fearing the belated approach of a bus or a cavalcade of taxis. After a few minutes the official came out from behind his counter.

'If you wish, señor, you can get on board now.'

As I walked out to the plane, I wondered if I would find the cabin stacked with freight. But it was empty except for the steward. Choosing a back seat, I strapped myself in. The engines started up and we moved down the runway. We made a sluggish take-off, but once in the air the plane climbed smoothly. It circled Guaymas bay, then, instead of heading for Chihuahua, its advertised destination, it swung off down the coast. I thought I must be in the wrong plane, so I called the steward. He explained that we were to make an unscheduled stop at Ciudad Obregón. Shortly afterwards we turned inland and within twenty minutes were over the town. As we nosed down to the airfield, I could see a crowd beside the runway. The plane had hardly stopped before the people came surging round it. A *mariachi* band, twenty strong, stationed itself at the foot of the steps and began playing full blast.

I imagined this to be the send-off arranged for some local dignitary and tried to spot him in the crowd. I picked on a man wearing a white suit standing in the forefront. When the band stopped playing, he stepped up to the leader and embraced him. But instead of climbing the steps, he drew back, and it was the *mariachis* who turned and clambered into the plane.

They were in full regalia with striped ponchos, tight pants and embroidered sombreros. These last were so wide that they had to remove them to get through the door. They were burly men with huge stomachs. Encumbered by their instruments and numerous boxes and bundles, they were soon locked down the length of the cabin in a heaving scrimmage. Half a dozen *aficionados*,* who were travelling with them, added to the congestion. The steward tried to sort them out, but when the plane started to move, half the band were still on their feet. They shouted and gesticulated as it taxied down the runway, but when it turned and bounced forward at full throttle, they were suddenly silent, and the only movement in the cabin was the flutter of their plump brown hands as they invoked in criss-cross semaphore the aid of the Virgin and appropriate saints.

At the very end of the runway the plane rose and staggered reluctantly into the air. Once it was well up, the *mariachis*, after briefly kissing the medallions round their necks, became as boisterous and noisy as they had been on the ground. The

---

* Knowledgeable supporters.

aficionados produced bottles of tequila which were passed from hand to hand. Between swigs, neighbours playfully hugged or buffeted one another, while friends who were separated shouted down the length of the cabin.

As the plane struggled higher, the land rose steeply so that we were never more than a few hundred feet from the pine-covered spurs below. With my cheek pressed against the glass of the porthole I could see the great rock wall of the Sierra Madre rising ahead, black in the shadow of storm clouds piled along its summit. As we drew closer to it, the plane began to rock and shudder, but the *mariachis* were unperturbed. Urged on by the *aficionados*, two bandsmen in the gangway took their trumpets from the rack and blared out the opening bars of a *ranchera*.* Others who could reach their instruments joined in, while the rest beat time with heels and handclaps. With this riot of sound racketing in its belly, the plane struggled higher, but the rocks and pines, the last haunt of the wolves and grizzlies of Mexico, rose with it. The sky darkened and lightning flashes flickered on brass and brown faces. A grey fleece swept over the wing tips and the plane plunged, bouncing, into a cloud. The only light in the cabin was the illuminated safety-belt warning, but that had been on ever since Guaymas. When we came out of the cloud, a saw-edged pinnacle of rock rose high above us less than fifty feet from the wing. Then the plane dropped, the safety-belt warning went out and the air was full of flying hats and musical instruments. A violent jolt sent us soaring up again. Now the *mariachis* were silent. All round me their hands fluttered in frantic crosses. As if in answer to their prayers, a sulphur yellow gap opened between the crest of the mountain and the cloud ahead of us. The plane edged towards it. As it plunged under the black fringe of the cloud, I could see the flanks of the mountains falling away on the other side. The safety-belt warning flicked on again. A moment later, as we banked on to our course, the sunlight streamed in through the portholes. Feverishly kissing their medallions, the *mariachis* sat huddled in their seats or crouched on their knees in the gangway. The two trumpeters

---

* Ranch song. Modern successors to the old *corridos* or folk ballads, they are full of references to passionate love, the bottle and the gun.

recovered first. Rising with their trumpets to their lips and their cheeks blown out, they looked like recording angels carved on the roof of an Indian church. As they shattered the cabin with a resurrection blast, the plane slid gently down through the smooth air towards the burnished prairies of Chihuahua.

On the Ground.

The green and black markings of a seven-foot rattlesnake sunning itself, on a track near Celaya. The swift liquid movement of a *fer-de-lance* as it slid across my path in the rain forest of southern Veracruz. Gay and bright as the beads round the neck of an Indian girl, the red, white and black of a coral snake curled in the grass above the bay of Zihuatanejo while in the surrounding bushes scores of butterflies tumbled on scarlet wings. A yellow, near-transparent scorpion, the most lethal of the Mexican species, with one pincer cut off, climbing every day at the same hour the terrace wall of a house near Manzanillo until it reached the height at which I could knock it down with a broom handle into the bushes below. Tarantulas by the thousand at evening on the road to Laredo, huge hairy insects raised high on their splayed legs so that the setting sun pointed their shadows in black triangles over the lake-like surface of the tar.

Shelter for the Night.

A vast replica of a Spanish baronial castle, complete with suits of armour, cannons and portcullis, pitched like a rich child's discarded toy on the stark, arid waste of the mesquit plateau. A windowless hole in a wall, rattling with cockroaches, in a Chiapas doss-house outside which two drunken truck-drivers had a knife fight at three o'clock in the morning. A whitewashed mission cell in Baja California, the door opening on to a courtyard garden of hibiscus bushes and flowering creepers stitched at by scores of brilliant humming-birds. A *conquistador*'s palace in Yucatan.

I came on the palace after being turned away from every respectable hotel in the town. A congress was in session and there was not a bed to be had. At midnight I ended up on a bench in the square. Glancing at the building opposite, I saw a hotel sign, so faded as to be hardly legible, inscribed above the high arch of its open doorway. I got up, crossed the road and walked in. The walls of a great courtyard loomed round me. A dozen or more Indians were stretched out on the cobbles. At the far end a magnificent flight of marble steps soared up to an arched loggia. A light burned dimly under one of the arches, otherwise the whole place was in darkness. I climbed the steps and found a wizened mestizo sitting at a table under the light.

'Can I have a room?'

'A room to yourself?'

'Yes.'

'For how many hours?'

'For the night.'

Hammocks lumped with sleepers were hung from hooks on the walls to the pillars of the loggia. The mestizo led the way, ducking beneath them. Keeping up with him was like competing in a school obstacle-race. He stopped outside a door, opened it and handed me the key. The room was very large with tall windows facing on to the square. It was furnished with a tin chamber-pot and, ranged round it, eight iron bedsteads each with a straw mattress covered by a narrow grey sheet. I chose the bed with the cleanest mattress and lay down without taking off my clothes. By the light from a lamp in the square I found myself looking up at a row of carved and gilded beams. They were not less than thirty feet above me and stretched over an area much greater than the room. I now saw that the walls which separated me from my neighbours stopped short some distance below the ceiling. From all along under the gilded beams came the wheeze of bed springs, fierce cries and grunts and, beneath these louder sounds, a continuous husky whispering.

Although I was tired, it took me a long time to go to sleep. Suddenly I was awake again. The place was almost quiet but there was a scuffling on the other side of the partition behind my bed. It moved slowly higher. I turned over. The bed creaked and the noise stopped. After a few moments it began again. Then a pair of small dark hands appeared clutching the top of the partition. I did not wait to see the face which was to follow. Jumping off the bed, I grabbed my belongings and bolted to the door. Outside in the loggia I crashed into the first hammock, swinging its occupant up to the ceiling. I ducked under the others with only a few bumps but knocked heavily into the table at the top of the stairs. The mestizo woke up and shouted at me as I ran down into the courtayrd. An Indian lay, head foremost, on the bottom step. I hurried across the yard and out under the archway into the square.

On the Road.

There was no through bus that day from Tuxtla Gutierrez to Veracruz. The one I took was going to Villahermosa, so I had to change at Acayucán. It was New Year's Eve and the weather was clear and not too hot. The bus, a first-class express, was comfortable and almost empty. The views coming down the mountains from Tuxtla were magnificent and the lush green of the isthmus of Tehuantepec was enlivened by the yellow and scarlet of flowering trees. We reached Acayucan at two o'clock in the afternoon. As in other small towns in the south, its suburbs were fighting a losing battle with the vegetation. Jungly thickets flourished wherever there was a vacant space. An abandoned car, its paintwork still in good condition, was already entwined by creepers and had a small tree pushing up from under its bonnet. The streets looked mildly festive, but it could have been some local Guy Fawkes day rather than the New Year that the inhabitants were about to celebrate. Outside almost every house there was a stuffed effigy of a man, the face painted white and the features crudely scrawled in a simpleton's grimace.

The centre of the town was surprisingly crowded for early afternoon in the tropics. The bus station was in a street so narrow that our tyres scraped the pavement on either side. At least a hundred people were waiting for the bus. As soon as it stopped, they closed round the door in a struggling mass through which the passengers who were getting off had to fight their way. The station itself was so packed that I had difficulty in reaching the office. When I asked for a ticket to Veracruz, I was told that I could only buy one on the bus. The next bus was due in half an hour.

Although the station served only first-class passengers, it was not a pleasant place in which to wait. It was much too small for the number of people crowded into it. One side was open to the pavement which reflected the glare of the sun. The

215

low ceiling imprisoned not only the heat, but the smell from the public urinal which took up half the length of the back wall.

The first part of the journey had been so relaxed that I was dazed by the sudden change and felt in no state to compete in a struggle for places when the bus arrived. Surprisingly, it came in on time. Although I had edged as far forward as I could, I was outclassed in the in-fighting which followed and was left with a score of other would-be passengers on the pavement. I went back to the ticket office and was told that there would be another bus in an hour.

The station was now almost empty, as most of the passengers who had been left behind had gone away. I placed myself against the wall at one end close to the pavement. I chose this position not only because it was as far away from the urinal as I could get, but because I would be within a few feet of the door of the bus when it drew up.

The building on the other side of the street had barred windows. There was nothing remarkable in this, as most of the older houses in Mexico are so protected. The window opposite was filled with mournful faces. They were all male. Some had their chins resting on the sill, others peered out from the sides. Two belonged to bodies which clung, monkey-like, to the bars, while one at the top was upside down, as though its owner was suspended by the heels from the ceiling. As soon as a face was withdrawn, it was replaced by another. There were clearly a great many people inside anxious for the chance to look out. The heads, which went with the faces, were all shaven. I was looking through a window of the town gaol.

However humane it may be to allow prisoners a view of the outside world, to the outsider, unaccustomed to the practice, the sight of caged humanity at close range can come as a shock. More disconcerting still, when they saw that I was looking at them, they began to call in wheedling voices and beckon with sinuous brown arms stretched out between the bars.

Further along the street beyond the prison the door of a house opened and some children came out carrying one of the guy-like effigies I had seen from the bus. They propped it against the wall and fixed rockets to its hands and feet. Then they ripped open the belly, filled it with bangers and patched it up again with a paper stars-and-stripes. After jiggling round it, laughing and shouting, they went back into the house. The abandoned dummy had slipped sideways so that its inane white face gaped in my direction. I stared back at it until I realized, straightening up as I did so, that I was propped against my own wall in an identical posture.

The attention of the prisoners had been diverted to a woman who was walking along the pavement on their side of the street. As she passed under each window, brown hands snaked out to dangle small objects, toys and trinkets, in front of her. She spurned them all until she came to the window opposite where a set of doll's furniture, suspended on a string, took her fancy. She stopped and asked the price. After a brief haggle she settled for a few centavos and, handing the money up to the prisoner, received the toys in return. Encouraged by her example, I crossed over and bought a box of bone dominoes from an old lag.

The station had already started to fill up and, on my return, I found that my place by the wall had been taken by a family party. As the hour at which the bus was due to arrive came closer, people swarmed up the street from both directions. No matter how much I struggled I was edged further and further back. This time the bus was half an hour late. As I fought my way to the door, I saw a second coach with a Veracruz sign coming in behind it. I slipped out of the turmoil, ran towards it and scrambled up the steps. But the driver threw up his hands at me. Only the first bus was continuing the journey. By now, of course, it was full. It moved off and I was again left on the pavement.

I went back to the office where I was told that the next bus was due in two hours. 'You could try the second-class,' the man added. 'There may be one leaving sooner.'

With conditions as they were in the first-class, the advice seemed of doubtful value, but I decided to take it.

The second-class station was in a large square. It was much bigger than the first-class and there were fewer people in it but, as most of them were lying down, the floor space was just as congested. I had to step over a score of prostrate bodies to reach the office. The man at the window sold me a ticket and told me that the bus would be arriving in a few minutes. I picked my way back to the pavement and reached it just as a large empty bus rolled into the square. I made a dash for it expecting all the people in the station to be on their feet and racing after me. Breathless, I asked the driver if he was going to Veracruz. He nodded and got out as I climbed in. I sat down on the back seat. Looking out of the window, I saw that no one in the station had moved.

The bus was clean and only a little less comfortable than the one in which I had travelled from Tuxtla. Again I was dazed by my change of fortune. I stretched out my legs, lit a cigarette and watched the people walking in the square. A young and very attractive girl sauntered past the window. She stopped by the door and, after a quick glance round, climbed in and sat down on the front seat. As I straightened up to get a better view, she turned and looked at me. Only the top of her face was visible, but from the expression in her eyes she seemed to be laughing.

'You're English!' Her voice was so natural and had so slight an accent that I hardly noticed that she was speaking my own language.

'Yes, how did you know?'

'You couldn't be anything else.' She got up and ran down the bus towards me. 'I love Englishmen!'

In a moment she was sitting beside me screwed round on the edge of the seat and laughing without a hint of mockery, as if at the sheer delight of being able to look into my face.

'You see, I had an Englishman as my teacher. He was wonderful. I adore the English accent. Now just talk, please. I want to listen. Tell me what you are thinking.'

'I was thinking that your teacher was very lucky.'

'Oh no, he wasn't! Poor boy! But I don't want to talk about him.'

'Neither do I. Would you like me to give you lessons?'

'Of course!'

'Are you going to Veracruz?'

'Why not?'

'Splendid! Shall I start right away?'

'Yes, please do.'

She pressed close to me and took my hand. She was not

laughing any more. Passionately adoring, her eyes gazed into mine. Then suddenly she looked out of the window and her face clouded with schoolgirl petulance.

I turned and saw three men, one middle-aged and two much younger, walking resolutely across the square towards the bus. She snatched away her hand, scuttled down the gangway and disappeared between two seats. The men, from the family likeness unmistakably her father and elder brothers, climbed in and started to search the bus. Discovered, she went with them without protest. In the doorway she turned to look at me and laughed, as if there had been between us a delightful intimate joke.

When the driver came back, I was still his only passenger. It was beginning to get dark as we drove out of the town. Groups of adults and children were busy setting up their guys in the roadway. By the time we reached the outskirts, the holocaust had begun and dozens of stuffed *gringos** were going up in flames with bangers bursting and rockets whizzing into the sky.

Once on the open road we drove at a tremendous pace. Even when we ran into sea fog at Catemaco, the driver did not slow down. We made no stops although in every village people waiting beside the road waved at us frantically. At Alvarado we caught the ferry across the river just as it was leaving. A few miles further on we overtook with a triumphant hoot the first-class bus from Acayucan. It was five minutes to midnight when we reached the terminus in Veracruz. As I entered the cathedral square, the bells rang out. Caught in a whirl of revellers, I was dragged to a café under the arcades and plied with drinks. Although I did not know it, the last year in which I was to live in Mexico had begun.

I booked a passage on a boat which was sailing for Europe in the first week of December. I was determined to make a final expedition before I left, but the fortnight I reserved for it dwindled to ten days. In choosing an objective, I was limited not only by the time factor but the season, for the rains had

---

* My assumption that the guys represented *gringos* was based on the fact that they all had white faces. One, as I have described, was patched with an American flag. I asked several people in the bus station whom the guys were supposed to represent, but none of them knew. It was just an old New Year custom in Acayucan.

continued late, and rivers, particularly in the south, were still too high to be easily crossed. This ruled out what otherwise would have been my first choice; a return to Kilometre Eighty-One and a second attempt to find Rio Bec. Two other Maya sites in Quintana Roo which interested me were Tulum and Cobá. Both are in the north of the territory, the first on the coast near Cozumel Island and the second just over the Yucatan border about seventy miles east of Chichén Itzá.

Tulum can be reached by plane or boat from Cozumel. I had already been to the island but had failed to make the crossing owing to bad weather. At this season I knew that I might easily be frustrated a second time. In any case I was more attracted by an expedition which would entail a ride or walk through the jungle, so I decided on Cobá.

After Tikál in Guatemala, Cobá is one of the largest Maya sites, but it is not often visited as it lies buried in jungle, sixteen miles from the nearest village accessible by road. The journey can be made during the rainy season, for there are no rivers in the area, the terrain being of porous limestone rock which absorbs the rainfall. Although the vegetation in northern Yucatan consists of monotonous bush, Cobá, on its chain of lakes, lies within the belt of rain forest which stretches east to the coast and south to Chetumal and British Honduras.

I met only one person in Mexico City who knew the site, but he had not been there for thirty years. At that time the area was uninhabited. The ruins were very extensive and so overgrown that he doubted if I should be able to get more than a superficial impression of them. There were two very high pyramids, numerous carved stelae and some causeways leading to neighbouring ceremonial centres. It was surrounded by high jungle and wild life was plentiful, including jaguar, monkeys and tapir.

An archaeologist who had more up-to-date information, although he had not been there himself, told me that there was a shelter used by *chicleros* close to the ruins. I should, however, be prepared to sleep in the open. He offered to lend me an enclosed hammock with a waterproof cover and panels of mosquito netting. I accepted this gratefully and he gave me a demonstration in his office of how it should be hung.

I flew to Merida by an early plane and called on a local

archaeologist to whom I had a letter of introduction. He had not been to Cobá himself, and knew of no one else who had been there. He suggested that I should go to Valladolid where I would be certain of finding someone who could tell me the best way to continue the journey. I spent the rest of the day visiting acquaintances in the town. They all agreed that Valladolid was the place to set out from but thought it unlikely that I should reach my destination. One of them lent me a copy of Dr Eric Thompson's account of the ruins,* remarking that he did not expect to see either the book or me again. Another was equally discouraging. It was dangerous, he said, to make the journey alone and unarmed. The Indians were notoriously hostile to foreigners, while the *chicleros*, the only other people I was likely to meet, were all desperate rogues and cut-throats. I would be extremely fortunate if I found anyone trustworthy to take me to the ruins. Only a few years earlier a German who had tried to walk from Cobá to Tulum had been murdered by his guides.

Cobá is, indeed, on the fringe of an area which has a bad reputation. It is inhabited by the fiercely independent Chan Santa Cruz Indians† who held out so successfully against the

---

* *A Preliminary Study of the Ruins of Cobá, Quintana Roo*, by J. Eric Thompson, Harry E. Pollock and Jean Charlot. Carnegie Institute Publications, No. 424.

† One of the present chiefs of the tribe was born in Cozumel. As a small boy he was shipwrecked on the coast near Tulum. His companions were killed by the Indians, but his own life was spared at the intercession of a Negro timber merchant from Belize. He was not allowed to return to Cozumel, but the fact that he was an outsider by birth did not prevent him from becoming a tribal leader.

Shortly before the arrival of Cortés in Mexico, a Spanish ship was wrecked in the same area. Two survivors were taken prisoner by the Indians. One escaped and joined up with Cortés, but the other stayed with his captors, became one of their chiefs and led them against the Spanish armies.

It has been suggested that Quetzalcóatl, the fair-skinned, blue-eyed, bearded god of culture worshipped by the Aztecs, who vanished across the sea to the east promising to return, was a Viking who had survived shipwreck. Though the idea has been scoffed at by archaeologists, recent discoveries proving the extent of Viking settlement in North America make it, at least, a possibility. The equivocal attitude of Moctezuma, the Aztec emperor, towards Cortés was due to his belief that the *conquistador* might be the returning god.

There are representations of African negroes in Olmec sculpture. It is difficult to explain their existence unless Africans reached the shores of America in pre-conquest times. If they did so, they may have become chiefs or been worshipped as gods. Since the Itzas of Tayasál deified the horse which Cortés left with them, it is possible that in ancient times exotic foreigners may have received the same treatment.

Mexican army in the War of the Castes. They had never been conquered and until the signing of the Great Peace in 1935, they had murdered all Mexicans whom they found on their territory except for a few privileged traders. The only foreigners they tolerated were the British, who in the early years of their struggles against the Mexicans had supplied them with arms from Belize.*

I had nothing to fear from these Indians and would have welcomed a meeting with them, but I knew that their villages lay far to the south of Cobá. The *chicleros* were a more doubtful factor, but I did not expect to encounter any as the expedition would only take me a short distance into the forest.

My main concern was to waste as little time as possible, so I decided to take the first bus the next morning to Valladolid. Thinking I would have to spend the night there, when I arrived, I went straight to a hotel where I told the proprietor the reason for my visit. Although it meant the loss of my custom, he assured me that it would be useless to make inquiries in the town and I had much better take a bus to Chemax, a village twenty miles further on along the Puerto Juarez road. As it was Sunday it would be full of country people and I might be lucky enough to meet a farmer from the Cobá district who would be prepared to act as my guide.

Among the warnings I had received in Merida there was one which had been pressed on me several times: that I should avoid arriving in a village on Sunday as all the inhabitants would be drunk and the *presidente*,† the only person who was likely to help me, would be away in Valladolid. I decided to take the proprietor's advice, however, and an hour later I left on a second-class bus for Chemax.

The village lay a mile off the main road. As the bus entered the square, I saw that my friends in Merida had been right

---

* When Morley visited Tulum in 1922, he was surrounded by hostile Indians who demanded that he should show them a document signed by Queen Victoria authorizing him to land. During my own time in Mexico, some archaeologists working on the coast learned that the Indians had a sacred book in one of their villages. Believing that it might be an ancient Maya codex, they sent two members of their party to the village. When they asked to see the book, they were told they could only do so if accompanied by an Englishman carrying a signed portrait of Queen Victoria.

† The mayor.

about the state in which I would find the inhabitants. There were dozens of them lying drunk on the ground. Those who were still on their feet came staggering forward to inspect the descending passengers. I hesitated before getting out.

The regular users of hallucinogenic drugs sometimes describe the experience as 'going on a voyage'. It is a good description, but the voyage has special characteristics: there can be no foreknowledge of the splendours or miseries to which it may lead and, once one is committed to it, there can be no turning back. Standing in the doorway of the bus, I felt the same kind of apprehension as I had experienced before eating the mushrooms and the peyotl. Once I had got out, the bus would drive away and I would be left in the power, as uncertain as that of any drug, of the intoxicated inhabitants of Chemax. Although I had a vague idea of my intended destination, I did not know how I should get there or what the journey might entail. I walked down the steps into the crowd.

As the village was a little distance from the main highway, only second-class buses stopped there and a visit from a foreigner was obviously an unusual event. The people were so curious and pressed so close to me that I could not move. Helpless, I stood smiling into the wild, drink-bemused faces which were thrust to within a few inches of my own. There was a babble of talk but as it was all in Maya I could not tell whether the people were addressing me or merely discussing my appearance among themselves. I asked a man who seemed more sober than the rest if he would take me to the *presidente*. Once again my friends in Merida were proved right. The *presidente* was in Valladolid. Next I asked for the priest, but, from the blank look I received, such a person might never have been heard of in Chemax. There seemed nothing else to do but wait until they got tired of looking at me and began to drift away. But as soon as any of those in the front rank moved, others thrust forward to take their place.

I was finding it difficult to keep my smile from turning into a nervous grimace, when the village guard, an old man in a faded khaki cap, pushed his way through the crowd and, frowning sternly, asked me what I wanted. I was relieved, in spite of his severe expression, to have someone sober to talk to. I said that I had come to visit the ruins of Cobá and would be grateful for any help he could give me. For a moment he looked so disapproving that I was afraid he was going to arrest me and lock me up. Then he turned on the crowd and, speaking to them in Maya, began to push them away. When they had dispersed, he nodded to me to follow him, and we set out across the square. We stopped at a stall which sold soft drinks and *tacos*. The guard explained to the owner that I wanted to visit Cobá and asked him if he could provide me with a guide and mules. He agreed to do so, promised to have them ready at seven o'clock the next morning and suggested a reasonable price. As I had been told in Merida that I might be asked as much as a thousand pesos for the journey, I accepted without bargaining. But the arrangement had been made so quickly and with so little fuss that I doubted if the man had any serious intention of carrying it out.

I thanked the guard for his help and asked him where I could spend the night. He suggested that I should put up my hammock in the village school. This was in the *presidencia*,* a handsome building, probably an old *hacienda*,† which took up one side of the square. Its central block was approached by a flight of steps which led into a loggia giving access to two outlying wings. The one on the right was occupied by the school; it consisted of a large room with a high ceiling and tall windows. The floor space was taken up by battered desks and benches. The guard cleared some of these to one side and showed me hooks on the walls from which I could hang my hammock. He explained that it was not an ordinary Sunday in Chemax but the second day of a fiesta to celebrate the installation of an electric light plant in the village. There had been some heavy drinking, and if I wished to keep out of trouble I should stay where I was. After giving me this advice, he wished me a good journey to Cobá and left me.

I decided to spend the rest of the afternoon in my hammock studying Thompson's book on the ruins. I had not unrolled the hammock since my friend had demonstrated its advantages to me in his office. Considerable as these would undoubtedly have proved in the open jungle, I soon realized that they made

---

* The building housing the local government offices.
† A landowner's country house.

it impracticable for use indoors. The waterproof cover had cords attached to it which were intended for tying to branches overhead so that the cover itself could be raised high enough to allow the occupant to lie in comfort beneath it. When I had hung the hammock, as there was nothing on the walls or ceiling to which I could fix the cords, the cover flapped over it to form a suffocating, airtight sheet. By standing four of the school benches on end and attaching the cords to them, I managed to raise the cover a few inches so that at least some air could enter through the mosquito netting at the sides.

I had been working so intently that it was not until I had finished that I noticed the group of astonished onlookers which had collected in the doorway. Feeling foolish, I explained that the hammock was intended for sleeping in the open. This made them even more curious and they crowded round to inspect it. Soon they were demanding that I should give a demonstration by getting inside, but I had not enough confidence in my knots to risk testing them in public.

To create a diversion I sat down at a desk and opened out a plan of Cobá at the back of Thompson's book. Only one of my visitors claimed to have seen the ruins but he could not understand the plan. He told me that the *chicle* camp had been abandoned and that there was now a settlement beside the lake. The people cultivated *milpas** and raised cattle.

I asked him if there were many wild animals in the area.

'No, there're too many people about. You won't see even a squirrel. The high jungle has been cut down. It's all *pura ramón.*'

This was disappointing. *Ramón* is a low-growing tree which makes excellent fodder for mules but is scenically uninteresting. I could only hope that his account was exaggerated.

Few of the men spoke any Spanish and, when they found that I could not understand Maya, they soon began to drift away. A youth who had been waiting at the door came forward after the others had gone and sat down at the desk beside me. He spoke fluent Spanish, had been to Cobá and was able to follow the plan. He pointed out the position of the settlement in relation to the ruins and told me that it was

---

* Maize plantations.

inhabited by Maya Indians from villages to the south of Valladolid. They were firmly established, rarely left the settlement and had little contact with Chemax. He doubted if any of them spoke Spanish. This again was disappointing, for I had hoped they might be Chan Santa Cruz Indians who had moved up from the south. When I asked him if he had ever met any of the *sublevados*,* he told me they never came as far north as Chemax. He had, however, been at school at Valladolid with the sons of one of their tribal chiefs. He had become close friends with them and they had invited him to their village. He would have liked to accept but he was afraid to do so because of the known hostility of the Chan Santa Cruz people to strangers. The boys had been intelligent and had done well at school.†

While we had been talking, I had noticed a very drunk Indian reeling about under the arches of the loggia. Suddenly he staggered through the door and threw himself on the floor at my feet. He announced in broken Spanish that he wished me well and called on God to bless me. Then, clasping my legs, he broke into a long harangue in his own language, only breaking off at intervals to exclaim: '*Chemax Maya! Pura Maya!*'

I asked the young man to translate.

'He says he likes you very much and wants you to know that Chemax is pure Maya.'

Another even longer harangue followed. Again I asked for a translation.

'He's still saying the same thing.'

He was a wild-looking creature with long smooth black hair, a finely curved Maya nose and fiery black eyes. After a little the young man, bored with the intrusion, made an excuse and

---

* The term used to describe the dissident Indians in the War of the Castes.

† Robert Redfield, the American social anthropologist, in his book *The Folk Culture of Yucatan* (University of Chicago Press 1941) remarks on the readiness of the leading Chan Santa Cruz families to send their sons away to be educated. Unlike other Maya Indians they regard themselves as the equals of the *dzulob* or white Yucatecans from the towns. Despite their desire to remain independent and exclusive, they realize the advantage of education in dealing with the *dzulobs*. The Mexican government has recently been allowed to open schools in the tribal area. This is certain to modify the exclusiveness of the Indians and bring about their eventual integration into the social system of the rest of Yucatan.

went away. I was left alone, trapped by the drunk's arms and subjected to his interminable gabble. Fearing that if I offended him he might become aggressive, I nodded as though I understood what he was saying and interjected an occasional noncommittal phrase in Spanish. But soon I gave up any pretence at listening as my attention became absorbed by the effect of the evening light on the façade of the church which, from where I was sitting, was framed by one of the arches of the loggia.

Since my arrival in the village I had been so occupied with its inhabitants that I had hardly noticed its architecture. The church, I now recognized, was a fine example of the colonial style in Yucatan. It was faced with plain stucco broken only by the moulding round the door and some baroque scrolls high up between its twin towers. On the crest of each scroll single vultures were perched like heraldic carvings. The sun was setting and its light striking full on the stucco made it glow so that the whole church, set against the violet sky, resembled a gigantic reliquary sheathed in gold. The sun sank, the shadows rose and the splendour faded. As the last gleam melted from the towers, the vultures, abandoning their decorative role, spread their wings and spiralled silently away. I returned to my predicament.

The Indian still held me by the legs and gabbled on. I was preparing to free myself by force when a door at the back of the room opened and an old gentleman with glasses at the end of his nose tottered in. At the sight of my hammock, he stopped and gaped in astonishment. The Indian let go of my legs and greeted him with a wave of his hand. I got up and apologized for my presence, explaining that I was spending the night in Chemax on my way to Cobá.

He was silent for a moment, then murmured in a descending scale: 'Cobá! Cobá! Cobá!' Turning away, he crossed the room and picked up a broom which was propped against the wall. Carrying it on his shoulder, he tottered back and with a final 'Cobá! Cobá! Cobá!' went out and closed the door behind him.

His entry had secured my release, and I strolled out under the loggia. Some Indians had collected on the steps waiting to see the lamps light up in the square. I slipped through them and walked across to the stall. The man who had promised me the mules had been replaced by a woman. I bought some *tacos* from her and ate them sitting on a bench under a tree.

After several false starts and one or two alarming flashes, the generator got going and the lights came on. There were murmurs of wonder and appreciation from all sides. The children, making the most of this novel extension of their playtime, raced about wildly under the lamps. I had just finished the *tacos* when I saw the Indian who had attached himself to me in the school approaching. He sat down beside me and, more sober now, addressed me in Spanish. He said that I had made a mistake in visiting Chemax for such a miserable fiesta. I should have come a month earlier for the great annual feast. There had been dancing, real drinking and bullfights. This year the fights had been very bad but last year there had been a wonderful *torero*, handsome, graceful and brave. So brave that he had taken one risk too many. The bull had gored him in the groin and had charged round the ring carrying his genitals on its horn.

The telling of this gruesome story appeared to have exhausted his Spanish, for at the end of it he lapsed into Maya. Suddenly, in the middle of what sounded like a sentence, he got up and walked away.

I returned to the schoolroom and wedged a chair under the door handle as a protection against intruders. After testing the knots, I swung myself into the hammock. It sagged almost to the floor and the waterproof cover drooped to within an inch of my face. I was not at all comfortable but I was too tired to get out to tighten the ropes and cords. I fell asleep immediately only to be woken within minutes by a nightmare. I was walking across a field near my home in England when I saw an enormous bull charging towards me. After that I lay awake for hours. There were scufflings on the floor and huge bats whirred in and out through the glassless windows. The old man in the adjoining room snored and groaned. Once I heard him murmur in his sleep, 'Cobá! Cobá! Cobá!' At midnight there was a violent storm. The rain roared on the roof tiles and great gusts of wind set my hammock rocking. When the storm died away, I dozed off.

It was after six when I woke up and I was still packing when

228

the children started to arrive for their morning class. I crossed the square to the stall where the woman served me with a bowl of tepid coffee spiced with cinnamon. I was still drinking it when the man arrived to tell me that my guide and mules were ready. He led me to a track on the outskirts of the village where they were waiting. The mules were lean and scruffy. Miguel, the sixteen-year-old guide, did not look intelligent but he spoke some Spanish. After packing my rucksack on to the larger of the mules, he mounted it himself. My own animal was a miserable creature, and the prospect of spending an indefinite number of hours on its wooden-hooped saddle was daunting. The stirrups, designed for Maya feet, were so small that I could only get the tips of my toes into them. The hoops of the saddle were slippery and too wide to grip.

The sky was overcast and the storm had left the atmosphere hot and clammy. As we started down the track there was a rumble of thunder. We passed a few scattered huts and maize patches, then the bush closed in on either side. The trees were about twenty feet high with trunks only a few inches thick, but they grew so close together that it was impossible to see for more than a few yards in any direction. The only signs of life were occasional humming-birds darting across the track, and enormous blue butterflies which spiralled round each other with a curious wobbling flight. Although the bush was as flat and featureless as it had been all the way along the road from Merida, its floor was uneven so that the limestone surface of the track, greasy after the night's rain, rose and fell in treacherous undulations.

From the start my mule had no inclination for the journey. I had to urge it along at every step, thumping its belly with my heels in a rhythm always a little in advance of its reluctant pace. It slipped and stumbled at every rock and pothole so that I was constantly heeling over on the hoops of the saddle. Soon there were no more humming-birds, but the blue butterflies continued to tumble round us in the gloom.

After three hours we came to a circle of huts in a clearing. Miguel pulled up his mule and suggested that we should rest. When I dismounted, I found that my legs were so cramped that I could hardly walk. A woman came out of one of the huts and Miguel asked her for water. She fetched a bucket and lowered

it into a well* in the centre of the clearing. The water she drew
up tasted brackish but I was too thirsty to be put off.

After ten minutes we mounted again. For half a mile we
passed scattered *milpas* and a few cows with bells hanging from
their necks. Then the bush shut us in and there were not even
butterflies to relieve its monotony. The track became narrower
and rougher and my mule more reluctant and clumsy in its
progress. The sky darkened and suddenly, without any warning
drops, the rain fell in a battering deluge. Within seconds my
clothes were drenched through. I found it refreshing at first,
but soon the clamminess in the air turned cold. My shirt and
trousers clung to me as the water streamed through them.
Every few yards the mule stopped, and I had to beat it with a
stick to make it move.

Chilled and saddle-sore, I was beginning to regret having
undertaken such a tedious journey when my guide halted and
pointed into the bush. About twenty yards away, what
appeared to be a low wall ran parallel to the track. I
dismounted, walked over to it and climbed to the top. I found
myself on a platform fifteen feet wide which stretched in either
direction as far as I could see. I realized that I was standing on
one of the ancient causeways which radiated from Cobá. This
strip of ghost-road, designed for great ceremonial processions,
unused for at least five hundred years† and now buried in the
dense gloom of the bush, produced a sensation of eeriness such
as I had experienced at no other Maya ruin.

I walked back to the track, and we rode on again. The rain
stopped and the sun came out. Gradually the vegetation became more varied and the trees taller. Brilliant blue-headed

---

* A hole in the limestone rock about three feet in diameter. Such wells, which are
almost the only source of water in Yucatan, are known as *cenotes*. They recur where
the limestone crust has collapsed, leaving the subterranean water level exposed.
Some are as much as two hundred feet in diameter and the water may lie a hundred
feet below the land surface. The famous *cenote* at Chichén Itzá was used by the
ancient Maya for human sacrifice. In the remote villages they are still regarded as
sacred. In Merida one of the *cenotes* is approached by a grotto which has been
turned into a restaurant and night-club. The food is excellent (the cooking in
Yucatan is the best in Mexico) and entertainment is provided by a ladies' band.
The musicians, who play with great verve, are all elderly and look like very respectable music teachers.

† Cobá dates from 623 and was occupied intermittently until the fourteenth
century.

230

jays flashed through the undergrowth and a flock of wild turkeys exploded from a clearing. Soon I heard cowbells and shortly afterwards we came to the first *milpas*. They were surrounded by trees of the high jungle, ciba, coaba, and zapodilla. The track sank into a shallow depression. As we topped the rising ground on the other side, I saw ahead of us, surrounded by a belt of savanna and edged with reeds, the lake of Cobá, its rippling surface* reflecting a cloud bank gilded by the setting sun. A line of long wooded hills rose on its further shore. Miguel pointed to them and announced triumphantly: 'The ruins of Cobá!'

We rode beside the lake until we came to a collection of huts scattered round a clearing. They were all built in traditional Maya fashion, oval in shape, with walls of slim vertical poles supporting high thatched roofs. We stopped outside one of them and dismounted. Miguel unhitched my rucksack and carried it into the hut, nodding to me to follow. There was nothing inside except a dying turkey which I took for a heap of feathers, until it twitched and I saw its head writhing in the dirt.

While Miguel went to find food and to cut *ramón* for the mules, I changed out of my sodden clothes and set about fixing up my hammock while it was still light. I tied the ropes to two of the stouter poles which supported the roof, but they were slippery and I had difficulty in securing the knots. I was more successful with the waterproof cover than I had been at Chemax and managed to arrange it in its correct position with the mosquito net panels on either side. When I had finished I went down to the lake and washed. On my return I found Miguel gaping at the hammock. I explained that it was intended for sleeping out in the jungle. Unimpressed, he shook his head and giggled. But he became solemn again when I asked him if he had found us any food. 'Only eggs,' he said gloomily. 'If you like, we can go and eat them now.'

The sun had set and it was almost dark as he led me across the clearing to a neighbouring hut. It was lit by an oil lamp and the glow from a charcoal fire. Its owner, Don Dionisio, a grave, dignified man with the sloping forehead and curved

---

* The full name of the place is Kinchil Cobá, which means rippling water. While I stayed there, even at dawn and the sunset surface of the lake was never smooth.

nose of the classic Maya, was lying in his hammock. Raising himself a little, he shook my hand without smiling. He was dressed in Indian folk costume, a white smock, trousers and short apron. His wife squatted by the fire. She too was pure Maya and wore the traditional *huipil*, a white, sleeveless shift with a square neck. A little girl sat beside her. Two older boys ran from the hut as I entered and stood whispering outside in the dark.

In contrast to the neat appearance and spotless white clothes of the family,* the hut and its contents were in the utmost disorder. Sacks, boxes, tins and domestic utensils were heaped and jumbled on the floor. Some rough shelves held a stock of salt, matches, candles, cigarettes and home-made cartridges. Miguel explained that Don Dionisio kept these supplies to sell to *chicleros* who passed through on their way to or from the forest. There was a low table in the centre of the floor with wooden blocks for seats. A bucket of water had been placed close to it so that we could wash our hands before eating. Our supper consisted of three eggs and an unlimited quantity of tortillas. The family remained silent while we were eating. When we had finished the woman handed us gourd-cups of water with which to rinse out our mouths. I followed my guide's example and spat the water on to the floor.

Don Dionisio, as grave as ever, began to question Miguel in Maya. There were long pauses in their conversation. When one of these had lasted several minutes, I joined in, using the boy as an interpreter. I learned that the settlement had been started twenty years before. All the families had come from a village to the south of Chichén-Itzá. The place was very isolated but most of the men went to Valladolid two or three times a year. They had neither church nor school. Don Dionisio regretted that his children lacked the opportunity to learn to read and write, but he did not appear to think the absence of a church important. The people followed the customs of their parent village, performed all the important seasonal ceremonies and lived decent and peaceful lives. Even when hunting, they rarely ventured more than a few miles to the south and had

---

* They bathed morning and evening in the lake. The woman changed into a clean *huipil* at least three times a day.

little contact with the Chan Santa Cruz Indians. In the past the *chicleros* had been troublesome but there were fewer of them now and they left the settlers and their property alone. He and his family were content at Cobá and had no wish to live anywhere else.

Miguel, who had proved a better interpreter than I had expected, soon began to yawn and suggested that it was time for us to sleep. He borrowed a hammock and lantern from Don Dionisio and we returned to our hut accompanied by the elder of the two boys who brought his own hammock with him. Miguel must have told him about my unusual sleeping contraption, for as soon as they saw it, they burst into the shrill tee-hee-heeing of Maya laughter. During our absence the sick turkey had dragged itself beneath it; swarms of insects crawled or hopped among its feathers. I would have liked to have moved it but I did not want to touch it and could find nothing in the hut with which to push it away.

The boys strung their hammocks quickly, climbed into them and lay grinning as they waited for me to get into mine. I regretted having tested the knots so superficially, but I swung myself in and they held. The disaster came when I tried to shift to the diagonal position which I found most comfortable for sleeping. Suddenly the hammock heeled over, the cords on one side of the cover broke loose and I found myself face downwards, staring at the turkey through the mosquito net. I expected the boys to burst into their shrillest laughter but they were silent. When I had extricated myself, I saw that they were hanging over the sides of their hammocks gazing at me in shocked astonishment. I fixed the cords and climbed in again. This time everything held. Miguel put out the lantern and we settled down to sleep without exchanging a word about my misadventure.

I remained for four days and three nights in Cobá, and would have stayed longer if Miguel had not insisted that he must return with the mules to Chemax. On the first day I explored the ruins with Don Dionisio's son. I climbed the pyramid of the diving god, which rose seventy-five feet above the court at its base and at least two hundred feet above the forest floor. From the sanctuary at the top there was a magnificent view of the lakes and the flat unbroken jungle stretching to the horizon. The pyramid of the *castillo* was even higher, but its view was masked by the trees growing on the ruins below. I managed to trace most of the building on Thompson's plan but some had been almost totally destroyed by the vegetation. In front of the few stelae* which were still upright, I found wreaths made out of twigs, heaps of copal ash and notched sticks yellow with candle grease.

On the second day I returned to the ruins alone. I spent an hour on top of the pyramid of the diving god and made a closer survey of some of the buildings round the *castillo*. Approaching the sacred cave, I disturbed a puma† which darted off, a fawn flash, into the undergrowth. I crossed the isthmus on which the ruins lay, bathed in the lake on the other side, and slept through the heat of the afternoon under a tree. Walking back in the evening, I met an Indian who spoke some Spanish. He wanted to know if I thought the *santos* of Cobá, since I had come such a long way to visit them, were more powerful than the famous Christian *santos*, the Three Kings of Tizimin.‡

---

* According to Thompson, the Indians believe that stelae and certain other stones are guardians of the forest. Formerly they were known as *tzimín tún*, the Maya for stone tapir. This was later changed to stone horse. They are supposed to be able to move about at night.

When I asked Don Dionisio about the ritual offerings I had seen among the ruins, he told me that some people believed that the stones had supernatural powers and if candles and copal were burnt in front of them they would protect crops and cattle and keep off sickness. He was not sure whether he believed this himself, but he considered the offerings a wise precaution.

Redfield gives an account of the duality of Maya religious practices in Yucatan. Those of Christian bias are led by the *maestro cantor* or prayer chanter, who invokes the Virgin and saints. Those of pagan origin are conducted by the *h-men*, who invoke the *yuntzilob* or spirits of the bush. The pagan rituals are essential to maize planting and other agricultural activities. The *yuntzilob* are close to men and belong to the earth, while the Christian God and his saints are fixed in the remote heavens.

The pagan Maya conception of the cosmos was a quadrilateral with each corner presided over by a different deity and associated with a special colour. Among the modern Maya it is represented by Christian symbols: a cross in the centre and one at each corner of the village. The central cross of the settlement at Cobá was outside the hut where I slept, and there was one at either end of the village beside the lake. I did not see the other two which made up the square. They must have been placed further back in the bush.

† I was told that puma and jaguar frequently hid in the ruins, attracted by the cattle in the savanna below.

‡ A village in Northern Yucatan. During its great annual fiesta in honour of the Three Kings, it is frequented by thieves and tricksters attracted by the pilgrims who gather at the shrine.

In the evening two *chicleros* arrived at the settlement and shared our hut. The turkey was still alive but it had not moved, so I fetched a stick from outside and pushed it into a corner against the wall. Until they realized that I was not going to kill it, the others all watched me with evident disapproval.* During the night I was woken by a loud splashing. One of the *chicleros* was pissing through the mesh of his hammock on to the floor.

On the third day, taking a track which ran south deep into the high jungle, I came on a tree full of spider monkeys. They chattered and screamed and threw twigs at me. When this failed to frighten me away, they scampered down the trunk and vented their feelings in frenzied copulation. Returning, I met the *chicleros* heading into the forest with shot-guns on their shoulders. They told me I had taken the wrong track, and walked back a quarter of a mile with me to show me the right one.

That night I was disturbed by a scuffling below my hammock and, looking down, saw in the barred moonlight which entered through the walls, the turkey moving in short jerks across the floor towed by a gigantic rat. At four o'clock Miguel woke me. After we had taken down our hammocks and I had packed my rucksack, we walked over to Don Dionisio's hut for the last time. He was lying in his hammock warmed by a pan of glowing charcoal placed on the floor beneath him. His wife was already squatting beside the fire preparing our coffee and tortillas. There was nothing I had enjoyed more during my stay at Cobá than the hour or so I had spent each evening with this Maya family and their neighbours. I was fascinated by the ritualistic order in their lives and impressed by their quiet dignity. Nowhere else in Mexico had I found people who treated each other with such respect or lived in such harmony with their natural surroundings.

In my previous Mexican travels, however attracted I had

---

* Mexicans are generally reluctant to kill dying animals. The *pistolero*, who thinks nothing of shooting a healthy fellow human, may recoil from finishing off a dog in its death agony. The Yucatan Maya, the *sublevados* apart, are the Mexicans who are least given to violence. Their pagan heritage teaches them to have a reverence for life. They consider it wrong, for example, to kill more game than is absolutely necessary as a supplement to their maize diet.

been by a place or determined to return to it, at the moment of departure I had always found myself content or even anxious to be moving on. I had come to think of this restlessness as one of my essential reactions to Mexico and a feature of my obsessive attachment to it. I had measured my liking for other countries by their towns or villages where I felt I would have been happy to have spent long periods of my life. At first I had looked for such places in Mexico and had been disappointed when I did not find them. But once I had stopped looking, had ceased even to believe in their existence, I quickly realized that a life of travel in Mexico appealed to me far more than any settled existence, either experienced or imagined, in other countries I had known.

When I had set out for Cobá, its ruins had only been part of its attraction. More important had been the journey itself, the prospect of exploring a little known stretch of country, of observing its animals and birds, and of encountering its reputedly wild or primitive inhabitants. In some ways I had been disappointed. The journey had proved too easy and more arduous than eventful. I had seen less wild life than I had hoped and, apart from the drunken Indians at Chemax, the people I had met had been neither wild nor primitive.

And yet I had been held by Cobá as by no other place in Mexico. The little settlement beside the brilliant, glittering lake, locked under a vast sky in the interminable expanse of level jungle broken only by the artificial hills of the ancient site, had the feel of true remoteness (it was, after all, on the edge of one of the largest blanks on the map of Mexico) and a profound tranquillity which owed as much to the peaceful, measured lives of its inhabitants as to its natural setting.

On this last journey I had found what I had least expected to find: a place where I would have been content to stay not for days but months, and a people with whom I felt at ease and whom, more than any other, I would have liked to get to know and understand. To this had been added the attraction of the wild country by which the settlement was bounded. In a land remarkable for its contrasts I can remember none more striking than that offered by the bird-view from the pyramid of the diving god: on the one side the community of huts with its stretch of carefully cultivated *milpas* along the lake shore and cattle browsing on the savanna, and on the other the expanse of flat untamed jungle stretching away without a break to fade into the blue rim of the horizon.

When we had finished our breakfast, Don Dionisio rose from his hammock and the whole family gathered at the entrance of the hut to see us off. The moon hung low over the lake and lit the path along the shore, but once we had turned into the bush, it was so dark that I could only see a few yards in front of me. After an hour the dawn broke and, with the track dry and the mules eager to be home, we were able to travel much faster than on our outward journey.

We reached Chemax at midday. A bus was waiting in the square and I had got into it before I realized that it was not going to Merida, but in the opposite direction to Puerto Juarez. I still had three days before I was due in Mexico City, so I decided to stay on the bus and cross over from Puerto Juarez to the Isla Mujeres.

Any bay or creek where a fishing-boat can put in may be called a port in Mexico. Puerto Juarez consisted of a dilapidated landing stage and a shack which sold beer and soft drinks. The jungle had been cleared for a hundred yards from the shore. The earth on this open space was deeply furrowed by the trucks and buses which had used it to turn round.

The woman who owned the shack told me that the boat was over at the island but that it would be returning in half an hour. I sat down at a table and drank some beer. This was the most easterly point of the mainland of Mexico and it felt like the end of the world. The ticks which I had picked up on the ride from Cobá were beginning to itch and I was longing to get out to the island. It was famous for its beaches and I looked forward to throwing off my clothes and plunging into the sea. I kept watching for the boat and at last I saw it heading out from the island. When it was half-way across the channel, I heard the noise of an engine and turned to see a first-class bus from Merida pull up beside the landing-stage. A middle-aged American lady, wearing a large yellow hat, ran down the steps and dashed towards the café. Red-faced and clutching her stomach she called desperately: 'Toilet! *Baño*! Toilet!'

The woman came to the door and pointed towards the jungle. '*No baño—monte.**

The lady gave a horrified cry and set off across the open space, stumbling in the ruts. When she reached the edge of it, she charged into the bushes looking round every few yards to see if she was out of sight. But the bushes were low and she plunged on and on, her yellow hat flopping above the bright green leaves like a huge butterfly. At last she bobbed down and disappeared.

The boat arrived and I got on board. The captain was anxious to be off but I told him that there was another passenger and that he must wait. After a few minutes the yellow hat reappeared and the lady came staggering back. But she had had enough. She crossed the clearing and, shaking her head at us, climbed back into the bus. The captain shrugged his shoulders. Starting up the engine, he swung the boat round and we headed out to the island.

1958–64.

---

* Forest.